Entrepreneuring Pakistan

27 Stories of Struggle, Failure and Success

Azhar Rizvi

Book:	Entrepreneuring Pakistan
Author:	Azhar Rizvi
First Printing:	2017
ISBN 10:	1986809994
ISBN 13:	9781986809993
Designed, Produced and Published by:	Azhar Rizvi AR@azharrizvi.com www.AzharRizvi.com www.entrepreneuringpakistan.com
	Email: ar@azharrizvi.com azharrizvi@gmail.com azharrizvi@cambridgeadvisorsnet.com 49/1, Lane 15, off: Khy-e-Badban, D.H.A-7, Karachi, Pakistan
	Facebook: Azhar Rizvi Tweeter @AzharRizvi Linkedin : Azhar Rizvi

Disclaimer:

The author has made every effort to ensure that the accuracy of the information contained within this book was correct at the time of publication. The author does not assume and hereby disclaims any liability to any party for any loss, damage, or disruption caused by errors or omissions, whether such errors or omissions result from accident, negligence, or any other cause. The information provided within this book is for general informational purposes only. While we try to keep the information up-to-date and correct, there are no representations or warranties, express or implied, about the completeness, accuracy, reliability, suitability or availability with respect to the information, products, services, or related graphics contained in this book for any purpose. Any use of this information is at your own risk.

Copyright © 2018 by Syed Azhar Afaq Rizvi

All rights reserved. No part of this publication may be reproduced, distributed or transmitted in any form or by any means, including photocopying, recording, or other electronic or mechanical methods, without the prior written permission of the publisher, except in the case of brief quotations embodied in critical reviews and certain other non-commercial uses permitted by copyright law.

Ordering Information:

Quantity sales. Special discounts are available on quantity purchases by corporations, associations and others. For details, contact the publisher at the address above.

DEDICATION

To my (deceased) Parents Najma and Syed Visaqul Hassan Rizvi
who made me what I am

To my beloved wife, Ayesha Menai and two daughters Mehreen Rizvi
and Najma Sabeen Rizvi
who stand patiently by my side through thick and thin

To all mentors, coaches, academia, professional and everyone who
came forward to help us with working with the young aspiring
entrepreneurs.

And, last but not least,
All the entrepreneurs who have the passion and commitment to fulfill
their dreams… this book is for you

About Azhar Rizvi

Azhar Rizvi is a consultant, trainer, mentor and coach who has worked with close to 450 fast-growth companies and 10,000 + student and almost 1000 researchers in the academia to develop their business plans and acceleration strategies since 2007. He is playing a major role in cultivating a new environment of promoting entrepreneurship at various universities as well as several business plan competitions, hackathons, innovation cups, startup weekends and other forums.

He is currently working as the CEO and director of Cambridge Advisors Network. He is also served as the Chairman, Standing Committee on Innovation and Entrepreneurship at the Federation of Pakistan Chambers of Commerce and Industries (FPCCI). He is the founding chairman of Pakathon Global – a platform for Pakistani students to engage in social development ventures-with chapters in 15 cities in the US, Canada, UAE, Australia and Pakistan; and the co-founder of Women's Digital League – established to educate and empower Pakistani women in digital livelihoods. Azhar is the founding vice chairman and a key architect of Massachusetts Institute of Technology Enterprise Forum of Pakistan (MITEFP), where he has been actively developing the strategy and direction of the chapter for the past eight years. He has also served on the global board of MIT Enterprise Forum Global for a period of two years.

In the IT sector, a serial entrepreneur himself, Azhar Rizvi has established several startups after a very fruitful industry career. He is the co-founder of THKS Technology Group and has previously served as the group COO and Director. Azhar has served at prestigious multinational organizations including NCR, AT&T and Unisys in Pakistan. He is involved in technology projects with the Sindh Ministry of Information Technology, the Federal Ministry of Information Technology, the National Information and Communication Technology Research & Development (National ICT R&D) Fund and the Karachi University.

In the social sector, Azhar is associated with DAISY for All, a worldwide project for Digital Talking Books for the vision impaired. He is also part of the advisory council of Rashid Memorial Welfare Organization, District Chair of Economic and community development committee of Rotary District 3271, Pakistan.

Azhar holds an MBA from the University of Houston, an M.Com from Karachi University and an EDP from the MIT Center for Entrepreneurship.

For More Information:
Website: www.azharrizvi.com
EMAIL: AR@azharrizvi.com
          azharrizvi@gmail.com

Foreword by Dr. S. Sohail H. Naqvi

In the 21st Century, we see a sharp shift of wealth and economic expansion in nations that have invested in knowledge creation, innovation and entrepreneurship. Japan, Korea, Singapore, Hong Kong and Taiwan have been able to generate more prosperity, jobs by entrepreneurship than any resource-rich country.

Currently, Pakistan is experiencing a youth bulge with roughly 60 percent of the population below the age of 30. By educating and equipping this younger resource with entrepreneurial skills and courage to startup, Pakistan can be a formidable force in the next 50 years. It is imperative to build policies, products and programs with a unified vision to take advantage of this paradigm shift.

It is, therefore, heartening to see the entrepreneurial grit and success demonstrated by the Pakistanis mentioned in this book. *Entrepreneuring Pakistan* documents the journey, challenges, successes and failures of entrepreneurs, who along the way create wealth, fame and jobs for others. These entrepreneurs, some of whom are LUMS graduates, demonstrate that hard work, combined with self-belief and a leap of faith that is the hallmark of all entrepreneurs, does lead to success. I am also pleased to read success stories of Pakistani researchers, ICT entrepreneurs, social entrepreneurs and, specially, silverpreneurs. This book documents the "method" behind the entrepreneurial madness that is engulfing Pakistan. It is the story of those who worked to build the ecosystem that allowed entrepreneurship to prosper in Pakistan. Azhar Rizvi, as one of the first ecosystems enablers, played an integral role in the entrepreneurial transformation process. In a short period of 10 years, we are able to see the fruits of developing entrepreneurship in Pakistan, particularly in the technology sector, where many promising ventures are now growing exponentially, as is the startup culture.

I met Azhar in 2007 when he came to us at HEC to sponsor the first MITEFP-OPEN (BAP) to be held the same year. Subsequently around 2010, his work with NUST and IBA gave a new dimension to entrepreneurial education and startup culture at universities across the country. Around the same time, we at HEC started establishing university ORICS (Offices of Research Innovation and Commercialization) in order to provide permanency through rules, system and processes for the process of commercialization of innovation that was now beginning to be a regular feature across campuses. Seeing the superb performance of MITEFP-OPEN Business Acceleration Plan, IBA-INVENT and NUST-DISCOVER business plan competitions with participants from 65 Universities across the country, Azhar was given the task to train the directors of these newly established centers on commercialization of research. Faculty from 50 universities was trained through different programs by him on successfully running these centers and promoting entrepreneurial culture at the universities. This gave the faculty a better perspective on how to conduct purposeful research and enhance industry-academia linkages.

I must admit that this journey of a decade has served us well as we can now witness many aspiring entrepreneurs from all walks of life creating successful ventures and becoming an example for all to follow. The LUMS Center for Entrepreneurship, established only a few years back, is one such example where over this period of time dozens of companies have been created with a combined valuation approaching PKR2billion. Ten years ago being an entrepreneur was a lonely job. Today several competitions, hackathons and incubation centers operate across the country through which these young people can get training, coaching and mentoring. The time to start up, though still challenging, has never been better.

I would especially like to recommend to heads of major corporations, financial institutions and policy makers to peruse this book to gain a better understanding of the winds of change engulfing businesses today and nature of work for the future. The stories are a tribute to those who accomplished so much with minimal support. With additional help, this same trickle can turn into a flood of change.

I wish the entrepreneurs the best of luck.

Prof. Dr. S. Sohail H. Naqvi, S.I.
Vice Chancellor
Lahore University of Management Sciences(LUMS)
April 2017

Dr. S. Sohail H. Naqvi has been the Vice Chancellor of the Lahore University of Management Sciences (LUMS) since July 2013. Prior to that he was the Executive Director of the Higher Education Commission (HEC) for eight years, where he oversaw implementation of an ambitious portfolio of programs that resulted in an explosive growth in research activity in the universities in Pakistan, quadrupling in the number of students, standardization of programs at the undergraduate and postgraduate level with clear quality related benchmarks along with the implementation of a comprehensive higher education quality assurance regime. He has extensive teaching, research and entrepreneurial experience both in the US and Pakistan, and has also been a consultant on higher education for the Asian Development Bank and World Bank. He was awarded Order of the 'Palmes Académiques' with rank of Chevalier, by the French Government, and the Sitara-e-Imtiaz by the Government of Pakistan for his services to higher education.

With a PhD in Electrical Engineering and extensive experience in institutional building, teaching and research both in the US and Pakistan. Dr. Naqvi has a number of patents to his credit. He has also worked with startups bringing high-tech inventions to the market place.

Author's Note

Entrepreneuring Pakistan

"Sow a thought, reap an action;
Sow an action, reap a habit;
Sow a habit, reap a character;
Sow a character, reap a destiny."

After a quarter century of working in leadership positions in the Information Technology industry as well as co-founding several startups, in 2007 I steered course to venture into the still mostly unchartered waters of nurturing the entrepreneurship ecosystem of Pakistan. This was a time when very little was known here about how to start and promote ventures.

In my 10 years of working in this space, my learning and experience has been simple: Some of the biggest solutions to the problems begin with a small idea and the will to make it happen.

My previous engagements had provided me the exposure to differences in markets and working in different types of firms: Working for multinationals was demanding but more organized with both local, global support and a very clear career track; whereas, the scenario for startups was unorganized with no support from any institution be it the government, industry or even academia.

It has been a long, hard and exhausting but equally rewarding journey. Rather, it has been more enriching and motivating than I would have enjoyed doing a nine-to-five at a corporate entity. In the past decade, I have mentored, coached and trained close to 450 entrepreneurs and ventures across all industries, as well as 10,000+ students and 1,000+ professors and researchers from 65+ universities all over the country. I have had the privilege to be part of the founding teams of many initiatives introducing business plan competitions, formal mentoring and coaching programs, and training and networking forums that are now pivotal parts of the industry.

A JOURNEY OF A MILLION MILES BEGINS WITH ONE STEP

In March of 2007, on a chilly evening in Trondheim, Norway, Ken Morse, his team from MIT Entrepreneurship Center, my friend Junaid Iqbal and I went for a walk after a conference to discuss a few things. How and why we were there is a story I will leave for another time and place. Our stroll took us to St. Olaf's mausoleum, the seventh holiest pilgrimage site in Christianity, where we pledged to work together to develop and promote the IT startups in Pakistan. Somehow, I had a premonition that we were being guided by Providence.

Upon my return to Pakistan, I established contacts with other MIT alumni. The first was Farrukh Captain, a philanthropist and President of the MIT Club of Pakistan. He officially became the captain of our ship as chairman of MIT Enterprise Forum of Pakistan (MITEFP). Because of our interaction with other MIT Club members, Dr Zahir Ali Syed joined the small team to set up MITEFP and start operations. He is a graduate of MIT and Stanford with extensive experience in founding and managing many IT organizations including Karachi Institute of Information Technology (KIIT). He was also the Director at National ICT R&D Fund, Avanza Solutions Pakistan and ABM Group of Companies. Dr Zahir's addition was instrumental in our finally becoming the co-founding team that set up MITEFP, Cambridge Advisors Network and Technology Angels Network. Other industry leaders joined us to become mentors, coaches and judges to establish the first Business Acceleration Program (BAP) and launch it in June 2007.

BAP has become the flagship program of MIT Enterprise Forum of Pakistan since 2007 catering to 450 IT companies in the process of learning competing training at MIT itself, followed by road shows in major cities of the US. As a result, in a short span of eight years, we have taken a large number of these companies from a few hundred thousand dollar revenues to multimillion-dollar valuations operating on a global scale.

The second part of the contribution in this journey was that of OPEN Global--the Organization of Pakistani Entrepreneurs of North America. A 3,000+ diaspora organization, it partnered with us to host a road show for the BAP. To be honest, the MITEFP would not have achieved success without this collaboration, mentoring and coaching support and the efforts to arrange roadshows for the winners. From Boston to Silicon Valley, our friends were instrumental in ensuring that the talent was mentored and coached on global opportunities. The results are evident from some of the stories in this book.

ACADEMIA STEPS UP TO INTRODUCE ENTREPRENEURSHIP IN UNIVERSITIES

IBA Invent: Dr Ishrat Husain is a great transformer in any organization that he serves. His role at the IBA, Karachi, was just as transformative. We met him during the 2009 BAP finals. Visibly impressed, Dr. Ishrat asked us to design a similar proposal for IBA for an inter-university competition. IBA-Invent started with participants from 15 universities, and in four years more than 65 universities from eight cities across the country participated in the program. During these years, we trained close to 5,000 students to set up startups from Invent's platform. Many of them have continued to pursue entrepreneurship as a viable career choice.

The competition created a fresh avenue of learning for the students and introduced them to alternate career paths. Thanks to the internet, many are running their businesses, as well as participating in both local and international programs to get the necessary exposure, trainings and funding for their initiatives. Through Invent, we discovered ventures such as Zaraei Ootaque that works with farmers to increase yield.

NUST Discover--Prime Minister's Entrepreneurial Challenge: National University of Science and Technology (NUST) was the second to embark on this journey. It was the vision of Admiral Muhammad Mushtaq, Provost at NUST, with the Director NUST Technology Incubation Centre (NUST-TIC), Dr. Qasim Sheikh, to design a program similar to IBA-Invent. We launched Discover and through the team's hard work, and the patronage of NUST Rector General Muhammad Asghar, we received endorsement from the then prime minister, Yousuf Raza Gillani, to designate it as the Prime Minister's Entrepreneurial

Challenge.

In this program, NUST also invited close to 60+ universities to participate, as it had a great advantage of having 17 campuses spread nationwide. This gave students the opportunity to explore new areas and collaborate with students at other campuses for their projects. Soon NUST's engineering students were pitching their projects to business school students to hire marketing and financing resources. The trend soon caught up at other cities. We witnessed NED Engineering University and Sir Syed University students shopping for resources at the IBA, Karachi. In Peshawar, Institute of Management Sciences and the University of Engineering and Technology (UET) students were collaborating to partner on projects. In Rawalpindi, Fatima Jinnah Girls University looked for business students at Iqra University's Islamabad Campus. While in Lahore, Lahore School of Economics (LSE) was teaming up with Lahore University of Management Sciences (LUMS), UET Lahore, University of Punjab and UMT Lahore students.

We were able to create intra- as well as inter-university teams and to get industry mentors to come to schools with us. Three of our researchers whose stories you will read in this book, Maha Yusuf, Tahira Khan and Faria Khan, were all spotted during Discover--Prime Minister's Entrepreneurial Challenge. Today, the three continue to follow their entrepreneurial journeys carving their paths to commercialization.

ECOSYSTEM IS MADE OF MANY PARTS

Once the ball had started rolling, many other local and international organizations joined Pakistani ecosystem to play their part in developing, supporting and promoting the startups. These included Computer Society of Pakistan's Islamabad Chapter and their dynamic leadership who volunteered at my workshops, trainings and marketing activities; The Indus Entrepreneurs (TiE) Global Lean Startup; JumpStart Pakistan; SeedStars, Startup Weekend and Peshawar 2.0.

On the government side, Pakistan Software Export Board (PSEB), Ministry of I.T, Ministry of Science and Technology and the National ICT R&D Fund are some of the amazing organizations that have helped build the awareness and entrepreneurship support system to what it is today.

However, our collaboration with Higher Education Commission (HEC) played a pivotal role in launching our efforts from day one till today. To our good fortune when we started our journey, Dr Attaur Rehman was the Federal Minister of HEC and Dr. Sohail Naqvi was serving as the Chief Executive. We got their unequivocal support in engaging with the universities to launch our programs– from BAP in 2007, to the NUST and IBA Business plan Competitions from 2010.

Furthermore, our firm Cambridge Advisors Network collaborated with HEC to provide business plan training to PhDs, chairpersons, deans and heads of research at universities. My five-day marathon hands-on workshop on *"Changing the Mindset--Commercializing Research"* is now a flagship product that promotes entrepreneurship in Pakistan's R&D fraternity. In the process, we have had the privilege of meeting and training faculty members from 65+ universities across the country. We have also had the pleasure of working on the policy framework for developing offices of Research Innovation and Commercialization at universities as well as for Business Incubation Centers. Through these offices, we hope to promote commercialization efforts among the academia.

With National ICT R&D Fund, we were able to train 60 PhD faculty members, who were working in 35+ universities across the country, on various projects for six months. This included training, mentoring, coaching and roadshows in the US.

The PSEB is another great supporter of our efforts. We have collaborated in quite a few projects including training workshops, boot camps, business plan competitions and acceleration programs. This platform has helped the Pakistani diaspora, not only with export opportunities but in also facilitating them with subsided real estate, bandwidth, tax exemptions and other measures for the IT sector. I am grateful for their support for almost 10 years now.

While many international organizations supported entrepreneurship, especially after 2010, this narration will not be complete without mentioning one more pioneering competition: Global Innovation through Science and Technology–Civilian Research and Development Foundation (GIST-CRDF), a US State Department initiative.

Following the US President Barack Obama's famous speech at Sharm-el-Sheikh in Egypt to promote entrepreneurship in the Muslim world, GIST was launched in 2013. At that time, CRDF, headed by Kathleen A. Campbell, and her strong team members such as Natalia Pipia and Ovidiu Bujorean, developed a platform inviting aspiring entrepreneurs, startup firms and scientist researchers to participate in ideathons and business plan competitions. It was a privilege to work with them.

In 2013 and 2014, Pakistani participants were major players and formed 35 percent of the total participants from 43 Muslim countries. Six or seven Pakistanis always featured among the top 12 announced each year. The platform helped groom Maria Umar, Maha Yusuf and Farhan Masood, who are all featured in this book.

The program was arranged around training events, pitching sessions and coaching by world-renowned entrepreneurs, angel and venture fund managers. These opportunities gave the young Pakistani teams an international perspective and immense motivation by judges and mentors. More importantly, it gave them the confidence to move ahead and never look back. At two of the events in Turkey and Abu Dhabi, our young men and women sparkled and made us extremely proud.

By 2009 several of the participants of MITEFP had started establishing their offices in the US thus generating revenue, creating employment and paying taxes to the US economy. This served as a good reason for USAID to consider supporting the program. In 2013 and 2015 USAID joined hands with MITEFP by sponsoring the participants for local training, coaching the winners at MIT and road shows in various cities in the US.

OPPORTUNITY SPEAKS

We started with a vision and with a dream to build the ecosystem so that the future generations do not have to struggle. God Almighty has been our most gracious guide. We, as a small group, set out to develop a few examples and were rewarded with immense success opening new opportunities for Pakistani talent.

As entrepreneurs–and later as ecosystem supporters–we have designed and executed many programs that have achieved successes beyond all expectations. Every day we learn new things from the brightest minds we encounter in our line of work, making us ever more hopeful about the future of this country and its enterprising people.

There was a time when entrepreneurs feared failure. Now they know that they can stand up again. There was a time when Pakistanis felt that research and innovation were impossible in the developing world. Today we are proud to have researchers that are working to solve big local problems.

It all starts with a drop in the ocean, an idea, but the ripples thus created turn the tide. This book is a humble testament to the strengths and abilities of Pakistanis and the resilience they have shown even in the absence of a support system. These are the thinkers, dreamers and builders who represent real hope for the country. They will create jobs, generate wealth and change Pakistan. This is our ultimate vision for entrepreneuring Pakistan.

I hope you enjoy reading these stories as much as I have living and reliving them. May God bless each one of these entrepreneurs and the many who we worked with. (Azhar Rizvi – April 2017)

Acknowledgements

It would be impossible to thank everyone who has made this decade long journey with me. There are too many mentors and silent ecosystem enablers who have helped us along the journey of a decade. However, I would like to mention a few who have been a source of great support, enthusiasm and help in reaching this milestone.

I would like to acknowledge the support and passion of the initial MITEF team that came together in 2006 to build the MITEFP in Pakistan; Ken Morse, Bill Aulet in USA and founders of the EDP program at MIT who supported this idea of establishing a business plan competition; with them Imran Sayeed, who put us all together in one room.

Hand in hand with the local founding team, our Chairman Farrukh Captain provided the leadership needed to establish this social venture. Dr. Zahir Syed, the co-chairman MITEFP helped in the strategic development and was the operations leader. Behind them was our small operations team: Asghar Azmi, Nehal Ahmed, Naveed Afridi and M. Mukhtar as well as the small army of university interns who supported us throughout our competition days.

I would also like to thank the many institutions and individuals who believed in us. There are so many that I would need to write a separate book just to name the people involved in each and every competition. But each has contributed a drop that has turned into a great entrepreneurship ecosystem today. Some of the people I would like to specially mention are: Dr. Arshad Ali and Dr. Mukhtar of HEC; Dr. Ishrat Husain and Zafar Siddiqui at IBA; Admiral Mushtaq, Dr. Qasim, Majid Maqbool, Air Commodore Salman Absar, and the NUST-TIC Team; Dr. Zafar Khan and Dr. Rafi Ahmed from Institute of Space Technology; Dr. Nisar Sheikh, Mr Ali Akbar Rizvi and Dr. Pervez Memon at IBA Sukkur; Dr. Rasheed of University of Malakand; and the Team at UET Lahore who honored me with inaugurating the first technology Incubation Center at UET Lahore.

I would also like to acknowledge the national and international organizations and the people that helped build the ecosystem into what it is today. The Pakistan Software Export Board has specially been supportive of our endeavors; this includes Asim Husain, Abbas Hasani, and Salman Ahmed; Adeel Sheikh from National ICT R&D Fund; and the team at NEW-G, lead by Rizwan Razvi.

Internationally, many people at TiE Global, OPEN USA, USAID and GIST-CRDF have helped catapult our entrepreneurs into the global entrepreneurship arena.

There are many others who have helped support our initiatives over the years and whose names I have failed to mention but am humbled by their assistance--the enablers, mentors, coaches, investors, volunteers--you know who you are who stepped up when they were needed. Thank you for your support.

Of course, this book could not have been written without the small army of people who helped put this book together. The editorial team was led by Syed Abid Ali, a veteran journalist of 45 years and his extremely capable deputy, Asfiya Aziz who brought the book to its final shape; Our design and publications resources were led by Mr Rasheed Butt and Najmi Ahsan Mirza; Faisal Shuja Khan, CEO of Ovex technologies for his professional and brotherly support.

A special mention to Shazia Yaqub, General Manager at CAN, who has been the team leader for this project. Along with Saadia Zaidi and Sherezade Samiuddin, she helped shape the initial stories and bring them into manuscript form. With them were the student interns from NED, IOBM, KITE and NUST Islamabad who have helped put together initial part of the book narration, specially Aiman Rehan, Aneeta Ochani, Ahmed Maqsood, Hassaan Choudhri, Mashal Dhamani, Sabah Amin and Maira Tahir.

I am also grateful to my family: My parents, my wife, children, brother and sisters. They have stood by me through thick and thin and in all times – God has truly graced me with a wonderfully supportive family.

Finally, this book would not have been possible without the support of the subject of the chapters, the entrepreneurs themselves. I am grateful to the 27 entrepreneur teams who agreed to participate in this project and took the time out to give us interviews, share their successes, failures and deepest thoughts. Later, they worked tirelessly responding to our countless requests, helping us answer queries, giving feedback, refining, reviewing and finalizing their stories, recording lessons for the future entrepreneurs.

Contents

	Page
Foreword by Dr. Syed Sohail H. Naqvi	7
Author's Note	10
Acknowledgements	17

Book 1: The Technopreneurs
Book 2: The Socialpreneurs
Book 3: The Silverpreneurs
Book 4: The Futurepreneurs

- **Book 1: The Technopreneurs**
  Technology Mavens Who Create New
  Products, Services and Businesses 29

1. **Genius Unlimited** 34
   SoloInsight Inc., Farhan Masood

   A precocious teenager with a passion for software programming, Farhan rose to run one of the fastest growing biometric companies working on advanced technologies. From a revenue of US$100,000 in 2012, his company grew exponentially and by 2016 was valued at US$30 million.

2. **Game On!** 46
   GenITeam and Tapinator, Khurram Samad

   When his first startup did not pan out as planned, Khurram decided to build android games. He was first time lucky and hit the gaming jackpot with Gang Wars. Since then, the GenITeam has grown to become the fastest growing game development company in Pakistan and has expanded its foortprint to the US Through its venture Tapinator. Today both the ventures are valued at USD 30 M.

3. **Quality By Design**   57
   Kualitatem, Virtual Force, CoVenture, Jamil Goheer
   Jamil Goheer caught the entrepreneurship bug while still a student fresh out of college. After several failed ventures, he went on to become the founder of an internationally recognized quality assurance firm. He is currently the founder of three ventures: Kualitatem, an independent quality assurance firm; Virtual Force, an early stage accelerator; and CoVenture, a seed investment firm with a funding of US$20 million.

4. **The Dream Chasers**   70
   Bilytica, Usman Ahmad

   Small town boys Usman Ahmed and his brothers from Sahiwal founded an international business intelligence firm Bilytica. Today, Bilytica serves markets across the US, Europe, the Middle East and other regions and has an estimated valuation of US$ 10 million.

5. **Communicating Business**   81
   Evamp & Saanga, Anwar Khan

   Anwar Khan started his IT services firm in 2000 with a vision to enable and modernize the local industry through technology. In 15 years, prudent partnerships and customer management have allowed this venture to bring in over US$3 million in annual revenues with a total valuation of US$11 million.

6. **Garage Startup Hits Big Time**   91
   Symbios.pk, Muhammad Saad Jangda

Unemployment forced Saad Jangda to start an ecomoerce company in 2006. Started with intitial investment of US $ 100, Saad now runs a large e-coommerce portal selling 40,000 products to more than three million clients in Pakistan.

7. **A Match Well Played** 99
   Cricket Companion, Arslan Khakwani

   Marrying their love for sports with their expertise in mobile app development, Arslan's team developed the Cricket Companion, which propelled them into the big league in the world of digital sports. Their software received 1 billion hits, 300 million downloads and a valuation of US$50 million during IPL cricket season of 2011.

8. **Sending Love Your Way** 111
   Tohfay.com, Shahzad Qureshi

   At the turn of the century, Shahzad Qureshi and Mehdi Hasnain started a small e-commerce store selling Pakistani handicrafts in the US. They spun off a gifting service for the Pakistani diaspora who wanted to send gifts back home. Little did they realize that they would be setting the pace of e-commerce adoption in their home country.

9. **Putting Urdu on the Web** 121
   Hamariweb.com, Abrar Ahmed

   Abrar believed that his Urdu-medium education would prove to be a hurdle in his career. Today he runs one of the largest Urdu-language portal Hamariweb.com in the world, which receives an average of 16 million hits every month and over 500 million visitors every year. Hamariweb.com ranks among the top 10 Pakistani websites and the top 1,300 in the world, serving millions of Urdu-speaking community members daily.

Book 2: The Socialpreneurs 129
Social Catalysts for a Better Tomorrow

10. **Dreaming of a Better Future** 133
    The Dream Foundation Trust, Humaira Bachal

    Born in a low-income, conservative community, Humaira Bachal dared to dream of a better life for herself and other girls like her. She now runs a multi-storey school for 1,200 students, an industrial home for women and a microfinance facility for 500 women in Moach Goth, a semi-urban settlement on the periphery of Pakistan's largest metropolis, Karachi.

11. **Connecting Women, Improving Health, Transforming Lives** 144
    doctHERs, Dr Asher Hasan, Dr Sara Khurram, and Dr Iffat Zafar Agha,
    Three passionate doctors founded doctHERs, which connects stay-at-home female doctors to the population in underprivileged areas through telehealth clinics. In eighteen months, they have set up eight facilities and treated over 100,000 patients, bringing quality healthcare to those who need it most.

12. **Opening Minds and Empowering Women** 158
    Women's Digital League, Maria Umar

    Maria Umar founded a social enterprise that mobilizes a home-based female workforce to earn digital livelihoods for economic empowerment. No matter where the women live, WDL ensures that they will always be able to find work, with just a computer and an internet connection.

13 **Effective Charity Systems** 171
PDX: Pakistan Development Exchange, Hassan Sami Ahmed
Philanthropists Hassaan and Sami always wondered about the leakages in donation systems and the lack of transparency. They piloted an alternative charity match system through a social exchange bank, based on crowd funding, hyper-connectivity and community development. Attempting to shift the paradigm, Hassaan and Sami are proving to the world that it is possible to move a community out of the vicious cycle of poverty, one family at a time.

14. **Connect, Educate and Evolve** 179
Rabtt, Imran Sarwar

A vacation time interaction with students from underprivileged schools inspired Imran to start a summer program for children that would break down barriers of education, class and attitude, through critical thinking, connecting with others and identity development. Through Rabtt programs, doors open for children from all kinds of backgrounds as they undergo life-altering early experiences.

15. **Reversing the Brain Drain** 191
Pakathon, Asad Badruddin, Zheela Qaiser
Asad and Zheela started a civic hackathon to brainstorm solutions that would help the Pakistani diaspora connect back home and develop products and solutions to Pakistan's most pressing problems. What started as a small hackathon has created a multiplier effect that has mobilized 45 universities in Pakistan, many universities abroad, students in five countries, 15 cities, five host countries and 1,000+ global participants.

- **Book 3: The Silverpreneurs** 203
  Entrepreneurs Who Leveraged Experience and Made Impressive

Comebacks

16. **Silver and Savvy** 207
Secure Tech Consultancy (Pvt.) Ltd.
Brigadier (R) Saleem Ahmed Moeen
A massive cardiac arrest changed Brigadier Saleem Moeen's career track. He retired from the armed forces, to serve as Chairman of NADRA. Following this, he came out of retirement a second time to set up his own firm Secure Tech. He took advantage of the lessons he had learnt in his previous careers and ramped up operations to grow a firm with annual revenues of US$10 million and approximate valuation of US$35 million in just six years.

17. **From Lab to Market** 220
Center for Advanced Studies in Engineering (CASE), Dr Shafaat Bazaz
A research team took on the challenge of transforming a PhD thesis and an eye disease diagnostic product from a mere blueprint to a commercial product installed in premium eye-care hospitals across the country. This story demonstrates the mutual benefits of industry-academia collaborations, saving millions for the industry and in the process creating two PhDs, 10 MScs, 12 research papers, many jobs for students and an MoU of US$3 million to build a state of the art Health Management and Information System for Al Shifa hospitals, Islamabad.

18. **Clinic on the Cloud** 231
Infogistic, Sajjad Kirmani
Respected IT industry leader Sajjad Kirmani's early experience in the corporate sector and as part of Netsol Technologies' core team helped him gain market knowledge. Post-retirement, Sajjad set up Cloud Clinik, a SAS-based

electronic management record system, to transform the Middle Eastern mid-size healthcare market. Cloud Clinik has captured close to a 50 percent market share in Qatar.

19. **Cracking the Reinvention Code** 240
    EGS, Abid Hussain
    Abid Hussain of EGS reinvented a pioneering IT services company to compete at a time when many national and international ventures went bust. Not only did EGS survive, it continued to grow through rapid industry changes. This story demonstrates the unique challenges of an established company that responds to the vagrant business cycles to manage growth for the last 35 years.

- **Book 4: The Futurepreneurs** 256
  Future Innovators and Entrepreneurs

20. **The Rickshaw Kings** 260
    Travly, Shahmir Khan, Talaal Burny, Mehmood Ali, Faizan Khan, Mohammad Zohaib
    When a group of students found public transportation unnavigable, they decided to create a rickshaw app that allows customers to connect to rickshaw drivers through their phones. Four years ago when they came up with this idea in a business plan competition, they were taken as young, overambitious, aspiring entrepreneurs. Today, the same concept is a vibrant industry with major players such as Careem and Uber operating on the similar model.

21. **Harvesting an Agricultural Vision** 273
    Zaraei Ootaque, Umair Malik, Abdul Samad Sahito
    The Zaraei Ootaque team proves that there is a huge scope for entrepreneurship in rural Sindh. They started from scratch at the IBA-Sukkur incubation center, working to develop higher yield farms through their one-window farming

consultancy and collective farming unit since May 2012. Today, the student led venture has graduated from the incubation center and is earning a revenue of PKR50 million annually (US$500,000).

22. **No Speed Limits**   282
    XGear, Muhammad Ahmad Khalid

    The XGear team revived a student project that collected real-time statistics about a vehicle and using that data can recommend corrective action. They improved upon the initial idea to create a product that extends the life span of the car, saves lives and saves millions of dollars.

23. **The Need for Speed**   293
    Omni Motorsports, Dr Syed Ovais Masud Naqvi

    A doctor by profession and an auto racecar driver by passion, Ovais dreamt of bringing professional motor sports culture to Pakistan. He is currently involved in a Greenfield project developing the first of its kind Formula One racing tracks in Pakistan. Today, he has proved that audacious dreams are the only ones worth striving for.

24. **The Bazaar of the Story Tellers**   302
    Emperor'Bazaar, Muhammad Ahmad Ibraheem, Usman Khan, Haroon Baig

    With extreme pride in their heritage and culture, three young technology entrepreneurs realized the need for highlighting Pakistani handicrafts to the global market. So, they built an online marketplace that not only connects artisans to the market but also provides training and development to bring them at par with quality expectation of internal customers .

25. **Cancer Killing Virus**   314
    ASAB-NUST, Tahira Khan

The cartoon show, Dexter's Laboratory, motivated Tahira to be a scientist. She is now working at the Atta-ur-Rahman School of Applied Biosciences (ASAB) at NUST todevelop a virotherapy cure for the 1.4 million cancer patients in Pakistan whose number is rising each year by 8 to 10 percent. Moved by her interactions with suffering cancer patients, one of whom was her own grandfather, Tahira was inspired to find a cure through her research-which has already shown in-lab success.

26. **Embracing Indigenous Knowledge** 322
NanoSmart, Faria Khan

A WHO internship set Faria on the research path. She is currently developing a nanoparticle-based hospital disinfectant-a patented product that will be commercially viable and more eco-friendly than other disinfectants in the market.

27. **Running Towards My Dream** 331
Stanford University, Maha Yusuf

A simple small town girl from Jhang, Maha dreamt of becoming the next Nobel laureate, like Dr Abdus Salam who also hailed from her hometown. This is the story of her struggle to reach Stanford University and become a doctoral researcher working in hydrogen-based fuels.

Glossary 340

Bibliography 353

Where to get more help 364

Book 1: The Technopreneurs

Genius Unlimited
    SoloInsight Inc., Farhan Masood 34

Game On!
    GenITeam and Tapinator, Khurram Samad 46

Quality by Design
    Kualitatem, Virtual Force, CoVenture, Jamil Goheer 57

The Dream Chasers
    Bilytica, Usman Ahmad 70

Communicating Business
    Evamp & Saanga, Anwar Khan 81

Garage Startup Hits Big Time
    Symbios.pk, Muhammad Saad Jangda 91

A Match Well Played
    Cricket Companion, Arslan Khakwani 99

Sending Love Your Way
    Tohfay.com, Shahzad Qureshi 111

Putting Urdu on the Web
    Hamariweb.com, Abrar Ahmed 121

Technology Mavens Who Create New Products, Services and Businesses

In early 2000s, America's dotcom bust caused ripples that resonated strongly with Pakistan's infant IT industry. Many startups that had mushroomed at the time shut down, or struggled to survive for the next five years, due to what financial gurus called a 'market correction'. However, after a number of remedial actions, the local and international IT industry was able to rise again.

Since 2012, a new wave of entrepreneurs and startups has been surfacing on Pakistan's business environment, because of the initiatives taken in the 2000s. This has resulted in the emergence of the technopreneurs in the Information Technology (IT) and IT-enabled Services (ITeS) sectors, who have been able to assess market signals correctly and reap digital dividends.

Major government players that supported the rise of the industry include the Higher Education Commission (HEC), the Ministry of IT and Telecom (MoIT), and Pakistan Telecom Authority (PTA). By investing in human resources, the HEC expanded the pool of universities, and developed a comprehensive strategy to improve the availability and quality of education. It also encouraged research through development of incubators and commercialization offices within the universities. The MoIT and PTA worked to create traction in telecommunication growth, particularly of digital services and mobile phone penetration.

Pakistanis are now the eighth largest mobile phone owning population in the world. Although internet infrastructure continues to lag behind, the IT industry was given first access to the latest advances and now 3G and 4G subscribers have reached close to 37 million. The industry has also received tax exemptions and other similar incentives.

Secondly, a diverse set of organizations-semi-government and private-grew to form the body of ecosystem enablers that we see today. Some of these are PSEB, National ICT R&D Fund, PITB (Punjab Information Technology Board) and KPK ITB (Khyber Pakhtunkhwa IT Board).

Lastly, pioneering industry platforms such as Pakistan Software Houses Association (P@SHA), Computer Society of Pakistan (CSP), I2I (Invest to Innovate), Pakathon, MITEFP, TiE Pakistan and OPEN are playing key roles in promoting strong entrepreneurial cultures in major cities. They are providing support to emerging entrepreneurs, as well as to Pakistan's academic institutions.

The change in direction has resulted in a mass-scale realization that the digital economy is here to stay and is increasingly being made available to the masses. This has created a wave of young entrepreneurs and is generating spillovers in other sectors. The support ecosystem is now maturing and is developing a wide range of young talent that is open to starting up. Not only are these energetic entrepreneurs benefiting themselves, and the economy, they are also becoming role models for the youth of this country- development crucial for enhancing entrepreneurial culture.

This section contains nine stories of technopreneurs and their organizations that have been able to grow successfully. The ventures are pure IT ventures or ITeS firms. All the entrepreneurs have had a close mentoring association with me during the growth stage. The first seven stories are of people with IT backgrounds, while the last two are firms whose founders had never thought of going for technology-related ventures, but still established excellent businesses. The variety and depth of these companies demonstrates that the niche player has a definite advantage. They initiated their startups at a time when there was limited support. These stories also demonstrate the importance of non-IT skills that are required to take advantage of technology. These inspirational narratives display the courage of their lead actors who are now distinct stars of the IT world.

Many of the people we met as part of the MITEFP-BAP represent both the pool of winners and those who did not make it to the final round. Nevertheless, each of them carried away learning that helped realign their organization with latest skills in the quest to become truly global players.

Key Learning for Entrepreneurs

A common thread in our work with the technopreneurs is they come with the perception of a lack of finances, contacts or global presence as key hindrances in their business growth. However, after going through a five-and-a-half month intensive BAP experience, they understand that the only barrier was their mindset keeping them from realizing their true potential. Today most of these firms have revenues of three, five, ten or even 15 million US dollars. Many have clocked in most of the growth after a few years of going through BAP, almost like getting an adrenaline boost.

What may seem surprising however is that BAP did not provide them any funding. It gave them a platform, and some basic training on coming up with a business plan. After that, we exposed them to the best mentors from OPEN Global in the US. A small intervention such as this was able to create tremendous impact on the national economy.

When we started on this journey, our vision was to create eight to ten firms, with a million dollars in revenue each, as a role model for young entrepreneurs in a period of eight to ten years. God has been very kind and we have been rewarded beyond our expectations.

This book contains many stories of successful firms with revenues or valuations exceeding three to five million US dollars. Many have also since listed their companies internationally, or have received funding worth millions of dollars to expand their organizations globally.

IT graduates usually aspire to break out and do something of their own at some point in their lives. Here is some general advice to young technopreneurs or aspiring techies who want to focus on growing rapidly:

Focus on a key market. Study its needs and identify opportunities before developing solutions.

Remember, customer's needs-not technology-come first. So do not fixate on a certain technology.
Ride the wave to get your product out fast.

- Build teams that have all kinds of people with all kinds of skills. A strong technical team is great, but the marketing, finance, fundraising and sales teams are just as important, as are mentors and a board of advisors.

- Be aware that external funding is not the only way. None of the entrepreneurs in this book received early-stage funding. They bootstrapped or funded their ventures through customers.

- Act fast. Fail fast. Learn from the failure and get up again.

- Best strategy is always to get a job, work, learn for three to five years and then venture out to prove your mettle.

1
Genius Unlimited

Solo Insight Inc.
Farhan Masood

Founder and CTO
Chicago, Lahore
www.soloinsight.com

"There is no passion to be found playing small-in settling for a life that is less than the one you are capable of living." ~Nelson Mandela **Farhan Masood, Solo Insight Inc:**

A precocious teenager with a passion for software programming, Farhan rose to run one of the fastest growing biometric companies working on advanced technologies. From a revenue of US$100,000 in 2012, his company grew exponentially and by 2016 was valued at US$30 million.

Author's Note: With his larger than life personality, Farhan Masood instantly attracts attention. I met him while launching the GIST-ITech Competition in Pakistan, when Farhan was running Solo Tech out of Lahore. His operation was small, but what I found noteworthy was his clear vision, great technical skills, passion and potential for growth. I spotted his lack of focus in terms of strategy and advised him to work in this area. Meanwhile, his hesitation in pitching himself to large customers and organisations was also clearly visible. He needed more confidence and experience to promote his products and services. I took him to the GIST program and we worked on these shortcomings. From that stepping stone, Farhan moved steadily and in the right direction. In six months, he entered BAP, where I and a group of mentors coached him in every aspect of business.

Farhan eventually went to the finals in Turkey and his firm was ranked amongst the top 10 at the competition. Later, in 2012 he came to participate in the MITEFP-BAP (Business Acceleration Program) and won it with distinction, against extremely tough competition. He also went to the MIT Entrepreneurship Center to attend the EDP (Entrepreneurship Development Program), and the rest is history. In just three years, the firm has gone from being worth under a million dollars, to a valuation of US$ 15 million with US$ 3 million in investment and with offices in US, Pakistan and China.

An entrepreneur and philanthropist, Farhan Masood runs one of the fastest growing Biometric and IoT (Internet of Things) companies working on advanced technologies in the world. With offices in the US, Pakistan and China, the company was set up with just US$100,000 in 2012. Today, it is valued at US$15 million, with seed investment of US$3.5 million.

Through willpower, hard work and sheer tenacity, Farhan was able to grow his company into a multi-million dollar business, demonstrating that one can achieve big dreams and ambitions, even while living in a developing country where all odds seem stacked against you.

Farhan was born in a middle-class family in Lahore, where his father owned an offset printing business. He was a cheeky and rebellious teenager, with a passion for computers. As a young boy, he bunked classes at his Urdu-medium school to spend his days at Hafeez Center, Lahore's hub for computers. His passion and talent remained unacknowledged by his parents and teachers, while Farhan eventually dropped out of college to pursue a career in software programming.

In 1997, just short of his 20th birthday, Farhan was recognized by the Voice of America (VoA) for being the originator of the Urdu, Persian and Arabic language word processor on the internet. This confirmed the prediction of a fortuneteller, who had told his mother that one of her sons would become famous. The VoA interview propelled Farhan on to his journey as a consultant to governments worldwide and a career as a serial entrepreneur.

When he is not pursuing his high-powered tech ambitions, Farhan pursues social initiatives close to his heart. He heads a volunteer outfit called the Go Green Movement (http://www.gogreenpakistan.com/) that organizes blood donations, fundraising and digital-activism campaigns.

Discovering A Love for Technology

Farhan was born in 1977 in Lahore to a family of migrants from India that had settled in the Punjab province of Pakistan. His father set up an offset printing business in Lahore after graduating from the prestigious Government College there.

Farhan always wanted to become an inventor. As a young boy, he loved playing with the Legotoys his father would buy for him. When someone pointed out to him that an inventor needed strong sketching skills, he spent a lot of time practicing drawing. His single-minded focus led him to become a well-known inventor and entrepreneur.

Farhan studied at the Divisional Public School, an Urdu-medium school in Lahore. A naughty child, Farhan was not much interested in studies, and neither his parents nor his teachers could foresee the awe-inspiring success that he would experience in the future. While his mother was expecting Farhan's younger brother, his great-aunt, a palmist, predicted that one of her sons would become famous by the age of 20. Since Farhan was not a great student, his mother concluded that the prediction must be for her unborn child.

Farhan attributes his love for technology to his father's passion, who was always the first to buy the latest and trendiest gadgets in the market. He purchased an XT computer when Farhan was just eight years old. The young boy was not allowed to play with the machine, but that did not dampen his spirits. He would satisfy himself by peeking through the keyhole, whenever his father played Digger on the computer.

Farhan got his first chance to explore the fascinating gadget when his father went away on a business trip. Seizing the opportunity, he looked for the computer keys and copied the key strikes he had seen his father use to play games. When his father returned from the trip, he was angry, but also impressed with the young boy's natural skill with the computer.

This event set the foundation for Farhan's tech career.

A Taste of Independence

In 1991, Farhan's father instructed him to commute to school by public transport so that he learns to be more independent. At the time, he used to get a meager PKR10 as allowance for that day's bus fare and lunch money. Farhan was strapped for cash and soon started to look for ways to earn more money.

Not particularly fond of school, Farhan would bunk classes and spend time at a bookstore at Hafeez Centre, Lahore's main technology market back then. The bookshop had all kinds of books, and Farhan made a beeline for the computer books. The shop-owner let Farhan read as many books as he wanted to and allow him use of his computer as well. It was there that Farhan created his first program-a drawing of a Volkswagen-using BASIC language. His passion for computer-graphics programming grew leading him to create a software for textile designing.

A friend offered to sell the software to a textile manufacturer for PKR1 million, of which Farhan would receive PKR200,000. The 14-year-old was ecstatic and agreed enthusiastically.

While Farhan was in Faisalabad installing the software, his parents discovered that he was skipping school. Furious, his father made it clear that school was not negotiable, he must attend school regularly and graduate from college. He enrolled Farhan into Haleem Institute, which had a strict educational environment, and would ensure that his son cleared his Matriculation examinations. In school, Farhan became popular because of his programming activities. He was unofficially the richest boy around for miles and the only one who earned his own pocket money.

A turning point came when Farhan's father received a call from the examination board office, informing him that his son had failed nearly all the exams in Matric. In a fit of rage, His father dragged him to the board office. Once there, they discovered that his Chemistry and Mathematics exams were almost completely correct. However, Farhan did not receive the marks that he deserved, because the shady examination official was looking for a bribe to pass Farhan, which his father categorically refused.

As a result, Farhan could not get admission into any of the degree programs of his choice or interest. He ended up in FC College studying for a general science degree. This was torturous for Farhan, who was forced to study theoretical subjects that he did not care for. He felt cheated out of his right to having a better degree. This made Farhan lose faith in the education system, but it also awakened in him the will to work harder to achieve his goals.

Endless Internet

Farhan started preparing for the National College of Arts (NCA) entrance exam. He wanted to leave the BSc program and get into a more hands-on design degree course. At the same time, he decided that he wanted to redesign Brain Net's website. Brain Net was Pakistan's first Internet Service Provider (ISP). A few nights before the NCA entrance exam, his father caught him programming and developing Brain Net's website.

Farhan recalls: "My father asked, 'What are you doing Farhan? Your NCA exam is tomorrow morning.' I replied, 'I am designing the Brain Net website.' My father queried, 'Did they ask you to design it?' 'No,' I replied. Infuriated and exasperated, my father asked, 'Then why are you doing it? And on a night when you should be studying for your exam?' 'Because I know they will want it' was my reply."

Ready to tear his hair out, his father dropped Farhan early next morning at the Brain Net office telling him not to come back until he was ready to study for the exam. At the office, Farhan had showed up so early that the guard did not let him in. He waited at the gates and as soon as Dr Shahid Alvi, Brain Net CEO, arrived, Farhan created a fuss saying he wanted to meet him. Curious to find out what it was about, Dr Alvi allowed Farhan to come in and show him what he carried in his floppy disc. Dr Alvi instantly liked Farhan's web design options and asked him what he was demanding in exchange for his services.

"I asked him to give me unlimited free internet as that was all that came to my mind," says Farhan. It was mid-1990s, when there were few ISPs (Internet Service Providers). Dial-up internet was charged by the hour making the price of a connection unreasonably high which had restricted Farhan's internet usage to a couple of hours per week. When Dr Alvi asked how much internet access he wanted, Farhan replied, "As much as I want and when I want." He struck a bargain with Brain Net and got access to unlimited internet in exchange for the development and management of their web portal. At 19, Farhan became the official webmaster of Brain Net.

On to Greater Things

Using the programmable engraving machine at his father's printing services bureau, Farhan created an Arabic-based character map and used it to develop the first Urdu font for engraving nametags. He did it for fun and showed it off to his father.

A client from Kot Addu liked the font and ordered thousands of bilingual nametags. The family needed the money, so Farhan rose to the occasion and developed an Urdu word processing software to complete the order. The same software tools were used later to print and engrave nametags in offices like NADRA (National Database and Registration Authority).

Once the project was complete, Farhan became comfortable with typography, calligraphy and software development in these languages. His research and subsequent development formed the basis of the Urdu, Arabic and Persian fonts. He also developed software for typing in Urdu, Persian and Arabic and made it accessible to the public for free. Later, he created a program that converted languages and displayed them on websites, laying the foundation for multilingual sites. Some of his initial work is still being used by the Emirates Airlines.

As Brain Net's webmaster, Farhan used the Urdu font to create the first online Urdu newspaper, which he called, *'Urdu ka Pehla Akhbaar'* (Urdu's First Newspaper). This portal was popularly accessed by international news agency sites and had relevant collaborations, including one with the Voice of America (VoA). Soon Farhan's work came to the attention of the global media and they contacted Brain Net to learn more about his work on promoting Urdu on the web.

Fame and Fortune

The Voice of America called Farhan following a review in the Washington Post about his work in web design and web writing fonts. They wanted to highlight his efforts in promoting Urdu on the web. The broadcast recognized Farhan as the originator of Urdu, Persian and Arabic fonts on the internet and thus opened many doors for him. The interview aired on June 23, 1997, a day before Farhan turned 20, fulfilling the palmist's prediction.

On the morning of June 24, 1997, Farhan's interview was published in all major Pakistani and Gulf newspapers. Later that year, he received the Presidential Award for his work on e-government from the President of Pakistan, Farooq Leghari. Farhan was offered an assignment by Shahbaz Sharif, the Chief Minister of Punjab, to provide support to the provincial Revenue Minister, Chaudhry Shaukat Dawood, and his team in computerizing land records. One after another, opportunities popped up for Farhan as he was offered many government and international projects, including some by Lt. Gen. (Retd.) Moinuddin Haider, then Governor of Sindh and later the Minister of Interior. Farhan worked on digitizing Karachi maps and on various other projects with the likes of Chenab group, Lakson Group and numerous other big companies.

This was when Farhan dropped out of his Bachelor's program at FC College, preferring to focus on his entrepreneurial journey. He believes, "You should not do ten tasks inadequately, when you can do one properly."

Becoming an Entrepreneur

From 2000 to 2005, Farhan worked in Dubai in senior positions on numerous projects worth over US$196 million dollars, including the e-government project under the leadership of Sheikh Mohammad. The digitization project streamlined the Middle Eastern country's immigration and judicial systems. Farhan became an expert consultant for the government and the companies that wanted to sell systems to the government would request him to evaluate their product critically.

Farhan's team in Dubai comprised exceptionally talented individuals involved in producing highly advanced technical solutions. With their collaboration, he designed facial and iris recognition algorithms and automatic recognition systems, as well as an analytics engine to measure employee productivity. Farhan became a valuable resource for the UAE government. Normally, non-graduate employees were not hired as managers, yet he became one of the rare exceptions. After gaining expertise through these projects, he founded his own organization called Quick Fix Advertising Technologies, operating out of Dubai.

The Light at The End of The Tunnel

The year 2005 proved to be a time for personal and career-related upheavals in Farhan's life. Alongside working for the UAE government and running Quick Fix Advertising Technologies, Farhan also got married that year. It was a short-lived marriage. He was divorced within a year and left to care for his baby girl by himself.

Things got even worse. While working on projects in Dubai and dealing with his personal loss, some of his staff betrayed him and stole his assets. Disheartened, dejected and overwhelmed, Farhan decided it was time to return to Pakistan.

Back home, Farhan sprung into action again. He felt that the logical extension for his family's printing business was to start a debit, credit and ATM card manufacturing facility as consumer financing was growing exponentially in Pakistan. Unfortunately, because of inadequate research and a vague business plan, the venture failed. In the process, Farhan lost all his personal savings.

While working on government projects, Farhan had built extensive expertise in security technologies and started working on refining 2D and 3D recognition tools. Influenced by the popular sci-fi movie Minority Report, Farhan wanted to create the technologies that he had seen in the movie, such as iris scanners. In 2006, he set up a company called SoloTech. Today the company is known worldwide by its global name SoloInsight, Inc., and is known for developing one of the most accurate 3D facial, iris and retina recognition and IoT (Internet of Things) technologies.

A Winning Streak

By 2010, Farhan was back on his winning streak. Having bagged the APICTA and P@SHA awards repeatedly, he felt hopeful when invited by an American investor after winning the Global Innovation through Science and Technology (GIST) competition organized and sponsored by the US Department of State, in Turkey.

"The first time I applied for a visa to the United States, I was refused. I was actually told, 'We don't want to do business with Pakistan. You can leave the embassy.' I was disappointed. My American dream was shattered and I thought I would never be able to accomplish it."

Little did he realize then that this was only a minor speed bump on the road to success. He met Azhar Rizvi at an event in Lahore. Azhar introduced him to the MITEFP-BAP program. Azhar also encouraged Farhan, telling him not to give up. He told him to find a way through which the embassy could not refuse him a visa.

Later that year, SoloInsight took part in the BAP. Four months of rigorous training at the business planning competition finally paid off and SoloInsight won the competition. Farhan received the visa and went on to join the MIT Entrepreneur Development Program in Cambridge, Massachusetts, where he was acclaimed as 'a brilliant mind' by the expert panelists.

After completing the training, Farhan joined a road show. He met an experienced Chicago entrepreneur called Carter Kennedy through a common contact. Farhan saw Carter's potential and made him his business partner and CEO in the US. Through his network, Carter introduced Farhan to many people, including one of his current investors Jai Shehkawat who had just sold his technology business to SAP for US$1.2 billion that year.

Many firms expressed interest in his products and were impressed with the level of technological innovation he displayed. Microsoft and IBM offered to assist as they felt his technology had far-reaching applications across several verticals.

SoloInsight Today

SoloInsight is a pioneer of a cloud-based global recognition platform called the 'Internet of People'. SoloInsight's flagship product, SmartXS was created in 2010 and was acclaimed as the fastest facial and retinal scanning algorithm. In 2005, when Farhan launched his first Facial Recognition Kiosk, a prototype of the current one, the hardware as large as a TV trolley. Now it has become smaller than a PC. SmartXS integrates workplace attendance management with security access. The hardware also has applications for the medical industry. Over the past few years, harnessing the power of machine learning and artificial intelligence, the technology has become the best in its class globally.

According to Winter Green Research, which provides strategic market assessments and research reports of the Internet, software, hardware, and telecommunications, the massive biometric devices' market is generating as much as US$6 billion in sales and this number is expected to triple by 2019, to become about US$17 billion. SoloInsight leads this market in its category. The product is currently deployed at many multinational companies like The Home Depot, PepsiCo and Nestle, as well as locally at the National Database and Registration Authority (NADRA).

In 2013, a three-and-a-half million dollar funding led to the transformation of SoloTech to SoloInsight. The organization started out as a small team of six members and now has a team of 67 employees working out of China, US and Pakistan.

Go Green-A Renaissance Man

Today Farhan is also at the forefront in philanthropy and social work. After reading numerous disheartening statements on social media about his country, Farhan was inspired to start the Pakistan Go Green movement. The organization engages active citizens who arrange blood donations, hold fundraisers and perform community service. Started in August 2009 through Facebook, it has more than 1.5 million Pakistani followers on its page.

Farhan is extremely patriotic. When you ask him what comes to his mind when he hears the word 'Pakistan', he says, "Pakistan is rising... Pakistan is not a piece of land. I am Pakistan. You are Pakistan. We are Pakistan.... We will change, and so will Pakistan."

Advice to Entrepreneurs

Talent in Pakistan: Farhan says our nation has many highly skilled individuals with ingenious ideas, who do not strive towards their implementation, unless they are in dire need. He believes that hard work outweighs talent and working smart is as important as working hard. Farhan suggests that young people should opt for careers in the software industry and should not lose hope when they are not immediately successful. This industry has a lot of promising career prospects, although it does not guarantee success overnight.

Business Planning: Farhan's visit to the US convinced him of the need to build his business by taking a backseat and hiring professionals. He describes himself as a 'scientist' and someone with 'purely technical knowledge'. During the trip, his mentors impressed upon him the need to look at other aspects of managing businesses, such as operations, finance, law and marketing. "It isn't enough just to build a world-class product with the hope that it would succeed. The business has to be managed professionally."

Being Confident when Diving into Entrepreneurship: Farhan believes that fear does nothing but obstruct one's way to greatness. Young entrepreneurs need to be confident enough to execute their ideas and not pay heed to naysayers for they create doubts and stop one from achieving anything.

2
Game On!

GenITeam, Tapinator
Khurram Samad

Founder and CEO, GenITeam
Co-founder and CTO, Tapinator Inc.
Lahore, New York
www.geniteam.com; www.tapinator.com

"The secret of success in life is for a man to be ready for his opportunity when it comes." ~ Benjamin Disraeli

Khurram Samad, GenITeam
When his first startup did not pan out as planned, Khurram decided to build android games. He was first time lucky and hit the gaming jackpot with Gang Wars. Since then, the GenITeam has grown to become the fastest growing game development company in Pakistan and has expanded its footprint to the US through his venture Tapinator. Today both the ventures are valued at USD $30M

Author's note: Khurram Samad's potential was unmistakable from the very first time I had met him. Therefore, when he could not make the shortlist for MITEFP-BAP at first, for the reason that his firm was generating less than US$ 100,000 in annual revenue, we had to do something. For the first and the last time in eight years, we waived that precondition for entry. His technical skills, business plan and hard work were fantastic, but what really impressed me were his human skills and humility, which he maintains despite the success he has achieved in the past six years. Today, he has gone global and is running two successful ventures: GenITeam from Lahore—a BPO and software firm—and Tapinator, a mobile game development firm based in New York. Both firms have a combined valuation of US$ 30 million.

Khurram Samad comes from a family of air force pilots. He dreamt

of becoming one in the Pakistan Air Force (PAF) just like his father. However, an injury crushed his air force dreams and spurred him on to create a new identity for himself.

Khurram enrolled in an MBA program. In his second year, he laid the foundation of GenITeam, a mobile app and game development company based in Pakistan that would develop games for the iOS, Google Play and Amazon platforms.

With Khurram as its CEO, GenITeam has gone on to become an award-winning game development company that has also been rated amongst the Top 100 Asian Companies by Red Herring 2012. He is also the CTO and co-founder of Tapinator, a global game development company listed on the New York OTC Stock Exchange. The total valuation of GenITeam and Tapinator is US$30 million. The company has development teams in Germany, Pakistan, Indonesia, Canada and the United States.

As of mid-October 2016, his company, Tapinator has publicly declared the following in its quarterly disclosures:

- 324 million cumulative player downloads, up by 141 percent from last year
- 272 active games as of September 30, 2016
- 81 games that have each achieved over one million player downloads
- 21.5 million average monthly active users (MAU) during the quarter
- 1.2 million average daily active users (DAU) during the quarter
- 626,000 average daily downloads across the network

Stumbling upon a Love for Programming

Khurram received his early education at Pakistan Air Force (PAF) schools, completing his intermediate from PAF Cadet College, Sargodha, in 1998. Born to an air force officer and brought up in a military environment, Khurram Samad's earliest aspiration was to become a pilot in the PAF. But an injury while playing football left him bedridden for almost a year and unfit for a military career.

Khurram talks about that trying time. "It was a difficult decision for me. I had to make peace with living life as a civilian unlike my military family. My father found it difficult to accept my decision."

After graduation, he enrolled in the Foundation for the Advancement of Science & Technology-Institute of Computer Science (FAST-ICS), Lahore. Khurram laughs, "I wanted to be a textile engineer. I am from Faisalabad, and always thought textile would be a good career. When my father saw FAST-ICS's advertisement for the first time, he told me that I should not enroll in a house-turned-into-a-campus university. He told me I should pursue computer science and apply to the University of Engineering and Technology (UET), Lahore."

However, his father soon changed his mind when a friend endorsed FAST-ICS as one of the most prestigious colleges for computer science. Soon Khurram received a ticket to Lahore from his father who told him to go and take the entry test at the university. "Honestly, I just wanted to visit Lahore for fun, since dad was paying for my travel. The entry test was just an excuse. I didn't even expect to clear the test," recalls Khurram.

To his own surprise, Khurram got into FAST-ICS and stumbled upon his passion in programming. He believes that there are two types of people: those who believe everything that is being taught to them, and those who have to do things themselves before grasping their essence. Khurram puts himself in the second category and believes it is one of the main reasons behind his love for writing code. "Some people like doing things with their hands. Some people can't relate to lectures. The process of writing code attracted me. So sitting in the lab, watching friends build programs, steadily built my interest in the field," he says.

Dabbling in Startups

Graduating from FAST-ICS in 2001, he joined an IT company called Techlogix. Khurram recalls, "My father told me that my first salary was more than his own salary at the time of his retirement."

However, a year-and-a-half later in 2004, he upset his parents when he resigned from the job. "Father was really mad at me. I remember him telling my mother that I had lost my mind, because I was leaving such a great job." Khurram allayed his father's fears when he told the family about the significant funds he had managed to save.

For a short while after leaving Techlogix, he worked with a family friend in a startup that did business process reengineering. At the same time, Khurram decided to develop his own IT product. He dreamed of setting up his own business, while still working at his day job. "I always wanted to run my own software house someday; have my own group of companies. I was so confident that I even wrote that in my yearbook." He now admits that starting his own software house was a leap of faith and a result of youthful confidence.

Unfortunately, Khurram ran out of funds before the product was finished. He had made the mistake that most technologists make. While building the product with the latest technology, J2EE at the time, he had not realized that it was already available in the market at a much cheaper rate. Khurram's product became unmarketable and the startup failed miserably.

With no funds left, Khurram was forced to find work; this time at LandSlide Technologies. While there, he realized the importance of reliable market research and, a year later, took the plunge again and launched another startup.

This time he set up an online venture in which an international company outsourced work to Khurram to design different products. Impressed with Khurram's work, the CTO of the company called him and asked if there were others like him in Pakistan. "I told him yes, they all are wandering in the streets, looking for jobs." The company started giving Khurram and his team more work and eventually established operations in Pakistan.

Khurram realized that he knew enough to be able to help other Pakistani entrepreneurs to run their operations. While he did consulting assignments with other entrepreneurs, he felt the need to understand business management himself. By 2006, he had enrolled in the MBA program at Lahore University of Management Sciences (LUMS).

Khurram received financial aid while studying at LUMS. Midway into his degree program, the university ran out of funds and told him that they could not support him in the coming year. On his request, his teachers allowed him to freelance at a few companies to raise the money he needed.

Around this time, Khurram secured a product development contract from a Middle Eastern company. He hired ten employees in Pakistan. A tight schedule ensued: attending MBA classes in the morning and managing his employees in the evening.

He also began to analyze the factors that had led to the failure of his first venture. He realized that a key mistake he made was that he had not established his company as a brand.

Setting Up GenITeam

In 2007, Khurram founded GenITeam while enrolled in the second year of his MBA. The firm was established to provide outsourced services to the international market. Work was good. Not only did Khurram earn enough money from GenITeam to pay his tuition fee himself, he also paid off all his previous university loans.

On seeing the initial signs of success, his father started urging him to continue the business. Khurram graduated in 2008 and started devoting full time to GenITeam. However, during the 2008 global recession, both the companies GenITeam was working with backed out, cutting off all the company's sources of revenue.

"My father asked me what my plans were. I told him I had money to take care of company expenditures for three months, and would then search for a job and hope for the best," recalls Khurram.

Khurram's father said, "Do not take on another job until all of GenITeam's members find employment elsewhere." Khurram discussed the situation with his team and they all agreed to do their best to keep the company alive for three months.

Around this time, someone recommended that Khurram meet Azhar Rizvi for mentoring. Khurram approached Azhar for product advice and subsequently GenITeam started working on Web2.0. This was a move towards mobile app development for the iOS (Apple) iPhone.

Later he met Imran Sayeed and Naeem Zafar the only two Pakistanis working in this area. Based in the US, both the mentors had been part of the US IT industry and had extensive knowledge of the market. When Khurram came to Karachi to present his company to them, they were surprised to learn that he was a Pakistani, mainly because the Apple app development was primarily based out of US. They also found him to be a good communicator. The response Khurram received during that visit motivated him to start creating his own products.

Entering The Gaming Industry

GenITeam eventually went on to create games for the Android operating system also. Facebook was gaining popularity back then; Zynga had just emerged as a Facebook-based gaming company and their text-based RPG games were trending. Khurram's team decided to innovate on this platform. They reasoned that even if the game did not sell well, they could develop it, then outsource and sell it.

Luckily, they hit the jackpot at the outset. GenITeam's first game, based on Gang Wars, became a huge success. "To be honest, it was not just me. The fact is that nobody in Pakistan invests in market research," says Khurram. Professional gaming companies based in Pakistan were just not taken seriously. Developers would make games, but only as a hobby. The game Khurram picked was in the text-based RPG format, and did not require much work in terms of graphics and animation. It was based more on the codes. With strong engineering background available to them, the team was smart enough to utilize their skills towards developing the game. The team did not do extensive market research, but Khurram had seen the mobile app market develop and a pattern emerged in his mind.

The game was successful and the team introduced advertisements in it to generate enough money to pay the office rent. They added more in-app purchases, and the game started paying off. Product revenue doubled. GenITeam employed another 30 people.

Talking about this sudden jump, Khurram says, "The good thing was that the profit margin was significantly higher, around 60 70 percent in 2010." GenITeam's outsourcing wing that now had ample projects, combined with the game revenues, was generating over US$1 million dollars in profits annually. These were fantastic returns for a small company that had started with an investment of a mere US$60,000 just a year ago.

The market evolved rapidly. GenITeam started receiving enquiries from Warner Brothers and other companies that wanted to invest. At the same time, the big studios debuted in the mobile games market. Competition became fierce and GenITeam felt the need to upgrade themselves. "Basically the gaming industry is 'hit-driven'. If a game becomes a success, the company generates heavy profits, otherwise it does not," explains Khurram. "We couldn't spend all our lives generating revenues from a single game. We had to evolve with the market."

The team also upgraded their portfolio approach. They invested the funds in their projects so that at the end of the day their cash flow was always positive. Its products were divided into three categories: low-risk low-returns, mid-risk mid-returns and high-risk high-returns. Annually, they also select to work on two projects that are high investment and have high (expected) returns.

Going Global with Tapinator Inc.

As the company grew, GenITeam started developing its own products. Predictably, the startup started getting offers to sell and eventually received a bid from serial entrepreneurs, who had had past success with Facebook applications and wanted to invest in mobile applications. Khurram decided on a partial exit. He did not sell the company entirely as they could not agree on the valuation, and the entrepreneurs ended up investing in GenITeam instead.

"There wasn't an exit," says Khurram. "I am still the majority shareholder at GenITeam. However, in 2013, we incorporated another company called Tapinator." The other two co-founders of Tapinator are American serial entrepreneurs who understood the market better. Currently, Ilya Nikolayev is the CEO, Andrew Merkatz is the President and CFO, and Khurram is the CTO of Tapinator.

Tapinator is listed on the Over-the-Counter Market at the New York Stock Exchange (NYSE-OTC). It owns the intellectual property rights of all the games. The NYSE-OTC is a launching pad for small companies that require capital, but are not ready for NASDAQ trade and obtain capital from the equity market. Khurram Samad is one of the shareholders in Tapinator. Legally, Tapinator's development work goes through GenITeam that also has a separate independent outsourced services division.

"I found that the team has reaped big benefits from listing the company. In order to list the company, we had to create a business plan that we give to any investor. Quarterly term sheets are routinely prepared, audits are filed and shares are traded. As a result, we know the value of our company."

"The advantage of being listed is that there is an accountability built into the company. For Tapinator, this means that there is pressure to deliver. I realized that this was important as the investor will talk numbers, the metrics for success. Management also understands that they need to answer the shareholders first. As a sole proprietor, you make many decisions based on gut feeling or interest. After listing the company, I feel I have become more responsible."

One of the co-founders sold his shares, valued at US$10 million in 2013. Two years had not passed when he realized that it was a mistake and came back to purchase his shares at a premium. Khurram estimates that the combined net worth of GenITeam and Tapinator are close to US$30 million now.

In 2016, GenITeam with a portfolio of 270+ games under its belt was generating around US$5 million in revenues. Next year, Khurram expects the figure to hit $10 million.

Tapinator is expecting revenues of US$4 million in 2016, according to some analysts in the global industry. This is in light of the prediction that the industry is slated to grow to US$90 billion dollars by 2020. According to Tapinator's third quarter press release in 2016, it surpassed 300 million cumulative player downloads and 20 million monthly active users (MAU). It has a portfolio of 272 active games as of September 30, 2016, of which 81 games have achieved over one million player downloads. Tapinator also has 1.2 million average daily active users (DAU) and 626,000 average daily downloads across the network. Since 2013, they have been showing triple digit growth in most engagement metrics.

Tapinator will be launching multiple Hollywood studio games, starting with the launch of the official game of Rocky in collaboration with MGM. The company is currently working with Sony Pictures and Discovery. There are development teams in the US, Canada, Indonesia and Germany also. In future, Khurram hopes his team will be able to do it all in Pakistan. As the company has some cash available, they have started looking for a few studios as well.

The outsourcing work at GenITeam is continuing and a future strategy is being devised in areas other than gaming space. "We've come a long way," says Khurram. Talking about the various specializations in gaming, he elaborates, "Actually games are divided into several categories; arcade, casino, text-based, etc. Although, our team has developed expertise in most of them, it specializes in six categories."

A Finger on The Market Pulse

A number of innovations are being introduced in the gaming sector. Khurram believes that virtual reality is an important space. Virtual reality is a computer technology that replicates an environment, real or imagined, and simulates a user's physical presence and environment to allow for user interaction. With specially designed headsets, virtual realities create artificial sensory experiences that can include sight, touch, hearing and smell. GenITeam is transforming all the company's games into virtual reality. Khurram believes that virtual reality will be received by the world, just like the iPhone was back in 2008.

He also predicts that educational games are going to be big in the near future, as the world now understands the importance of using games to add fun to learning. GenITeam recently worked on a project for Dubai government using games to educate children about road safety. He with shorter attention spans of children, and changing expectations from schools, Khurram is preparing his team to explore the fast-changing dynamics of learning.

Advice for Entrepreneurs

Building A Successful Team: In Pakistan, Khurram is the sole owner of GenITeam, but in the US his Tapinator business partners have proved to be an asset. Khurram says, "I have learned a great deal from my partners in the US. Since the Tapinator team consists of seasoned entrepreneurs who have done one or more successful exits, our roles and responsibilities are clearly defined." Khurram strongly advises having a board based in the US to be the early bird in the market, as that gives a company time to mature.

Some of Khurram's employees are also key players in his businesses. An incentive structure has been devised for key players, so that they eventually become partners. "They were with me during the highs and lows of business. They were in the initial team and they are still dear to me. To be able to take them along, and to give them priority, is extremely important."

He is proud that the company has reached a level where its processes are streamlined and where individuals and personalities have ceased to influence its performance. Tapinator employs people in strategic locations all around the world. There are five employees working in New York, five in Toronto, eight in Bangkok, and 40 in Pakistan. GenITeam employs a further 60 people, based in Pakistan. There are multiple reasons behind hiring employees in different countries. The biggest one is as Khurram explains: "…because at the end of the day Pakistanis still need to improve some skills. We have fallen behind in a lot of areas, especially in RT graphics."

Needing Advisors: Khurram endorses the requirement to have more than one advisor. It was only after he established his company on this model that he understood that his advisors should be from different areas. Some can advise emotionally, while others should be from the relevant field and understand company dynamics.

Financing Style: "My mother told me to never take a loan. So I never used any financial leverage for my ventures. Even if you have to sell your car or your house, do it. Try to arrange your own money as long as you can," shares Khurram. GenITeam grew from the profits it made and from the internal funds. Cash flow was never a problem as there were no delayed payments.

"It is really easy to take money from investors, but in the long run it isn't worth it," says Khurram. He advises raising money only when one really needs it. If one is aiming to get into a multi-million dollar venture, and expecting someone to buy out, only then can external investment be recommended. Otherwise, he advises, it is not going to work. In retrospect, Khurram thinks that he could have taken his products further if he had spent time and money on marketing. Even when money was coming in, he was more inclined to save it for a rainy day.

Acquiring Other Companies: Khurram feels that he took a hasty decision on his first acquisition. It did not have the best evaluation, but Khurram felt that it was an experience worth going through. "I agree that it would have been better to have stopped then. But I'm saying this now." He also feels that in that acquisition, he added to the mistake with his micromanagement.

Planning Well: Planning is a very significant process in any venture. "It is more important than execution that your plan must be well-devised," he says. He recalls that developing the business plan for BAP competition was a difficult exercise. He understood its importance later when running his own company. He had made a very skeletal document back then. Realizing this gave him a sense of the gaps in the management planning. He now regrets rushing with business ideas and going ahead solely on his gut feelings.

Khurram believes that his MBA made all the difference and helped him succeed. During his course work, he had analyzed case studies and gauged them against his experience to assess how he could apply the learnings in future. However, at heart he remains an engineer and can still write code. This enables him to have a better understanding of the industry.

3

Quality by Design

Kualitatem, Virtual Force, CoVenture
Jamil Goheer
Founder
Pakistan, UAE, US
www.kualitatem.com; www.coventure.vc

"If you always put limits on everything you do, physical or anything else, it will spread into your work and into your life. There are no limits. There are only plateaus, and you must not stay there, you must go beyond them." ~ Bruce Lee

Jamil Goheer caught the entrepreneurship bug while still a student fresh out of college. After several failed ventures, he went on to become the founder of an internationally recognized quality assurance firm. He is currently the founder of three ventures: Kualitatem, an independent quality assurance firm; Virtual Force, an early stage accelerator; and CoVenture, a seed investment firm with a funding of US$20 million.

Author's Note: During the first decade of 2000, Pakistan's software industry was nowhere in terms of products and services, mainly because of quality issues. When I met the Kualitatem team, my first thought was that if they succeed in their venture, they would add great value to the whole industry. During the five and a half months long mentorship at BAP, we worked together on achieving focus and boosting their confidence in meeting customers, in addition to adding depth in their products and services. Here was a firm that was pitching itself as Pakistan's first independent quality assurance and testing firm. They were already working for and tapping an international clientele. Jamil is now co-founder of three successful firms: Kualitatem, the quality assurance firm, with an illustrious Fortune 500 clientele; Virtual Force, a mentoring and incubation center and CoVenture, an early stage VC fund with a US$ 20 million investment, all in a period of six years. They are a clear role model for others to follow.

Jamil Goheer stumbled upon his career while in the final year of his Bachelor's program in Computer Science. He did an internship in Speech and Language Processing that set him on the entrepreneurial path. Jamil and his team set up Kraysis that started as a speech company and went through multiple pivots before offering an independent software testing and quality assurance service.

A series of unfortunate events caused the team to reboot and set up Kualitatem, a venture focused on executing independent Quality Assurance Projects. The course correction paid off and today Jamil and his team have made Kualitatem an award-winning company that provides independent software quality assurance and testing services. During the last eight years, the company has expanded from Lahore to the Middle East and the US. In 2015, Kualitatem was featured in the Top 10 list of 'Pure Play Testing Companies' by Gartner.

Jamil and his team have also contributed significantly to the country's IT sector by demonstrating that Pakistan is not only a low-cost offshore outsourcing destination, it is also one that can provide world-class services verified by quality independent providers.

Jamil and his co-founders have spun off developing and supporting a few other ventures. They have also initiated CoVenture, a venture fund for startups that works for pre-launch ideas, based out of New York.

An Idyllic Childhood

Jamil Goheer was born in December 1979. His father taught Mathematics at FC College, Lahore, and his mother was a deputy director at the Department of Education. As an only child of parents working in the education sector, his early life was keenly focused on education and learning. Jamil fondly recalls, "Education was central in our household. I still remember the way my mother used to teach me. It was a lovely childhood and a lot of fun because of the close association with my parents. We had a very friendly environment in the house."

After his O levels from the Salamat School Systems in 1996, Jamil completed his A Levels from the Keynesian Institute of Management & Sciences (KIMS) in 1998. Inspired by nuclear physicist Abdul Qadeer Khan, Jamil was interested in joining the Metallurgy department at the Ghulam Ishaq Khan Institute (GIKI), Pakistan. Unfortunately, due to high entry requirements and limited seats, Jamil could not enroll in the Metallurgy program, and went on to pursue Physics at undergraduate level at FC College.

One day, his father said to him, "I have heard FAST is a prestigious institute. A lot of my colleagues were congratulating our principal on his son getting accepted there." Jamil was not too keen on joining FAST as he wanted to go abroad for further studies, but being the only child it was a hard decision for his parents. Eventually, they made a deal with him: He could complete his undergraduate studies in Pakistan and go abroad for his Master's degree.

Jamil joined FAST, switched his major to Computer Science and became very active in a wide range of extracurricular activities. He was part of the football team, the volleyball team and played a lot of table tennis. He also co-founded the Creative Society and was editor-in-chief of the annual students' magazine, Interface. He was elected, first as the vice president and then as president of the Creative Society, and was actively involved in organizing SOFTEC, the biggest software competition in Pakistan for students at that time.

Towards the end of the second year, Jamil was enjoying himself at FAST, but he found that his GPA was sinking. He realized that in order to get into a postgraduate program or land a better job, he needed to do better in academics.

Internship At The Center for Language Engineering

During the summer break in Jamil's junior year, Dr. Sarmad Hussain started The Center for Language Engineering that would research language processing. Dr. Sarmad was looking for junior researchers to join him at the center and do work that could be used as their final-year projects. Jamil was attracted to the idea of doing something extra during the summer break, so he volunteered.

This proved to be a turning point in his life. "The hard work that we did during our summer break made us complete a final year project even before starting our final year semester. That made all the difference in my senior year."

"We were actually making a component for speech and language processing. The software was able to identify multiple languages upon receiving speech signals, and was aimed at supporting the global call center industry," he explains. Jamil and the other students worked on six different languages. In addition, they were also able to co-author two IEEE journal papers on the technique.

"Due to this research, we were able to do our final-year project even before we were supposed to start it officially. This gave us time to participate in competitions. We went to Karachi for a software competition at a university and subsequently went on to win a competition at GIKI. This opportunity gave me the direction that I needed to complete my degree. At the same time, it opened up a venue for me to innovate and develop my own ideas."

After graduation, Jamil started thinking seriously about the career path he wished to pursue. The IT job market was limited to two or three employers and the rest of the students were getting internships at very low pay. It was a difficult time for IT industry in Pakistan. The locals were highly dependent on outsourced projects from the US. But in the aftermath of 9/11, it seemed like everything was collapsing, and there were fewer jobs with opportunities for future growth.

The final-year project had given Jamil, and his fellow team members

Mustafa, Bilal and Fahd, the confidence and drive to continue working on their idea and turn it into a business venture. They were still unclear about the commercial aspects of the research on Speech and Language Processing. Dr. Sarmad gave them the opportunity to pursue the commercialization of the technology, as a research project.

"At the same time, I started exploring ways to do something on my own. I started to ponder over the technology transfer and commercialization plan. We met different people from Islamabad and Lahore to seek help in building our venture," remembers Jamil.

A Master's Degree From LUMS And Research

After nine months, all the team members got admission in the University of Edinburgh in Scotland for their Master's in Speech and Linguistics. While the others pursued their degrees, Jamil had to stay because his mother had fallen ill. "My parents had given me so much over the years, including the room to grow. Their old age was the time when they needed me to be with them. I realized that if I left then to go abroad, there would be nobody to look after them."

He decided to stay in Lahore and pursue a Master's degree at LUMS, where he continued to put his fingers in many pies. He immediately became a teaching assistant and helped as a research assistant. This enabled him to work on a couple of startup ideas.

Funding Through Competitions

Meanwhile, Jamil and his two teammates, Bilal and Fahd (who were at the University of Edinburgh), prepared their idea for a business competition in Scotland and won a GBP50,000 grant.

Their next goal was to raise another GBP50,000 from venture capital firms. He believes his team did not face many issues in finding investment because the idea was powerful. The team raised around GBP100,000, to kick-start the company, which was called Alivox at that time. He recollects that one of his professors had once said, "If you really want to do something from the core of your heart, money is never a problem."

After building the product for two years, the team lost track of the changing business dynamics. By the time the product was ready, other players in the market were offering simpler and cheaper solutions. The team ran out of the financial runway and had to shut down the company. They lost almost GBP400,000 in investment. Jamil has a positive take on the experience and believes the learning was valuable. "We were full of ideas and wanted to go back to the industry," he says.

Incubation at LUMS

After graduating from LUMS in 2005, Jamil had many lucrative offers, including a Fulbright scholarship. However, he felt that there was a lot to be done in Pakistan. For one, university incubation was a concept still alien here.

Brimming with ideas, he approached the Vice Chancellor of LUMS, Dr Syed Zahoor Hassan, and requested support for university incubation. Dr. Zahoor asked him to do some homework instead, which Jamil did. Dr. Zahoor kept asking for more. For six months, Jamil kept going back and forth to convince the management of the viability of his idea. Eventually, they agreed and gave him and his team the space and resources to innovate and build on their thoughts.

The foundation for the LUMS incubation center was laid and Jamil and his team were the first formal test case. He still remembers the Head of Finance being brought in to negotiate with them about how to pay for the services, the retainer and the terms and conditions to spin out as an independent firm.

"The first idea I worked on was a continuation of the speech and language processing research. We had to build a search engine for speech files and index all the databases. In addition, we had to search it matching a speech signal," explains Jamil. "For example, I say 'search Toyota Corolla' or search some song and that speech query would give us a list of files corresponding to that sound bite."

The team tried to generalize this in the Jungle Business Plan Challenge, sponsored by Fenwick & West and Intel Capital at that time. Out of 200 entries, Jamil's team was placed in the top 25. One of the team members who had an American passport, Nosheen Akram, travelled to the US to compete in the final round as none of the other team members was able to get a visa. The idea was ranked among the top six, during the final round in Santa Clara, CA.

"While there was a lot of interest in the product, it was hard to get visas and relocate to the US. In the aftermath of 9/11, visa policies were tough. We were able to invite a couple of venture capitalists to Pakistan for due diligence. They flew in to spend time and learn more about the team, the company and the possibilities of growth. But unfortunately, our inability to relocate to the US was a deal breaker," Jamil remembers.

360 Degree Pivot to Quality Assurance

"Ultimately, things did not pan out the way we had wanted them to. We were left with only two options: to close down or do something else. We decided to do something else." Jamil and his team opted to work for the local market to earn their bread and butter. They decided to pitch customized open source ERP solution (Open Taps) to domestic industry.

The team did a couple of presentations and some demos. One of their prospective clients was the largest fan manufacturer in Gujrat (Pakistan). The team did a gap analysis and identified that there was PKR80 million worth of inventory lying in the warehouse. The inventory was five or six years old, rusty, rotting and had never been brought out of the backyard. "We spent a lot of time on pre-contract work to win the project," says Jamil. "When it was time to sign the contract, we asked for PKR500,000. The counter offer was PKR25,000. That was it for me! I decided that I would not work for a local *seth* (business owner)."

Kraysis

"Next we came up with the idea of independent software testing and quality assurance. We were desperately looking for something that could sustain us. I had done some management audits for Nike in Pakistan, and my partner Khurram Mir had solid experience in the field of software testing. We thought of offering Quality Assurance (QA) solutions to the local IT industry."

Teaming up with Khurram, another LUMS MBA, Jamil launched the service and got a client right away. It was Moonis Rahman's Rozee.pk, which was about to launch. Problems arose because they had more than 20 engineers building the app, but no quality assurance team. The launch was delayed because of the bugs and issues in the app. Jamil and

Khurram offered to develop an independent QA team.

The team worked for Rozee.com and within two months, was able to identify and help fix majority of the issues. This resulted in a successful launch. Jamil regards this as his first successful experience. The team began marketing their services to international companies and started getting business in executing independent QA projects that translated into a healthy revenue stream for Kraysis.

Exposure to international market proved vital in boosting confidence about their capabilities. They were able to earn money, as well as train themselves. "We groomed ourselves at LUMS. We had nine people crammed in a small room. People would come to see how we were managing this feat."

Soon the team took over the PhD lab, a much larger space. They earned good money and successfully completed the incubation model in 2007, at a time when no university incubation existed in Pakistan. "The test case at the campus incubation center was successful, and we moved out as a team of 25 to the local industry, as well as to the international market."

This was the first successful spinout from the LUMS incubation facility. Kraysis went on to win the Best Startup Award by P@SHA in Pakistan, and the Best Startup in Asia Pacific by APICTA in 2008 in Jakarta. They were also the finalists in the MITEFP-BAP 2008.

Many naysayers had believed that an independent software quality assurance firm was not viable. However, the team believed in the idea and kept on working. They started building up momentum and became the talk of the town. "We were also one of the panelists for the Global Entrepreneurship workshop by MIT at Cape Town, South Africa, in early 2009," adds Jamil.

Unfortunately, in 2008, after three years of operations, and five months after winning these accolades, the company fell apart. The three partners developed serious differences.

The team had some cash flow issues: the founders were not able to earn, the legal foundation of the organization was not strong, doubts cropped up about the business model, and there was no exit strategy for those who did not believe in the idea. A deadlock occurred that ultimately ended in shutting down Kraysis.

Separating Thorns from Roses

In 2009, Jamil went back to the drawing board and along with Khurram decided to restart the Quality Assurance business under the brand name, Kualitatem. Even though low on cash, they quickly hired a new team. There was no money for the salaries and they were also hustling to get more contracts.

The team remained mostly intact and things kept evolving. They put the contracts in place and set up a more robust legal and contract framework. They also got senior advisors and honorary directors to oversee the team. An industry leader was brought in to be an honorary board advisor. "The key difference was that this time around we made better decisions and managed stakeholders' expectations better," says Jamil.

The credit for rebuilding the quality assurance firm goes to advisors like Abdul Razak Dawood, Jamal Arif and Dr. Zahoor Hassan. Razak Dawood advised them, "Either you be negative, or fight it out with a positive attitude and build it all over again. The choice is yours."

In the last eight years, Kualitatem has grown exponentially. They currently employ 80 people-all consultants and engineers-working out of Lahore, Dubai and the US.

Jamil feels that Kualitatem is experiencing organic growth. He also believes that independent Quality Assurance has infinite potential. It is a huge industry, and with all the evolving technology innovations, both in hardware and software, there is growing demand for independent software testing companies.

Kualitatem was ranked amongst the Top 10 'Pure Play Testing Companies' globally by Gartner in 2015. From its humble start in a small 650 square foot office, the company has grown to ten times its original size. They have a strong footing in the Middle East, where Khurram is leading operations personally from Dubai.

Virtual Force, CoVenture and More Startups

In addition, due to their interest and passion in the entrepreneurial space, Jamil and his partners have also started to move out into some very exciting spaces. Two such ventures are Virtual Force and CoVenture.

Virtual Force spun out from Kualitatem, as a pure product-innovation team (www.virtualforce.io) in 2011. It is an innovation-and-production center for technology solutions that seeks to change the world. Talking about learning experiences, Jamil says, "Within the DNA of our organization, we have learnt about product development. We learnt, experimented, made mistakes, saw and heard of others making mistakes and eventually rolled out our very first product. That was a failure. The experience helped us pivot and eventually become successful with the byproducts. We didn't give up."

Virtual Force works with founders to think their product through and helps them with initial market validation. The experience has been valuable for new founders. "We used our learning and worked with over 40 startups and ideas, launching them successfully. Most of the companies are US-based with a few from the Europe and the Middle East. The iterations of product development have continuously refined our ability to make the right decisions and reject things that wouldn't work."

The business charges for their services. "We have about 60 engineers and product thinkers working as a team. All the innovative technologies are explored in Virtual Force. Over time, Virtual Force has collaborated with various acceleration programs globally, including IDEA Labs, Techstars, UK Lebanon Tech Hub, Etohum, Frog leap and CoVenture. It is working with founders, innovating in spaces like healthtech, edtech, fintech and alternate lending," says Jamil.

As the company started picking up steam, Jamil and Khurram brought in a third partner, Tanzeel Ur Rehman, to lead the operations at Virtual Force. Tanzeel graduated from LUMS and Babson College, and brought with him experience of working with technology enterprises.

"We prefer working with great founding teams. Anyone can have a fantastic idea, but not every founder is a techie. An investor puts money in the technology, finding the right team, industry, technology,

technology stack and the right feature sets. With an experienced team, we can do in ten months what it would take a new team almost two or three years to do. We can accelerate any founder with technology support and market advisory teams. That is the kind of optimization we can achieve for our clients at Virtual Force," says Jamil.

CoVenture Llc

Jamil also helped set up CoVenture, a New York-based early-stage venture fund, established in 2013. The platform invests in technology startups. Non-tech founders are always on a lookout for tech co-founders who will build their initial products. CoVenture invests in founders in the form of cash and equity. They help founders design and build their first or second product release, in exchange for equity.

The idea of CoVenture came about after Jamil attended a UN conference in Kenya. He met his Co-founder Ali Hamed, still a sophomore student at Cornell University, and they started exploring ways to collaborate. Gradually, they matured the concept and formed CoVenture after a year.

The seed-funding round was arranged internally by the founders. The second round of investment came from family and friends, and the third round consisted of close to 57 limited partners. Many of these partners now read like the Who's Who of venture capitalists.

CoVenture invested in six companies in their first round. The second time, they invested in about eleven companies. For the third round, the company is closing deals with prospective investors to invest in about 22 companies. The fourth round is ongoing and they are raising US$20 million in software for equity business. Other CoVenture funds are also in place now in the form of debt funds. They have scaled their general partner team and have brought in senior partners including Thatcher Bell and Mike Beller. The pool is still growing.

Typically, CoVenture invests US$25,000 to US$50,000 in cash, and provides guidance to help validate product-market fit. Then they help the companies raise follow-on capital and bring their tech teams in-house. Often, while a company works with CoVenture, they pair the founders with senior engineers in their network, to act as advisors along the way.

Other Initiatives

Another initiative that Jamil is working on is an acceleration program in Pakistan. It is called Virtual Force Accelerator Plus. The accelerator accepts founders, who have seen traction in their business and are ready to accelerate, but are directionless. VFX+ will offer them a year-long program for growth readiness and funding readiness. Through this intervention, founders are offered space, technology consulting, business and marketing help. Deal flow is from current incubation programs, as well as individual deal hunting. VFX+ has already invested in health-tech, media-tech and e-commerce ventures.

In future, Jamil wants to continue to play an active role in developing the entrepreneurial ecosystem, especially in technology and high-impact spaces. "Khurram and I have seen the ecosystem grow over the last 16 years. We have been the test case and beneficiaries of this ecosystem. We are determined to pay it back through initiatives like VFX+ and others."

Advice for Entrepreneurs

Failure as A Learning Experience: Jamil recalls that each time the team had failed, it was a great learning opportunity. "We were building a product using the waterfall model, and we were able to make one with an accuracy level of 95 percent. Nevertheless, we failed to launch it because we did not focus on the market and the customer. Other players ventured in with a simpler and cost-effective solution while we were busy building, and overtook us in capturing the market." Now our mantra is: "Sell first, build later and fail fast."

Mentoring: A mentor is one of the best things for any venture. A good mentor will make life much easier. You piggyback and learn from their experiences to avoid fatal mistakes.

Going International: Traveling is very important. It opens up your perspective and brings you closer to opportunities. Travel should be taken as an investment for an organization, not as an expense. We have travelled extensively to GITEX since 2007. When Jamil and the team got business from Dubai the first time in 2007, they had money for travel, but not for the hotel. They stayed with friends and saved cash for food during the event.

Jamil recalls, "Getting a visa on a green (Pakistani) passport is not easy. However, one should never give up and never lose hope. My UK visa application was rejected five times. We had business and we had to go there to close the deal. Our sponsor was with us the whole way, giving recommendations and covering all expenses. But the visa officer just rejected us, thinking we were young males with insufficient ties to Pakistan."

Those faulty perceptions are the ones we have to fight as Pakistanis. However, for an entrepreneur it is important to keep going and keep solving problems. "I kept trying and got enough visas eventually. For the last few years, I have been traveling five or six times a year," says Jamil.

Facing Challenges Head on: Every challenge should make you resilient. Never give up. Every rejection opens new doors. That is part of the entrepreneurial journey.

"The silver lining was that I won a fellowship, an Endeavor Executive Award right after my fifth visa rejection. I was given a temporary resident visa in Australia. Later, I won another fellowship from the Prince of Wales Trust in the UK and got the visa, followed by the US, the Schengen and other visas," says Jamil.

4

The Dream Chasers

BILYTICA PRIVATE LIMITED
Usman Ahmad
Co-founder and CEO,
Bilytica Private Limited
Lahore (Pakistan),
Melbourne (Australia)
www.bilytica.com

"Intelligence without ambition is a bird without wings."
~ Salvador Dali

Small town boys Usman Ahmed and his brothers from Sahiwal founded an international business intelligence firm Bilytica. Today, Bilytica serves markets across the US, Europe, the Middle East and other regions and has an estimated valuation of US$ 10 million.

Author's Note: Usman had assembled an excellent team but bad experiences with partners had shaken their confidence. We helped them to expand their marketing capabilities, product development and develop a sound business plan, so they could replicate their success in the region. As a result, they are now expanding in the Middle East. During my association with them, we worked on expanding their vision, market reach and plan. The team of brothers started with a small order in Finland and a one-room office at their uncle's residence in 2008. Today, Bilytica has offices in six countries around the world and negotiates million dollar deals regularly. The story is a testament to strong family values and offers a difficult lesson about deception in business.

Usman Ahmad and his siblings own a multi-million-dollar IT company with tens of international offices and IT products with over

100,000 users. Their core domain is Business Intelligence, Data Science, Machine Learning and Smart IT products based on data. The startup, grown to a multi-national, has an interesting story.

Born in Sahiwal, a small town in central Punjab, Usman Ahmad and his siblings were raised in a middle-class family that placed strong emphasis on good education. His father owned a small electronics shop and his mother is a homemaker. Usman and his siblings worked hard to get admission into good colleges in Lahore.

After graduation, Usman worked in the technology sector with multinational companies like Teradata, Vodaphone, Logica and Nokia. While living in Finland in 2008, Usman and his brothers, Nauman Ahmed, Muhammad Awais and Muhammad Moin, launched Bilytica, a Business Intelligence and Applications company.

By 2016, eight years since its inception, Bilytica has grown into a multi-million-dollar business. The company serves 12 international markets including Pakistan, Australia, Peru, Russia, the UAE, the UK, Qatar, Saudi Arabia, Canada, Indonesia and Turkey. From a three-person home office in Lahore to a global presence that employs over 150 people, Bilytica's growth and Usman's journey have been extraordinary.

Today, Usman and his siblings believe that the family's sacrifices and their parent's single-minded focus on their education have been repaid several times over.

Small Beginnings

Usman was born in the 1980s in Sahiwal about 200 km from Lahore. He was the eldest of four brothers, born to an electronics shop owner. Their early education was at a government school, the only education the family could afford. However, a strong emphasis on schooling and learning was always a priority for the family.

"My father sometimes struggled to make just enough for monthly expenses. Yet he never compromised on our education, doing his best to give us the best. There were times when making ends meet would be a real challenge. But my parents always wanted us to get top education. They have the key role in getting us to where we stand now," says Usman beaming with pride.

After completing his Intermediate from Government College, Sahiwal in 2000, Usman joined the University of Engineering and Technology in Lahore (UET). Later, his brothers also moved to Lahore and joined FAST University. "My father could not afford to pay PKR20,000 per semester. Every semester, I would write letters to the vice chancellor to waive some portion of this amount. Similarly, all my brothers were also studying on scholarships."

"I studied Electrical Engineering and graduated in 2003. I had a natural affinity for programming languages and software." Usman was an outstanding student. While at UET, he wrote three papers that were published in IEEE magazine, a leading journal of electrical engineering. He was also the joint holder of a patent for Optical Character Recognition (OCR) technology.

Nurturing Entrepreneurial Dreams

Usman's first job was at Techlogix, a leading software consultancy, as a software engineer. He dreamed of starting his own business. However, as the eldest child of the family he was averse to taking risks.

"I would read Paul Graham's articles avidly. The English computer scientist and founder of Y-Combinator was a source of motivation for me. His articles inspired me to take risks and start my own business.

However, I could not take risks. I had just started my job and was responsible for supporting my family. My three younger brothers were studying at FAST-National University of Computer and Emerging Sciences (FAST-NUCES) and I was helping them financially," he says.

Usman put his dream on hold for the time being so that his brothers could finish college. He was ambitious and hard working, traits that helped him steadily climb the career ladder. When he switched jobs to work for Teradata in 2005, he joined as a senior business intelligence consultant. The position allowed Usman to travel abroad extensively. "I was always travelling to Turkey, Finland, Italy, the United Kingdom. Once while in Finland, Nokia offered me a job which I could not resist," he reminisces.

Usman took the offer, moved to Finland and started his dream assignment with Nokia.

Bilytica

Usman found the environment in Finland supportive of startups. Entrepreneurship was highly encouraged. "I just could not suppress my inner urge to launch a startup. I talked to a few people, including my manager at Nokia. At the time, Nokia was streamlining Human Resources and strategically outsourcing. The manager was very encouraging. He offered me a small project on the condition that I set up an offshore office with at least three people. I immediately grabbed the opportunity," recollects Usman.

Thus, Bilytica (the company name is an abbreviated form of Business Intelligence and Analytics) was born in Finland, in 2008. It was incorporated as a services company, offering a range of business intelligence and analytics services. Usman set up an offshore office in Lahore, in a room in his uncle's house, with just a chair and a table, and worked towards forming a suitable business model. A year later, he asked his brothers to join him.

"Initially, we had two options: Either to look for investors and make our own products or to provide services. We chose the latter, as it provided a steady stream of revenue and was the safer route for us. We also thought it would provide us with more knowledge regarding the business," explains Usman.

First Time Unlucky

Just after Usman had set up Bilytica, a businessman approached him with a proposition for a partnership. The man owned a development company in Saudi Arabia and sought BI (Business Intelligence) resources for the Saudi market. Usman was so excited at the prospect that he immediately made a deal and started working with his first partners. Still young and trusting, he did not worry much about legal paperwork.

The work progressed at lightning speed, with Bilytica and the company signing five projects in Saudi Arabia, worth over US$1 million each.

"It was all moving very fast for us. We were excited and revved up. We quickly employed 60 people and had good revenues lined up within six months. We would train BI analysts and place them in Saudi Arabia to work on the project. We had everything worked out."

Unfortunately, some things are just not meant to be. In six months the partnership went sour, as Usman found the invoices sent to customers not filtering back to Bilytica. Around Saudi Riyal3,500,000 (US$100,000) were due for a year. The entire team became frustrated as bills remained unpaid.

Whenever Usman confronted the partner, he would complain that the work was not satisfactory and the customer had not released the payments. Frustrated, Usman contacted some of the customers directly and found out that the payments had been made months ago. Usman was stunned when he discovered that his partner was holding money back. He realized he had been used.

"Learning to start a company was a roller-coaster ride for me. What you plan doesn't necessarily happen, and you have to be ready for new circumstances that evolve spontaneously. I learnt that we trusted people a lot-a lot more than we should have," a wiser Usman says now.

Usman broke off the deal. To date, he has not received the pending amounts. He had no written agreement and documentation and hence, could not approach the courts.

He recalls, "We learnt the hard way. Now, whenever we start an initiative, even if it is between the brothers, I always make sure we do our paperwork. Having a written agreement is necessary to avoid any problems in the future."

"Legal documentation is necessary at any level. Take all the time you need, but go over the entire legal framework very carefully so that if you ever have to go to court, you have solid proof in your hand."

Making Headway

The partner's betrayal caused huge losses and was a major setback for the team. While Bilytica was just able to keep its head above water through previous billings, the situation was challenging. Usman moonlighted on Finnish projects, which got the company out of the rough patch.

Meanwhile, he started approaching other Saudi contacts. Fortunately, Bilytica was popular in the market and their reputation enabled them to land a contract with another Saudi telecom company, Mobily, enabling a two-year business relationship.

However, they were in hot waters again within two years. They had placed all their bets on just one client. "I learnt that in business you must target multiple partners, vendors and customers. A technology company needs to be working with more than one local vendor or partner, to ensure that if one relationship fails for some reason, the company is still able to survive. Our earlier partners decided to overtake our business. We realized that we had made another mistake," laments Usman. "Thankfully by 2011, we had enough of a footprint to walk away from the partnership with the help of our other Middle Eastern clients and vendors. So this setback had little effect on us."

Usman and his brothers decided to diversify and explore other markets in order to avoid over-dependence on a single partner, a single client or a single market. "You make more enemies than friends in entrepreneurship. The lesson learnt is: Do not put all your eggs in one basket," quips Usman.

Bilytica Takes Off

By 2011, Bilytica had accumulated enough experience and the company was now successful with a good revenue stream. The founding team decided to reevaluate their services strategy. They realized that being a service provider they were only as good as the next project that they had in hand and that both the relationship and the market were generally fickle. They also felt that the time was right to start coming up with their own products, as it would build the company's brand and streamline operations.

"An entrepreneur has to work in multiple dimensions. I learnt that for sustainability we had to provide better, more standardized products, in order to serve more customers in the market," says Usman.

Bilytica changed course and started building its own products. Already working in the BI sector, Usman knew about data analytics and dashboard presenting. Most importantly, he was aware of the customers' and the market's requirements. The next set of projects the team worked on were based on Enterprise Resource Planning System (ERP), a business management software. Usman knew about the challenges in ERPs and, in order to remain in the market, Bilytica offered end-to-end solutions for both ERPs and analytics. He worked with ERPs, studied their problems and customized the systems according to the clients' requirements. With a large happy customer base, their revenue generation increased. They offered a free ERP with the service. Soon Bilytica acquired a larger clientele.

They created their flagship product, Erpisto, a cloud-based ERP that currently has over 30,000 users globally. The target market was oil and gas, microfinance, sales, trade and the retail industries. Erpisto is used in companies across Thailand. Shell Saudi Arabia (held by Al Jumia Holding SA) was among the first customers for whom Usman designed their retail Point of Sale (PoS) system. From three retail PoS systems, Bilytica has grown and now automates a few every year. They have automated close to 100 PoS systems by now and will continue to operate them for the next 10 years. "In fact, worldwide Shell is using another ERP system, but because we were able to satisfy Shell Saudi Arabia, they are using Erpisto," shares Usman.

Full Throttle

One of the early learnings at Bilytica was that they must have their own marketing function. Usman's brother Nauman Ahmed heads the division and his team has been working on an extensive e-marketing campaign for the last eight years. As a result, Bilytica has been generating, on an average, ten queries per day.

One of these queries was from an insurance broker, looking for a company that could work on an industry-specific project. His organization was looking for a vendor for over a year and none had been able to win it over with an appropriate solution.

"I said: 'Let's give it a shot. No one else is doing it. We can'. We started the project with a skeleton team. We also gave the client ownership of the results. Consequently, Bilytica developed a system that served the market better than other existing products," says Usman with pride.

As a result of this dedicated approach and the foresight to develop a product, Bilytica was able to reap rich rewards. After the first project, seven other insurance brokerage firms installed their product. "In Jeddah once, we were able to finalize a US$70,000 deal in under 30 minutes," remembers Usman.

The other strategic decision Usman took was to concentrate on cloud-based systems for small and medium-sized businesses. In the Middle Eastern markets of Turkey, Saudi Arabia and the UAE, individual subscriptions and the cloud business brings in more clientele.

Spreading Their Wings

Next, Usman targeted the microfinance and health sectors. They have done well in microfinance, while they are just beginning to make their presence felt in the health sector.

The health sector product called Cloudpital is cloud-based. Bilytica approached MITEFP for this product line. There were flaws in their product strategy, the marketing research and the associated marketing strategy. They wanted to automate hospitals, but there were holes in the plan. Tweaking Erpisto for hospital management was not the right solution. Usman decided to go with an e-clinic system, which turned out to be a better approach. Deployments are currently underway in Europe.

The team has found its focus. Usman says, "Customer is king and even with three successful ventures, we could not succeed without the customer. An entrepreneur should be flexible, he should focus single-mindedly on a project, ensure its success. Then only should he move on to another project."

A Long Road Ahead

By 2016, after a journey of eight years, Bilytica has grown into a multimillion-dollar business. Starting out as a three-person home office, Bilytica currently employs over 150 employees and has a presence in over 12 countries, including Pakistan, Australia, Peru, Russia, the UAE, the UK, Qatar, Saudi Arabia, Canada, Indonesia and Turkey. As the development campus is in Pakistan, roughly half the employees are based in Lahore, while the rest are in offices around the world.

Bilytica will continue its expansion into international markets through partnerships, and will continue to serve these markets. They plan to focus solely on products by 2018. They have also developed strategic partnerships with financial institutions, to help SMEs (small and medium-sized enterprises) deploy their systems, and to streamline operations.

Usman recalls, "We made many mistakes and miscalculations early on. We also learnt from our setbacks. There is a 99 percent chance that you will fail one day. The earlier you fail, the better it is for you, as you will learn faster. You gain courage and experience from these things. Before this, we had never imagined earning US$1 million and now we are playing with this number every day. That is the power of taking risks and learning from experiences."

Advice for Entrepreneurs

Choosing Your Partners: Be very careful. It is important to look closely at their profiles and ensure that you select established individuals, who have good reputations. Having learnt the hard way, the management now ensures that each business relationship is well defined.

Importance of Proper Legal Agreements: "Always be careful when it comes to legal documentation and agreements," warns Usman.

"It saves the company and its management a lot of hassle in future if the terms and conditions are well defined. It also protects them legally. It is imperative to take the required time to go over the legal framework. So that, if the company needs to go to court in future, the proof of the legalities for the projects or partnerships is readily available."

Legal agreements are also necessary, even if the parties are related. It is important to realize that personal relationships are tricky to navigate. When you mix business with them, you tread a fine path.

Building A Loyal Team: "For me, the team is very important. I have a services company and I focus on my colleagues a great deal. Find the right people and ensure that you retain them. Customers come and go but employees will remain. If they are not loyal, the reputation of the business will suffer. We aim to develop a flat structure in the organization. This enables us to reorganize very quickly and communicate at the speed required by clients. It also empowers the employees to speak their mind," says Usman.

Funding Through Customers: During the initial phase as a startup the best investors are your customers who would be willing to give you a chance and try your product. This means you should focus on your customers from the word go and keep them in the loop while developing your product and services. When the time comes to launch the product, they will be willing to give you a chance and by buying your products and services, they will be giving you the required liquidity for your venture. Therefore, finding investment is not important, customer focus is more important, and people often overlook this fact.

Branding the Company: "For an entrepreneur, the first thing to keep in mind is that your business name is your identity, and you should never let it die. If you are a third-party contractor, ensure that the final customer knows your name as well; otherwise you will feel as if you are nobody. You may be getting a certain amount of money, but your dignity and identity will have been stolen by your partners. Keeping the identity of your company is vital," advises Usman.

Markets and Marketing: "Explore multiple markets. You should not focus on one market from the start. Within a market, start with the right customer. Potential customers will not ask what your product is, but who you are and who your customers are. This will give them the confidence to decide whether to work with you or not," he says.

"To serve a specific market, always build products for industries that you are familiar with. I suggest you choose an industry or find a first customer willing to work with you to give customer insight, even if it is free. The product that you build will help you get the next customer," he recommends.

Financial Management: "One of my major shortcomings was focusing solely on a one-vendor relationship. Had we been careful, we could have avoided a year of instability. One important thing I would like to add is that anyone who wants to form a startup should first work somewhere else to learn the market's cultural norms. It is necessary for anyone who wants his own setup. Financial management is the best thing one can do. After our first financial loss, I hired a financial advisor, because only he is equipped to give a true picture when it comes to numbers. No matter how much I want to embark on new projects, my financial advisor provides a feasibility report which I use to take decisions," Usman concludes.

5

Communicating Business

Evamp &Saanga
Anwar Khan

Founder, Evamp & Saanga
Pakistan, UAE
www.evampsanga.com

"Twenty years from now, you will be more disappointed by the things that you didn't do than by the ones you did do. So throw off the bowlines. Sail away from the safe harbor. Catch the trade winds in your sails. Explore. Dream. Discover." ~ Mark Twain.

Anwar Khan, Evamp & Saanga:

Anwar Khan started his IT services firm in 2000 with a vision to enable and modernize the local industry through technology. In 15 years, prudent partnerships and customer management have allowed this venture to bring in over US$3 million in annual revenues with a total valuation of US$11 million.

Author's Note: Anwar is a true entrepreneur who makes quick decisions, takes risks and changes plans as and when required. Evamp & Saanga's rise is a great example of growth through mergers and alliances. Together, we worked on broadening their vision, enhancing their product lines and securing a more international focus. Their perspective and marketability were areas that demanded attention. With emphasis on proper team building, they benefited from taking their products and services to new markets, while acquiring new skills to serve their initial market segments.

When Anwar Khan returned to Pakistan to work from the UK, he had no idea that he would become one of the founders of a leading web, mobile and telecom solutions developer, serving major blue chip clients in over a dozen countries. What started as a quest to find the ideal employment, ended with Anwar setting up his own venture called Evamp in Islamabad. He later merged his profitable business with another company to acquire their mobile development expertise, becoming Evamp & Saanga in the process.

Launched with a team of just five employees, by 2016 Evamp & Saanga has grown into a 120+-member squad specializing in web, mobile and telecom applications, with a presence in Pakistan and commitments in six countries in the Middle East and East Africa. In just 15 years, the initial investment of PKR400,000 has multiplied, and today the company's top-line revenue is over a couple of million US dollars.

Evamp & Saanga has become a force to reckon with. Through strategic partnerships, mergers with other companies, the firm has an edge over their competitors by offering a one-stop shop. Today they are developing mission-critical systems for some of the largest telecom applications. With meticulous planning, Evamp & Saanga has been able to grow in Pakistan a market typically seen as difficult and challenging, but one that holds unlimited potential for those who stand their ground.

A Tryst with Banking

Anwar Khan comes from a family of agriculturists and ardent travelers. His father served in the Pakistan International Airlines (PIA) and the family relocated frequently to different parts of the world. His fondest memories are of traveling around the world, exploring diverse cultures and meeting people from various backgrounds. His early childhood was spent in Libya, Saudi Arabia and Pakistan. He completed his high school from the International School of Islamabad and pursued a degree in international business and economics at the Richmond University, London, graduating in 1995.

After graduation, Anwar lived in Germany, where his father was posted at the time. He trained at a private German investment bank, BHF (Berliner Handels-und Frankfurter) Bank that focused on agri-loans. During this time, he set up a commodity and trade financing relationship between the National Bank of Pakistan (NBP) and the BHF Bank that lasted several years.

In 1997, Anwar returned to Pakistan wanting to pursue a career in marketing. He had always admired Coca Cola as a brand, and joined the company in Lahore on an internship, with the goal of getting inducted as a management trainee. During his probationary period, a Singaporean bottler took over Coca Cola Pakistan and Anwar was invited to interview with the new HR head to figure out whether he should be taken on under the new management.

On the plane to Karachi, Anwar sat next to a slightly large, middle-aged man. The two ended up nudging each other for the armrest. Anwar laughs as he recalls, "I was going berserk, because we were in a silent war to take over the territory rights of the armrest."

On the fourth or fifth duel, the gentleman turned around and said, *"Aap kya kartey hain?"*[1]

A weary Anwar misunderstood the question, "I thought he had asked me, 'What are you doing?' So I impatiently started explaining that I was uncomfortable, and that he was monopolizing the armrest!"

The man clarified, "No, I am asking what you do. As in, what is your occupation?"

Embarrassed, Anwar explained to him that he was going for an interview at Coca Cola. Introductions were made and Masood Hashim, who worked for Standard Chartered Mercantile Leasing (SCML), insisted, "You should interview with us tomorrow instead."

Anwar went to the interview and was selected by Rana Humayun and Masood Hashim. Working at SCML's Corporate Finance department was an eye opener for Anwar. He learned a lot from Rana Humayun, one of the industry leaders; and Masood Hashim, a perceptive marketing professional good at evaluating people. Later, when Masood Hashim moved to HSBC Bank in Islamabad, he invited Anwar to join him there, which he did, staying there until 2000.

"It is funny how fate decides where to take you, even when you are headed in a different direction," reminisces Anwar.

---

[1] *translation: 'What do you do?' but can also mean 'what are you doing?'*

E-Business Beckons

It was the turn of the century, and e-business was the new phenomenon that was beginning to excite Anwar. Only a few universities were offering degrees in e-business, and the City University in London was one of them. Anwar left his job to enroll in the degree program. Once there, he realized that there were no textbooks for the e-commerce program.

"When I found out that we were going to be studying from photocopies, I felt I was paying too much money for learning things that I could probably read in my spare time. I decided I would make my tuition fees work."

As e-business was all the rage, Anwar asked his father to help him invest in a business, instead of sending him abroad to study. Fortunately, his father agreed.

Anwar started his venture in Islamabad in 2000, around the same time when the dotcom bubble was bursting in the West. In Islamabad however, the telecom sector was just starting out. PTCL was being privatized and new mobile telecom licenses were ready to be auctioned. Anwar realized that the mobile industry was going to be the next big tech sector in Islamabad.

"It was very interesting to learn how things were run. At the time, Pakistan's IT industry was in its nascent stages and the Pakistan Software Export Board was being run out of a small bungalow. The whole industry was learning on its way. If you asked for an NOC (no objection certificate) for something, PSEB officials would simply tell you to write it down, or bring a printout, and they would sign it."

Evamp is Born

In 2000, Anwar launched Evamp. He recalls that at that point the entire e-business and e-commerce boom was just beginning. There was no payment gateway, technology adoption was slow and websites were deplorable. However, he saw the potential in the market and was intrigued by the success of his Uncle Abid Abrar Hussain's IT company that served customers nationwide. Anwar decided that he would start with the basics and tap a niche that was not addressed. The purpose of Evamp was to "revamp" businesses and turn them into e-businesses, explains Anwar.

One of the prospective customers Evamp approached was the cell phone operator Mobilink. At the time, Mobilink had a very basic brochure-ware type of company website, that had simply converted their printed marketing and advertising material into an internet format. It was upgraded once a year.

Evamp pitched to Mobilink offering to build a portal that would engage their customers. Back then, the portal layouts were still evolving and in their initial evolutionary phase. On Evamp's third presentation to Mobilink, one of the two vice presidents liked the idea and gave his approval. Mobilink became Evamp's first account.

Their next project at Mobilink grew out of Evamp's own needs. At that time, if anyone applied for SMS short codes (special phone numbers that are shorter than full phone numbers and can be used to address

MMS and SMS messages from service provider's phones) the approval would take as long as 30 days. Anwar knew that the process should not take more than 30 minutes.

He connected with a friend who was starting a mobile application development company, specifically for Nokia phones. The available sets had limited memory. They pitched to the Mobilink CIO, Tariq Rashid, to streamline the SMS short code process. Tariq was amused, but not very interested at first.

"Tariq Rasheed was very patient with us. He heard us out and asked me a couple of questions for which I had no answers. He said, 'Don't worry. Go work on it and come back'. Ten days later, I had an updated presentation, and after a few meetings, Tariq Rasheed okayed the project. He made it clear that he would not pay us for the application. However, if we built it successfully, he would buy it."

"This was a great opportunity. We built an application that performed perfectly and is still active at Mobilink. Recently, Mobilink asked us to upgrade it. Evamp has also sold the same system to other telecom providers since."

Evamp went on to work for the SME Bank, as well as all the major telecom providers in Pakistan.

Going Global

At the beginning of their second year in business, Anwar decided to go to the US for a vacation. It was supposed to be a leisure trip, but Anwar ended up observing the pace of business in America. Instead of spending two weeks relaxing, he spent five weeks gathering assignments worth US$50,000-a considerable amount back in 2002. He spent his vacation learning: what customers needed, what vendors were charging and what areas to focus on to get better projects.

The dotcom bubble was bursting and while tech companies were packing up in America, Anwar saw an opportunity. He is quick to explain how: "One of the main reasons it was easy to gather these projects, was that our rates were extremely competitive. I was offering a solution that many established companies were unable to offer, as they were downsizing by the hundreds."

Anwar requested his US-based clients to commit to working with his organization for six months at a time. "I was young and did not fear that I would not be able to deliver. I felt that since I have a team that I pay on time, there was no fear. I committed, confident in the knowledge that I could deliver. The direction of my business was literally set."

New Partnerships, New Opportunities

The same year, while Anwar was working on web development, a friend was developing mobile apps at his company, Saanga. After discussing the strategy with him, Anwar decided that he also needed to work in the mobile space and the two companies merged to become Evamp & Saanga. With an investment of PKR450,000, his friend (who wishes to remain anonymous) became an equity partner.

The next merger happened in 2004 while Evamp & Saanga were located at the Software Technology Park in Islamabad. A new tenant, Nasr Sadruddin, whose company was just starting out in Islamabad, had taken the office next door. Anwar recalls, "I had an eye on the office and on the computer equipment, and I thought maybe he would consider packing up and leaving. I wanted to set up a call center and I made Nasr Sadruddin an offer. If he was interested we could use my contacts in London to provide business." Nasr agreed readily, saying, "Why not? I have the required basic infrastructure: computer equipment, the employees and the internet. Let's do it!"

Nasr and Anwar put together their funds and upgraded the infrastructure. However, they lost their first two customers because their calls could not get through to Pakistan. Subsequently, they invested more funds into the business and found a partner in the UK to work with. For the next seven years, they ran a small but successful back-office contact center. Anwar bootstrapped his software business' growth from the money he made through this venture.

By now, Evamp & Saanga had around 15 employees in the services team and around the same number at the BPO set up separately. The nature of the customers and the telecom boom from 2006 to 2010 became the catalyst for the company's growth.

An old-time friend, Ali Shah, became the go-to person for

technology and strategy decisions. He had good exposure with European startups and some of the leading tech companies, and was always a step ahead of the technology trends. During the startup years of Evamp, Ali was a valuable advisor and despite being located in Europe, never hesitated to support Anwar as a friend and a resident technologist. After being asked by Anwar several times in the past, Ali finally decided to join as a partner in 2012, and took the organization to the next level by focusing on a new set of solutions, improving software processes and quality.

The Way Forward

Evamp & Saanga has grown from a five-member team into a 120+-member squad. Outside Pakistan, the organization is currently providing solutions to telcos and enterprises in the Middle East and East Africa. Pakistan remains a major source of revenue streams.

"I started the business with just PKR400,000 in 2000. Today, our top line revenue is in excess of (US$3 million over PKR300 million). [2]*Alhamdulillah*, we have a very strong profit base in our services, call center and mobile applications," says Anwar.

---

[2]*Thank God*

As the telecom sector was evolving, Anwar felt that they had to change as well. The Telcos were evolving into mobile financial services creating a natural direction for Evamp & Saanga. Anwar has now invested in this area. In the last two years, Evamp & Saanga have modified their business model and added product strategy. They are working on developing ideas for various products. Anwar regrets not focusing on service delivery from the beginning.

The other area Evamp & Saanga wants to develop is their mobile app portfolio that can be quite profitable and will help them increase advertising revenues. The organization has created content for its telecom customers, both locally and outside Pakistan, and the team intends to leverage this in the near future.

Advice for Entrepreneurs

Funding: Anwar's father invested personal savings to help him set up business. Anwar kept these funds separately and managed them very carefully. However, with the initial debacle, he ran short of funds and ended up "...selling everything including my stereo system and my DVD player. At one point, I also sold my car. Luckily, my father was changing his car, so I 'borrowed' that for some time. I put this collective money back into the business."

Anwar says they always had business, but stayed short of funds because of outrageously long payment cycles. He advises being prudent with the cash flows of the organization. The revenue cycle for IT companies in Pakistan has not improved much in the last 15 years. Software houses constantly come under pressure, because the software development business is cash hungry. One must quickly generate invoices and follow up aggressively to settle receivables.

Work Before Entrepreneurship: Anwar has two pieces of advice for those considering becoming entrepreneurs. If a person has a clear idea of the business that one wants to get into, one should not waste time. However, one does not have to force oneself if she or he is not completely ready. Anwar advises, "Just because you feel you have what it takes to become a brilliant entrepreneur, it doesn't mean that you should leave everything immediately. Many successful entrepreneurs didn't start their own businesses until much later in life, and statistics show a higher degree of success for people with several years of work experience."

In retrospect, Anwar believes working in an organization instills the required discipline and know-how. From how you talk to how you manage your documentation; how you meet people to how you schedule your day, all becomes very important and can be learnt while working in a corporate environment. He believes experience and a good professional network boost productivity and effectiveness.

"I was never and, I think, I still am not great at managing my schedule. However, if I had not been in Standard Chartered, I would probably not have had the financial discipline required to become an entrepreneur," he says.

Strategy and Planning: In his first year of business, Anwar really planned the way forward with detailed notes on everything. The next 18 months, he spent running around. He did everything: from business development, to changing bulbs and fixing computers. That time was mostly spent firefighting. After the third year, Anwar realized that having lots of business was not translating into additional value. This led him to re-strategize.

In 2012, Anwar attended the MITEFP's business plan competition, where he met Azhar Rizvi and learned the value of planning and strategy. Anwar underwent a strategic planning exercise with his partners.

"The mentors that I met on the way really helped me. Taking advice is not a common practice. Most tech entrepreneurs tend to be arrogant and do not bother listening to people who are more experienced. I often seek advice from the people I trust. I share ideas openly with them because I believe this exercise is always beneficial," says Anwar.

Personality Traits of Entrepreneurs: Perseverance, trust, keen observation, taking calculated risks based on instinct at times and energy are important traits for entrepreneurs. Anwar says that entrepreneurship is a marathon, not a sprint, and it is important to stay in the game.

6
Garage Startup Hits Big Time

Symbios.pk
Muhammad Saad Jangda
Founder and CEO
Karachi
www.symbios.pk

"For e-commerce, the most important thing is trust." ~ Jack Ma, Founder, Alibaba Group

Unemployment forced Saad Jangda to start an e-commerce company in 2006. Started with an initial investment of US$100, Saad now runs one of the largest e-commerce portals in the country, selling 40,000 products in ten different categories to more than three million clients across the country.

Author's Note: Saad Jangda is another great visionary and symbios.pk can be considered a pioneer in Pakistan's e-commerce sector. He came to us in 2013, won the BAP competition and went to the MIT entrepreneurship center for the EDP program.

Initially, the company had restricted itself to the local market. We trained them in collaborating and creating joint ventures with international partners and primed them to take advantage of regional growth opportunities. I am pleasantly surprised to see the change in his vision and capabilities in the past year-and-a-half. He is now moving ahead with global partnerships and investor interests. Symbios.pk is in perfect position to be a major e-commerce engine in Pakistan. Saad's story is a testimonial to his hard work and marketing skills. I recommend that all startups read and learn from his wisdom. Saad gives priceless advice in simple language and is a great source of learning.

"I am sorry, but we are not hiring," came the reply from the other end of the phone line. Once again, Saad Jangda repeated the standard line, "Okay, please let me know when you have a vacancy."

With another job application turned down, Saad shook his head in frustration. "Why won't anyone hire me?" he wondered, distressed and discouraged.

E-commerce was still in its early stages in Pakistan when Saad finally decided to set up his own business in 2006. Symbios.pk quickly became one of the country's leading online shopping portals.

Today, Symbios.pk deals in a variety of electronic goods, home and kitchen appliances and offers 40,000 products in ten different categories. Saad's unique selling proposition is the Cash on Delivery (CoD) policy. Set up with an initial capital of just PKR10,000, symbios.pk is close to hitting annual revenues of PKR100 million.

Ten years down the road, Saad stands proudly in his own office, contentment radiating from his face as he oversees a team of over 60 employees. With more than 300,000 customers and half-a-million completed orders, he is silent for a moment before he reminisces, "It all started when everyone said 'No' and I said 'Yes!'"

Starting Out in The Garage

In 2004, Saad Jangda completed his Bachelor's with a major in Computer Engineering, from Sir Syed Institute of Engineering and Technology, Karachi. Getting an IT degree had become the latest trend in education and several thousand graduates poured into an already saturated job market every year. Armed with a degree at a time when jobs were scarce, it was not surprising that Saad faced considerable difficulty in securing suitable employment.

Facing countless rejections, Saad decided to make productive use of his time. Turning his father's garage into a makeshift workplace, he placed a computer system on a table and started working from home as a freelancer. To sustain himself, Saad created websites and took on graphic design jobs from his friends and family, creating logos, banners and web pages for small companies.

Three months into the business, he met a supplier of Franklin Digital Dictionaries, a renowned American brand that shipped its product from the US. The supplier asked Saad to make a website for the product for PKR4,000. While working on the assignment, Saad circulated an informational message to his email contact list on how to purchase electronic digital dictionaries via email and get them delivered to one's doorsteps. He requested his friends to forward this message to their friends and contacts. He received five orders for the dictionaries; three from Karachi and two from Punjab.

Saad requested the supplier to provide the dictionaries which he refused to do without payment. Therefore, Saad bought three dictionaries, worth PKR5,000 each, off his own money and delivered them to his Karachi clients. For the clients in Sialkot and Faisalabad, Saad was faced with a challenge, as the clients did not want to pay another PKR3,000 for the courier service. Saad turned to his father for advice, who directed him to Pakistan Post's Value Payable Post (VPP) service (now called Cash on Delivery. Saad sent the digital dictionaries to his clients in Punjab through VPP. Both the customers were thrilled, since in 2006 placing an order through email and having the product delivered to the house was practically unheard of.

Saad's first customers in Sialkot and Faisalabad turned out to be major influencers in the region, and drove more clients to him. From five, Saad's customer base soon grew to 20, and he began planning the launch of a website specifically to sell an array of electronic gadgets. Thus, the foundation of Symbios.pk was laid. Today the e-commerce website sells a wide range of products in over 40 categories.

Simplicity is The Name of The Game

Saad faced several challenges when he launched symbios.pk in 2006, since the service was a pioneering one. He counts attracting customers as his biggest challenge. "until you find a customer, you do not know whether your business is good or bad. All of that happens after you have customers," says Saad.

He realised that simplicity was the name of the game. He did not waste money directly on branding nor did he hire a marketing firm. Instead, he started working for his family and friends. By marketing his business in his own circle of influence, he grew the business gradually and steadily and did not worry about biting off more than he could chew.

Talking about the customer base, he says, "Your first customers should be from your friends and family. Give the best goods and services to them and they will open a pathway to the market, providing you with more customers." He felt that if he had a Minimum Viable Product (MVP) that satisfied his customers, finance would not be an issue.

Saad's initial investment was his pocket money. He says that making a minimum viable product like developing an online store did not require much finance. This was what attracted him to the industry. The other criterion for picking inventory was the utility of the product. The product should provide a solution to the target audience.

While overcoming his challenges, he recognized that there was a vast gap in technology in Pakistan and that new startups could fill in that void. In the absence of competition from big companies, young entrepreneurs could easily flourish in the country.

Saad believes that because IT and technology are changing rapidly, there is room for new types of online services. He predicts that this is how technological advancement will occur on a national scale.

Going The Extra Mile

According to Saad, the first law of success is: "Focus on customer service." *Symbios.pk* was born because of his compelling desire to provide his customers with the best. He points out that maintaining customers is harder than making new customers and it should not be taken lightly. Over time, Saad found that with the right products and flexible payment options, customer needs could be addressed. Very early into setting up his business, he had decided he would address other market issues only after his customer base was satisfied and that he would do his best for them. True to his word, he has introduced more than ten product ranges and now reaches nearly every city in Pakistan. He has a team of customer-service representatives who are always active on the website and constantly brainstorm innovative ideas to increase their customer base.

While launching *Symbios.pk,* Saad had targeted students and professionals who were more tech savvy. He feels that word-of-mouth recommendations are an important form of influence in this particular market. In his own words, "Students are easy to market to. If you provide good services to them, they will provide positive word of mouth marketing." He actively marketed to different universities by sponsoring student events. He also markets his products aggressively on social media.

Since he is catering to the Pakistani market, Saad has also introduced instructions in Urdu for better understanding. *Symbios.pk* also uses a business management software, Enterprise Resource Planning (ERP), to monitor the performance of the sales team, marking efficiency through the number of orders and customers. Other departments are also integrated with the ERP to monitor performance and to ensure that no orders lag behind. "We utilize technology to improve the user experience," says Saad.

On A Quest to Find Solutions

Back in 2006, Saad had started providing a service that would create convenience in the lives of many. This became the secret behind *Symbios.pk's* success. Saad focused on discovering what people wanted and then set about delivering it to them. He was also aware that before testing anything on family and friends, he himself would have to test-drive the product.

Speaking about test-driving, Saad says, "The most important question any entrepreneur should answer is whether he himself would use his service. You should step into the customer's shoes and ask yourself if you would pay the said amount for a product, and whether it would be worth it."

Saad recalls that initially he used his pocket money as investment. As the customer base grew, he realized that he would require access to larger sums of money just to keep up the supply chain. Only after he had received a good response from his customers, the suppliers agreed to give him the products on credit. Thus, his supply chain was streamlined and he managed to keep both his customers and suppliers happy. His receivables and payables cycle function this way even today.

After receiving his profits, he invested slowly and did not immediately spend on furniture or office fixtures. He believed that a good quality product and service would keep generating revenue so he deliberated on the way forward.

It is only now, when his business has expanded manifold, that Saad has started looking for external investors. He is predicting that sales will hit PKR100 million in the next five years and feels that this is the right time to accept investors.

Think Solutions

Saad sums up the entire business model of *Symbios.pk* in these words: "The formula for success is providing the ideal solution to the problem."

Starting in 2006, when dial-up internet was the norm, *Symbios.pk* was a pioneering service, the first of its kind in Pakistan. It addressed the needs of customers in smaller Pakistani cities by providing them the gadgets that were only available in big cities like Karachi and Lahore.

When Saad started his business, he did not set out to compete with any of the big companies. He simply pursued his goal of enabling clients to purchase branded gadgets and accessories from their homes.

Initially, he had created a simple HTML page and, for the next three months, only sold digital dictionaries. Selling any item via e-commerce in Pakistan a decade ago was considered a major success, as one happy customer would recommend Symbios.pk to another hundred people thus creating more potential customers. Saad says sales were more important than marketing in the early years and, hence, he focused his energies on generating sales.

In its first year, with an investment of just PKR10,000, Symbios.pk had earned revenues of up to PKR1,000,000.

Saad has a great insight on the importance of sales. "Marketing only gives you customers once. Sales mean that you have been able to retain those customers." That remains his motto to this day. He believes his best strategy was free delivery of products, that attracted a lot of interest and significantly boosted sales. Subsequently, Saad did introduce nominal delivery charges. This, he says, have not really impacted the customer base.

Slow and Steady

Symbios.pk was initially a one-man show. Saad soon hired his cousin at a salary of PKR5,000 for packaging and processing orders. He also hired a rider for purchasing items and for six months, the three team members worked well. Then Saad realized that he needed a sales person and an accountant to manage payables and receivables.

He did not hire too many people at once and chose to strengthen his team slowly but steadily. Currently, *Symbios.pk* has five different departments, with their respective managers and heads. There is a supply-chain department responsible for fulfilling orders, procurement, inventory management, packing, dispatching and quality assurance. The sales department verifies orders and manages customers relationships through a call center. The technology team maintains a user-friendly website, oversees ERP, call center technology platform and its operations. The catalogue team develops products, manages online inventory and vendors, while the finance team is responsible for all financial matters. There are 60 people in the *Symbios.pk* team.

The team is young with Saad being the most senior. He motivates his employees and guides them at every step. He conducts daily meetings to improve productivity and cultivate a friendly environment at the workplace.

Positive Influences

The entrepreneurship journey can be a scary and wild ride at times. It is during such moments that right mentoring can help light up the darkest of paths. A number of people have mentored Saad during his journey and he says, "Entrepreneurs are generally very emotional and passionate, and there are many areas in which we need guidance from experts."

Having a mentor from the same field is very important, as similar background and experience help with the management and resolution of issues at hand and help one avoid mistakes.

Saad won the MITEFP's Business Acceleration Plan and went to MIT for a two-week Enterprise Development Program in 2014. He believes MITEFP played a crucial role in mentoring his startup. He calls it 'the best program to plan and fine tune a business idea'. He feels that the forum was able to help him with pitching, business planning, beta testing and networking in particular. That year he was also a noted member of the prestigious All World Pakistan, an initiative led by Professor Michel Porter of Harvard Business School recognizing upcoming firms from the developed world, 100 Fastest Growing Companies.

Through his pioneering website *Symbios.pk,* Saad Jangda has had a significant impact on e-commerce in Pakistan. His work ethic has helped him achieve a high level of customer satisfaction.

Advice to Entrepreneurs: "Take care to satisfy your customers from the outset. That way you will be able to save the money to be spent on marketing. Instead, use that money to accelerate your business."

On Investing: "Your customers, portfolio, services and ideas are the major way to attract funding from any investor."

7

A Match Well Played

Cricket Companion
Arslan Khakwani
CEO and Founder,
Tricast Media-Cricket Companion
Lahore
www.cricketcompanion.com
www.tricastmedia.com

"First of all, convince yourself that you are the best, because the rest of your life is going to go into proving this to others." ~ Wasim Akram

Marrying their love for sports with their expertise in mobile app development, Arslan's team developed the Cricket Companion, which propelled them into the big league in the world of digital sports. Their software received 1 billion hits, 300 million downloads and a valuation of US$50 million during IPL cricket season of 2011.

Author's Note: Arslan's story is an example of a Pakistani company that developed a great service, got billions of hits and millions of downloads; Yet, it failed to reach its potential because of the absence of a funding vehicle for startups. I believe that if he were in Silicon Valley and had created a similar product for the NBA or Major League Baseball, the firm would have been a Unicorn – a billion dollar firm. I recommend that investment firms and ecosystem players study his story carefully. My role has been to help Arslan's company in formulating a broader vision for their future. We also worked on monetising their efforts and adding new product lines.

Arslan has displayed grit and willpower, as he has battled and overcome cancer to renew his commitment to his dreams. I respect him for his courage and determination. Individuals like him are role models for our youth to follow, not just for their career, but also for their social service. This is one area that has not been highlighted in the story, but I have worked with him quite closely and have seen his efforts to improve the livelihood of common farmers around his area.

The CEO of Cricket Companion and Tricast Media, Arslan Khakwani was born and raised in the rural outskirts of Multan and earned a degree in Computer Science (CS) from Lahore. His CS qualifications proved to be significant in his life, as they led to his co-founding Tricast Media, a mobile app development company.

Marrying their love for sports with their expertise in mobile app development, Arslan's team developed the Cricket Companion, a digital ecosystem that served cricket fans all over the world. With the Cricket Companion, Arslan and his team were propelled into the big league. The extent of his success can be gauged from the following facts and factoids:

At the height of its popularity during the IPL season, the Cricket Companion app was downloaded almost 100,000 times a day. There were 23 million downloads during an IPL season.

The Cricket Companion app and site have been used in 109 countries.

During IPL season, the Cricket Companion site received 1.2 billion hits in a span of 42 days.

The Cricket Companion established partnerships with a number of leagues and cricket boards as the scoreboard of choice, including the Sri Lankan Premier League (SLPL), the Bangladesh Premier League (BPL), the West Indies Cricket Board, as well as the International Cricket Council (ICC).

In 2011, an investment group tentatively valued Tricast Media at US$50 million.

Arslan Khakwani now wants to generalize his learning from the cricket ecosystem into other sports.

From Multan to Massachusetts

Arslan Khakwani is from a wealthy agricultural family and lives on the outskirts of Multan. Since his parents were settled at a farm far from the city, he lived with his paternal grandparents during the school year. Arslan completed his O Levels and Intermediate Science (FSc) in 1995 from Multan Public School.

Arslan enrolled in the Institute of Leadership and Management (ILM) in Lahore and graduated three years later in 1999. While studying for his undergraduate degree, he decided to pursue further education in the United States and transferred his credits to Arizona State University. "After I completed my Bachelor's in Software Engineering in 1999, I enrolled in a Master's in Computer Science program at the University of Massachusetts, graduating in 2003," says Arslan.

Maiden Over at Tricast Media

Arslan joined the consulting firm EMC^2 in Boston as a Systems Analyst. While still at EMC^2, he met Imran Khand, a businessman of Pakistani-origin based in Glasgow. Khand owned a group of companies called the Picsel Group. In 2000-2001, he had developed the Apple technology for mobiles that enabled "zooming in and zooming out" by pinching fingers, as well as flipping through pictures.

Arslan asked Khand to partner with him, and a mentor whom he trusted. An institution in himself, Dr. Hasan Sohaib Murad, Founder and Director of the University of Management and Technology (UMT), had been Arslan's mentor and guide and helped Arslan to set up a software house Tricast Media in 2006 at Lahore.

"In the early days, we focused on developing an SDK (software development kit) for Symbian (Nokia) mobiles. We developed small utility widgets, such as the one that would enable moving personal data from one phone to another. We believe that Tricast Media was the first software house to bring mobile software development to Pakistan. Tricast Media developed the Symbian platform for Nokia and Sony Ericsson using our proprietary SDK," says Arslan.

Tricast Media set up an office in the United Kingdom. Dr Salman and Dr. Ehsan Riaz looked after UK interests, while Dr. Majid Anwar and Imran Khand became partners. In Lahore, Dr. Hasan Sohaib Murad and Arslan looked after Tricast Media Development.

"Dr. Hasan Sohaib Murad is my mentor. He is a great institution in himself. I always look forward to his guidance. I consider myself lucky to have Dr. Hasan in my life", say's Arslan.

Becoming A Mobile Application Mogul

"I dreamt of us becoming the Google of mobile phones; developing free mobile applications, distributing them in the market in order to develop a community, and earning through them. This is the model Google uses for its web presence," recalls Arslan.

With one eye on the goal, Arslan gathered young enthusiasts and nurtured a 65-strong team of developers. Pakistani universities were still not teaching mobile application development; and so the Lahore office trained the new hires. After mastering the process, the new team members would be assigned to Tricast Media UK and Picsel Technologies. Passionate about sports, the team developed 15 sports mobile applications in 2005. These included Football Companion, Cricket Companion and Office Companion, all of which met with limited success.

Things turned around when the team developed the Boomerang app which suddenly propelled them into a different league altogether. Boomerang facilitated mobile phone contact transfers from one phone to another. Back in 2006, this was an innovative idea as transferring contacts was still a cumbersome task. Boomerang allowed contact information to be easily transferred to another phone.

Tricast also came up with the Unicornapp, another innovation. "We developed the Unicornapp in 2006. This was a consolidated chatting software. The instant messenger space was a craze back then and many desktops had separate chatting apps such as ICQ, MSN and Yahoo Messengers. We developed the Unicornapp that aggregated all feeds to open on one screen. If you logged in through Unicorn, you would automatically be logged into all these messengers and could chat through one window. However, due to a lack of funding, the project could not take off."

Nevertheless, it was an exciting time for Tricast Media. "The services we offered were perfectly timed as mobile technology was new. The opportunities for service providers to develop apps and small programs for mobile use were immense. We were developing in Symbian technology, the operating platform for the popular Nokia phones," explains Arslan.

Losing Khand

Even though these were heady days for Tricast and Picsel, the companies were not generating revenue. Tricast was a product-development company and in 2006, earning through mobile apps had become difficult due to stiff competition. However, the founders continued to harbor big dreams and ambitions.

Tragedy struck when Imran Khand, the mastermind and mentor of the team, was diagnosed with colon cancer and his health deteriorated. This had a devastating effect on Tricast media and the team as they lost their mentor and investor. At the same time, Picsel filed a lawsuit against Apple over IP infringements. This was a heavily cash-intensive exercise."It was like an IT earthquake had hit us! Imran was ill, his company lost credibility and value and the onslaught of new technologies killed many of our products. We required an immense amount of funds to sustain us, as our cash burn was significant," says Arslan, wincing at the memory.

Cricket Companion

It was during this upheaval that the team met Sardar Muhammad Ghalib. He was a Pakistani businessman based in Dubai, who owned a technology company called Tech Access-the sole distributor of Sun Microsystems in Dubai. Sardar Ghalib was a passionate cricket enthusiast and a patriot to the core. He knew Arslan's father and wanted to discuss business opportunities. Incidentally, Arslan had Cricket Companion with him on his phone when he met Sardar Ghalib.

"I was honored to have met Mr. Ghalib. He is a towering personality. At that time, ESPN-Cricinfo was the leading company with a strong web presence. The Cricket Companion was a simple app that could be used to follow the team scores on the go-a scorecard available on the mobile and the only sports application in Pakistan at the time," says Arslan with pride.

"I presented a demo to Mr. Ghalib, who immediately realized the value of our product. He introduced us to Telenor that partnered with us to launch Cricket Companion during the Cricket World Cup in March 2007," remembers Arslan.

What happened next was something no one had expected. "Cricket fans went wild! This was the first-ever sports mobile app in Pakistan."

The team's fortunes turned around and snowballed. Sardar Ghalib invested US$1 million in the Cricket Companion, and created a separate sports media company based in Dubai. The IT services and app development was managed by Tricast in Pakistan. The Cricket Companion was positioned as a sports media company focused on digital cricket.

With the Indian Premier League (IPL) launch in 2008, things were going to get even better. The first season was about to go live when BCCI (The Board of Control for Cricket in India) was ditched by their digital vendor, just two weeks before the launch on April 5, 2008.

"The Founder of IPL, Lalit Modi, found out about us and got in touch," Arslan beams at the memory. "He asked us if we could establish a web and a mobile portal in two weeks."

"Yes!" replied Arslan knowing that a less decisive answer would just not do. "Taking on the BCCI as a client was a brilliant opportunity." Arslan is visibly elated as he talks about the IPL breakthrough, "The whole world goes to Bangalore for IT development and Bangalore was coming to Lahore. It was a huge honor for us."

The Cricket Companion was declared the official mobile cricket scorecard of IPL for three years, from 2008 to 2010. The complete solution-design, development, hosting and maintenance of the IT infrastructure of the IPL was outsourced to Tricast Media.

"We started development immediately and the young team did incredibly well. I moved into the Cricket Companion office along with many members of our team. We had our beds put in there before the launch. We were sleeping and eating at the office, we were on a roll!" remembers Arslan.

"Of course this would not have been possible without my team, Muhammad, Ibrahim, Adnan, Waqar, Rizwan Haider, Bilal Alam, Saqib Shahzad, Mehdi Raza, Sajjad Awan and others. They are all absolutely amazing team players."

As the official mobile cricket scorecard of the IPL, the Cricket Companion was now on the world stage. It was the leading mobile software and the go-to site for IPL, and the team's efforts were recognized internationally. Cricket fans loved the app as it enabled them to track scores in real-time. Sony Ericsson gave the Cricket Companion an award for the best mobile application in 2008 and 2009. Tricast efforts were also rewarded in India, when the Cricket Companion appeared at number three on the Top 10 best mobile applications list. The Cricket Companion went on to become the best sports mobile application the most followed sports mobile application, and the most downloaded sports mobile application in India. Even today, after the contract between the IPL and Tricast has ended, the architecture of the IPL Digital presence remains the same as the one the Cricket Companion team had developed.

Scoring High

Partnerships with telecom operators, cricket leagues, endorsements and advertising, generated revenue for the company. "I remember, I would proudly tell everyone that as we sip our cups of coffee, Cricket Companion will have been downloaded 15,000 to 20,000 times. We reached 23 million downloads in 109 countries, and this was not only during the IPL. We had become the cricket scorecard of choice for 109 countries and were featuring all international cricket matches, be it a T20 or any other match," reminisced Arslan about those exhilarating days.

The traffic throughout the IPL was tremendous. During the 42 days of the season, there were 1.2 billion hits on their site. There were hundreds and thousands of concurrent hits. The Cricket Companion CTO (Chief Technology Officer) worked closely with CTOs of Facebook and Yahoo to ensure that the site remained responsive and did not buckle under high traffic, that could go up to millions per second.

"We worked out a solution and divided the traffic into three regions based on geography. Then we distributed the traffic load into three different servers from different regions. From a technology point of view, we evolved as the most modern digital cricket company," explains Arslan, and quickly adds, "Perhaps we still are."

Where There is Cricket, There is Cricket Companion

After their initial success, the team continued to develop new products and services. Their basic mobile on-the-go scorecard, the FirstSlip app, evolved into a comprehensive site for cricket fans worldwide. The first add-on to the service was a web portal. In 2008, the Cricket Companion featured highlights of IPL matches on YouTube, along with a live-stream option. Later three technology platforms, WAP, mobile and web were added.

"To streamline all of this, we developed a customized Content Management System (CMS) to cater to the various interfaces, protocols and regions that we were serving. We added an IP intelligent ad server, Brandwitise, to the CMS. This technology made it possible for different companies, such as Pepsi, to show different ads in India and Pakistan. The IP-sensitive technology ad server was programmed to deliver advertisements at different times and at different places. For instance, we would show a Coke ad in Pakistan and a beer ad in South Africa. Even in one country (e.g. Pakistan) it enabled us to run different Coke ads to different audiences," elaborates Arslan.

Next, the team developed Cricket Genius, an app that could throw a sponsored quiz at run time to the audience.

In 2009, Cricket Companion collaborated with Nokia to launch a game called Fantasy Cricket League, in which the players could create, sell and monitor their dream teams. This required 13 different systems and apps for web and mobile in order to reach audiences worldwide. A new nomenclature was coined to define this system that was becoming all the rage: the Cricket Sports Ecosystem.

After IPL had picked Tricast for the development of the entire ecology of the digital cricket industry, the Cricket Companion went into partnership with several other cricket bodies, including the Sri Lankan Premier League (SLPL), the Bangladesh Premier League (BPL), the West Indies Cricket Board, and the International Cricket Council (ICC). Various local and global cricket clubs, such as the Canadian Cricket League, were also using the Cricket Companion. Currently, Tricast has 17 such clients that read like the Who's Who of international cricket.

Wide Ball

By 2011, the Cricket Companion was dominating the digital cricket industry. "A number of investors were eyeing our startup. An Indian investor offered to buy us out for US$4 million the same year, a reasonable offer given that our contract with IPL was about to end, and BCCI was also looking for reasons to disassociate with all things related to Lalit Modi."

"An investment group tentatively valued us at US$50 million in 2011. We were just about to go to Silicon Valley to seal the deal, when a series of mishaps struck."

In 2011, Lalit Modi was accused of corruption. BCCI (Board of Control for Cricket in India) started cancelling contracts prematurely with all previous contractors. The World Cup was to be held that year in India and IPL was in a state of flux. Then Nokia started facing stiff competition from emerging iOS and Android technologies. "As we were primarily working with Symbian technologies, we failed to estimate the impact of Android and iOS technologies. All of a sudden, from being market leaders, we were left behind trying to catch up with market trends. The Silicon Valley deal died and the Indian investor also withdrew his offer," Arslan remembers. The experience taught him that for an IT entrepreneur, the first offer is always the best, no matter what it may be.

Soon thereafter, Arslan went through an upheaval in his personal life when he was also diagnosed with cancer. Between 2011 and 2014, he fought for his health and the viability of his organization.

However, the team continued to work hard. Between 2012 and 2014, the Cricket Companion received numerous accolades including the Best Mobile Application Award at the national level P@SHA ICT Awards.

Arslan also participated in the MITEFP- Business Plan Competition in 2014 and 2015 and was one of the finalists in the category.

From Cricket Companion to Sports Companion

All major telecom operators in cricket playing countries have associated with Cricket Companion to launch or package the apps and services. In Pakistan, they are associated with Mobilink, Zong, Telenor, Warid, Ufone and Wateen; and internationally in Dubai with Du, in the UK with Orange Telecom, in India with Airtel, and in West Indies with Vodaphone, among others.

Cricket Companion is looking to develop revenue-generating streams. To monetize existing apps and digital assets, the team plans to market Brandvertise, the online advertisement exchange, for sports events. The team is also developing a generic sports portal to address global sports fans. They are also planning an online merchandising store for fan paraphernalia.

In addition, the team is developing a generic app called the Sports Companion for all sports fans. The Sports Companion will enable fans to develop communities around the team sports they play. The Sports Companion will go beyond a few thousand international players to the sports being played on the streets and in parks. The idea is to help fans and sports people track their interests, their scores, their matches and much more. The team is also working on the screen integration of the mobile app with an app that allows sports fans to chat while watching a match. Talking about the roller-coaster ride of the last few years, Arslan says, "The best thing is that my core team has remained intact. Mehdi Raza and I were especially invited by the Facebook CTO for a meeting in Dubai, as he wanted to meet the technical wizards behind Cricket Companion."

Advice for Entrepreneurs

Participating in Competitions and Mentoring: Arslan has participated at the MITEFP Business Plan Competition thrice and each time the experience has energized him and opened his eyes to new possibilities. He has been mentored by many, including individuals from Silicon Valley, people he met through OPEN (Organization of Pakistani Entrepreneurs and Professionals), entrepreneurs and prominent

Pakistanis, such as Azhar Rizvi, Zahir Syed and Jehanara. In Arslan's opinion, these individuals are Godsend for the IT industry, as they are passionate about their work and patient while mentoring and guiding their protégés to achieve the next big thing.

Following Passions and Thinking Big: Arslan strongly advises entrepreneurs to follow their passion, rather than money. He believes if you have an idea that you are passionate about, the money will follow. He advises pitching ideas at every opportunity, whether in Silicon Valley, San Francisco, or at the Sydney Silicon Valley. "Go and pitch the idea in the market, even if property needs to be sold, or directors' salaries need to be cut, do it. Venture into these markets and buy that plane ticket."

Big Ideas: Arslan considers all passionate ideas to be big ideas, no matter how small or simple they may seem. "Every passionate idea is a big idea, every passionate idea is a stellar idea. And every passionate idea will fetch you funding. But it should be an idea with real passion behind it," stresses Arslan. He recommends developing a solid prototype to turn the idea into a hit.

Engaging Customers Through a Coherent Marketing Strategy: Arslan recommends engaging the customer only when a product is fully developed, matured and funds are available for marketing. A comprehensive marketing strategy is imperative to acquire a significant amount of funding.

"First you should be totally sold on your idea," Arslan pauses and thinks about his statement before continuing, 'No, not just sold on it, but beyond that. For instance with the Cricket Companion, I would tell people that with this idea, I will become the Google of mobile phones. I was so passionate about it that I used to believe and say that there is no business in the world other than this."

The Dream Team: Arslan approached investors only with his passion. He did not develop a go-to-market strategy for investors to review. Arslan maintains that a dream work-team needs "manic marketers, along with manic engineers." He feels he made a mistake by not hiring aggressive marketers earlier on. He now knows that having a marketer on the team right from the beginning helps drive the company's passion according to the market hunger or needs.

Having a financial expert on the team, who makes projects financially viable and can stand up to the CEO for certain decisions, is a brilliant asset. He also recommends inducting an experienced entrepreneur in the team as everyone can learn and build on his or her knowledge. Arslan suggests that all team members must socialize to build their network and interact with new individuals, creating new contacts wherever they go, as this helps develop the company's business. He advises that the CEO has to depend on and trust the team, and remain calm under pressure.

When asked what he thinks are the ingredients that make a business successful, Arslan is quick to reply, "Passion and teamwork."

8
Sending Love Your Way

Tohfay.com
Shahzad Qureshi
Co-founder
Karachi
www.tohfay.com,
www.mamooinpakistan.com

"It's not how much we give, but how much love we put into giving."
~ Mother Teresa.

At the turn of the century, Shahzad Qureshi and Mehdi Hasnain started a small e-commerce store selling Pakistani handicrafts in the US. They spun off a gifting service for the Pakistani diaspora who wanted to send gifts back home. Little did they realize that they would be setting the pace of e-commerce adoption in their home country.

Author's Note: This is the story of two friends who developed an e-commerce portal in the pre-Google era. Our collaboration resulted in their training in logistics, marketing and attracting investment. My association with them continued even after BAP was over and we worked together on areas like partnerships and branding.

Tohfay.com is a great example of servicing a market. It is a business model that has matured into a great platform and continues to evolve. The team's other company is mamooinpakistan.com, a concierge service which handles sensitive paperwork for its clients. Their efforts show that Pakistan offers tremendous opportunities to explore and build dream ventures.

While enrolled in a textile engineering course, Shahzad Qureshi had never imagined that one day he would be changing the face of e-commerce in Pakistan with an online gifting service.

Tohfay.com was born when Shahzad, Mehdi Hasnain and their

partners decided to source handicrafts from Pakistan to the US, Canada and the UK. In an unexpected turn of events, the venture failed, but a small branch of the business, which allowed overseas Pakistanis to send gifts back home, started generating a healthy revenue and grew rapidly to become a well-known name in the market. What started as a small investment of US$10,000 between the partners has swelled into a pool of over half-a-million dollars. The entrepreneurial startup now employs 35 people, with many others on contract.

Today the partners consider Tohfay.com as their gift to the Pakistani diaspora connecting them to family and friends back home.

An Uneasy Homecoming

After studying Industrial Manufacturing for two years at the University of Oklahoma, Shahzad Qureshi decided that it was the wrong major for him. He transferred to the Philadelphia College of Textile and Sciences, where he completed his BE in Textile Engineering before returning to Pakistan in 1996.

Shahzad came back to difficult times, as his hometown Karachi was in the throes of endless rioting and the general law and order situation in Pakistan was deteriorating rapidly. Many questioned the sanity of his decision, but Shahzad chose to stay quiet, mainly because he was nurturing a burning desire to give back to his country, to contribute to its progress, well being.

His first job after coming back was in Société Générale de Surveillance Pakistan (SGS Pakistan), a quality and inspection company that he joined in 1996. Shahzad worked with the company for about a year. During this time, his family established a factory in collaboration. The company would be the first of its kind to manufacture calcium carbide locally. It functioned for a year, before there was a falling out between the partners. Shahzad spent the next eight years visiting courts to settle the issues with partners.

Guided by Passion

Textile had always been his passion and in 2000, while still working with an organization, Shahzad started a sourcing company for Canadian and US buyers of textiles, garments, fabrics, curtains and a variety of clothing as a side business. He managed all the resources and arranged to ensure successful fulfillment of orders. In the US, his partners would manage the marketing and sale of the products. He was sending a variety of Pakistani goods, such as textile garments, marble and onyx handicrafts, cushions, covers and several other items to the US.

It was mid-1990s and nobody had heard of e-commerce retailing. Amazon was launched in 1995 while e-commerce was still limited. The concept of banking and online payments was not widespread, but was fast gaining acceptance. In 1996, Google was born and online advertising became easier.

Encouraged by the trends, Shahzad and his partners created a website for selling handicraft in the US. He wanted to give his business an eastern flavor and settled on the name Tohfay, which means 'gift' in Urdu. The original website displayed the inventory that was available for export. Initially the plan was to attract Americans and foreign customers with local handicrafts and other items. However, in one corner of the homepage, there was a link to an option to send items back to Pakistan. Shahzad wanted to sell beautiful traditional items to foreigners through Tohfay.com, simultaneously providing Pakistanis living abroad a service through which they could send gifts back home.

Shahzad worked hard for his venture. He personally photographed all the items perfectly and stocked up on the inventory. The original website had an eastern, specifically Pakistani vibe, and even the first logo depicted eastern values. High product quality and prompt delivery were two prime objectives.

Adjusting The Sails

Soon, feasibility issues began to crop up and the partners realized they could not maintain a large inventory in the US, as warehousing and inventory buildup was costing a lot. The items were becoming a liability. Those were still early days of the internet and search engines like Google had not yet taken off, marketing also became an issue and the handicraft venture collapsed. However, the corner of the website catering to non-resident Pakistanis wanting to send gifts back home was attracting attention steadily. What was supposed to be Tohfay.com's secondary source of income was growing faster than anyone had expected.

This was a pivotal point for the fledgling startup fast becoming a major source of revenue for the venture. The team decided to change its audience and started targeting Pakistani expatriates. They promoted their business via international newspapers, news channels that catered to the Pakistani population and set up stalls in different parts of the US and Canada. This new focus of the business was growing organically but rapidly. People would approach Shahzad's company in the US and deliveries would be made in Pakistan.

Initially, Tohfay.com used existing courier services. However, with the rapid growth of orders, they inducted their own on-ground staff in various cities. They realized they could not rely on other organizations to satisfy their customers, and began to deploy their own riders. With the previous courier services, they could reach up to 30 or 40 cities within Pakistan, but with their own riders in place, they were able to extend their reach immensely. His partner, Mehdi Hasnain and team in the US would collect the orders and Shahzad's team in Pakistan would ensure their seamless execution at this end. The deliveries were a crucial part of the task as customers tended to be selective and very sensitive about this matter.

Customer is King

Tohfay.com's new riders were working solely for them and following their protocols of quality assurance to the tee. Shahzad had to work hard to groom these new people. They also signed contracts in different cities and so Tohfay.com started expanding slowly and steadily. All modes of transport were thought through, and the transportation process was scrutinized minutely.

The intense focus on customer service and delivery has paid off for Tohfay. To date, the site has handled over half-a-million customers and Shahzad does all he can to ensure their satisfaction. The website receives around 3,000 to 4,000 orders monthly, and the team remains vigilant and steady in their work.

Another important benefit of Tohfay.com was the wide variety of products it offered. Unlike other gifting sites, Tohfay.com offered a multitude of items and created offers that were very attractive to the public.

All in A Day's Work

As a pioneering venture for expatriate Pakistanis, the service was well received. However, not all orders were customized gifts. Some orders that the team handled were somewhat unusual, such as one by a cab driver in the US who wanted to gift his son a bike in Sukkur. The team executed that order with perfection. When a customer wanted to send a refrigerator to his family, Tohfay.com proved to be the ideal choice.

The team offers services like flexible payment plans, midnight gifting, meal coupons and time-specific deliveries as an added bonus for its customers. While Tohfay's mantra is to serve expatriates to the best of its abilities, the team has also learned to say no to customers who ask for services that are not available, without sounding rude.

In 2004, three years into the business, what used to be a trickle of customers soon turned into a flood. As e-commerce took off and customer awareness increased, online orders flooded in. Earlier people would call in to enquire about the different products, but now the website was becoming popular. The balance sheets became a lot happier too.

What had started out as a personal passion for Shahzad and his friends was now blooming and changing their lives. They had unconsciously created something that would touch lives across the globe. Tohfay.com developed an immense bond of trust with its loyal customers. Shahzad recalls a story:

"One day I got a call from the US asking, 'Do you have roses?' We replied, 'Yes, of course.' The customer asked, 'Do you have riders available in Pakistan?' We said, 'Yes, of course' Then he said, 'I have been in the US for 25 years, and I haven't been able to go back to Pakistan. My father has passed away, so can you please arrange a wreath for my father's grave?' For two minutes, we were in a state of shock, but since we had absolutely no tradition of refusing the customer, we replied, 'Yes sir, of course we will do it.' So, we got hold of an Imam (religious cleric), reached the graveyard and searched for his fathers grave, as the customer did not know where it was. We found the grave, arranged the flowers and said a prayer. We even took photographs to satisfy the customer."

The Sky is The Limit

In 2007, Shahzad discovered that all of a sudden, they were receiving many odd-sounding orders. To cater to these, he decided to create a separate website and business unit called mamooinpakistan.com.

It was a concierge service for hiring of maids, applying for passports, travel-related documentation, property management, marriage verifications, birth certificates, attestations and translations. Mamooinpakistan.com took on these tasks as a personal priority, carrying out the work faithfully and leaving customers thrilled.

Shahzad laughs as he recalls processing a few orders of divorce notices too. Mamooinpakistan.com has also arranged wedding ceremonies and birthday parties, as well as found nurses for old parents. They have gifted and installed air conditioners too. To up the game, Shahzad contracted a legal team to vet the process.

Mamooinpakistan.com became extremely popular with expatriates, for a wide number of services their relatives back home could not find time to handle. Talking about the potential of this business, Shahzad says, "Sky is the limit."

Focusing on Pakistan

While orders from abroad were steadily growing, it took time for e-commerce to really take off in Pakistan. People only started recognizing its convenience in 2012, that is when its popularity skyrocketed. With the introduction of EasyPaisa, credit card systems, online banking and most importantly Cash on Delivery (CoD), potential customers showed immense interest in online gift services.

Earlier, Pakistanis were not used to online payment methods. With the boom in e-commerce, the team set up a portal for customers in Pakistan adopting a fresh brand strategy and newer and effective marketing techniques. Tohfay.com reentered the Pakistani market with pomp and show. This proved very effective. Corporations reached out and asked for their services.

Tohfay.com introduced new packages and promotional offers and set up stalls in parks and malls, distributing pamphlets and setting up flexible payment methods. Word of mouth and referrals popularised the service. They were using Google adverts and television ads in the US, the UK, Canada and the UAE and successfully tried similar approaches in Pakistan.

Due to extensive marketing, the orders came in huge numbers. Mother's Day became the biggest and the most hectic season, followed by Eid and Valentine's Day.

Shahzad says, "I mark 2012 as the start of the e-commerce industry in Pakistan. That was when rocket internet ventures came to Pakistan with US$10 million and earned up to US$50 million."

In Shahzad's words, "My take is that no knight in shining armor is going to come from outside. More and more of the world is realizing that viable businesses have to be funded. The value of e-commerce is now apparent; and it is rapidly expanding in the South Asian market."

He believes that the unicorn era, during which startups were valued at US$1 billion or more, is not always adaptable. That can only happen where there is deep penetration and acceptance. A business must be viable and stable. Shahzad started the venture as a one-man army. He, along with Mehdi, worked extensively and later brought in two more partners. By 2012, they also took on an equity-based investor, but Shahzad and Mehdi continue to be hands-on about their business.

Now with over half-a-million products and a promising new year, Shahzad says they have enough revenues to be happy and their profits are increasing.

Key Advice to Entrepreneurs

Vendor Relationships: Shahzad keeps pressure on vendors not for price but product quality. He always seeks innovative vendors who have to be trained extensively to be keep up with the trends. Speaking about relationships with vendors, Shahzad says that the relationship should always be respectful; however, any compromise on quality should lead to immediate termination of the contract. Payments must always be on time and everyone must be aware of the values of your company. One must always be connected.

Customer Satisfaction: Customer satisfaction is a key area of focus for Tohfay.com and every member of the company, whether in logistics or sales, pitches in, especially during peak seasons, to ensure prompt deliveries. Despite being the Chief Resource Officer, Shahzad himself goes out for deliveries, sometimes even in the middle of the night to portray the best image of Tohfay.com and new recruits are first inducted in the customer satisfaction department. While hiring, Shahzad is careful that the new entrants will understand their roles, fit the job description, have a professional attitude to work and display a strong work ethic. Mehdi and Shahzad sacrifice their holidays and festive occasions for Tohfay.com and are in the office till late night and early morning, loading trucks, wrapping gifts and making deliveries. They expect their employees to do the same. They do manual work alongside other workers when required, and keep an open environment at the workplace.

Recipe for The Perfect Partnership: Shahzad did not start his venture alone. He has four partners. Mehdi Hasnain is the Chief Executive Officer (CEO) of Tohfay.com and Shahzad is its Chief Resource Officer (CRO). In a world where navigating partnership, whether it is with spouses, friends or business partners is tricky at best, Shahzad has had a successful partnership for about 20 years now and has kept his dream alive.

The remarkable thing about Tohfay.com is that Shahzad and Mehdi were functioning on different continents; one was in Pakistan, while the other was in the USA, yet they never had a falling out.

It is critical that there are never any communication gaps between partners. It is imperative that there be blind trust between partners along with open and honest communication. He believes that finding the right partner and testing him is something that should be done in the early phase of a business.

Importance of Written Contracts: With 30 regular employees and several under contract, Shahzad says that it is important to find the right person in time and put everything in writing.

Networking and Cultivating Relationships: When Shahzad returned from the US in 1996, he joined the Rotary Club and remains an enthusiastic member to date. He fondly shares that his social circle at the Rotary Club is still his primary circle of friends. He says that all his energy, habits and skills are a result of the training and atmosphere at the club. He attributes his personal growth, self-confidence and social skills to being a Rotarian. Being in the Rotary Club was also beneficial for networking and the club has been supportive of Tohfay.com.

Entrepreneurship is Like Planting A Tree: Shahzad believes that businesses should be allowed to grow organically. He believes that every business' story is unique. In Tohfay.com's case, all the partners had different primary jobs and the gifting service was like a pet project, which they let grow at its own pace. They were, of course concerned about the revenues, but did not rely on this passion for their bread and butter, and would only pitch in whenever the need arose. The supply and demand chain is something that he believes should be the focus of the business, and cash inflow should be accordingly.

9

Putting Urdu on the Web

Hamariweb.com
Abrar Ahmed
CEO and Founder
Karachi
www.hamariweb.com

"If you just work on stuff that you like and you're passionate about, you don't have to have a master plan with how things will play out."- Mark Zuckerberg, Founder of Facebook.

Abrar believed that his Urdu-medium education would prove to be a hurdle in his career. Today he runs one of the largest Urdu-language portal Hamariweb.com in the world, which receives an average of 16 million hits every month and over 500 million visitors every year. Hamariweb.com ranks among the top 10 Pakistani websites and the top 1,300 in the world, serving millions of Urdu-speaking community members daily.

Author's Note: My friend Abrar's story is a classic road map for aspiring entrepreneurs. He came to our program (BAP) in 2015 and although he did not win, he was among the finalists who impressed all the mentors and judges. We helped him monetize his massive clientele of 500 milllion using the portal, worked on revenue growth, and on adding product lines specific to customers' needs. Working with Abrar, we helped him identify new and more profitable customer segments and add new services resulting in increased financial and customer growth.

He has now ventured into e-commerce and in six months has established a great website that sells women's clothing and home products. I am sure all those who want to start a venture and lack funds, will learn from his story. Abrar has clearly demonstrated how clarity of vision and hard work can help you achieve your goals and become a top star in your field. Today Hamariweb.com stands tall among local portals in Pakistan and is ranked among the top 1300 in the world.

The CEO and Founder of Hamariweb.com, Abrar Ahmed, started his entrepreneurial journey in 2001 while Pakistan's online industry was still in its infancy.

After a stint at a technical marketing firm, Abrar Ahmed joined an e-commerce startup called Herbsmd.com and helped it reach US$3 million in sales. In 2006, Abrar laid the foundations of Webiz Media and Hamariweb.com. Today, Hamariweb is proving itself to be the leading web portal in the country with a user base of 12 million and 18 million visits every month. The website is ranked amongst the top 1,300 websites of the world, and also features on the list of the top 20 Pakistani sites, according to Alexa Rank. The company was also ranked on the list of the 'Top 100 Fast Growth Companies of Pakistan' in 2012.

After managing info-portals, Abrar and his team has ventured into online retail also. In late 2015, he and his team launched ShopRex.com, an online store that delivered 35,000 consignments in its first year.

Against All Odds

Abrar was Born in Jhelum and grew up in Karachi where his father was laying the foundations of the family's transport business. He was just 12 years old when his father suffered a heart attack and passed away. The extended family took over the business and took on the responsibility of educating and bringing up Abrar and his siblings.

Abrar cites his father as the greatest inspiration behind choosing the entrepreneurial path. His ambitions motivated him to develop his interest in emerging technologies. Abrar fueled these aspirations by creating simple home automation systems before jumping into the online space.

He was educated in an Urdu-medium government school, which helped him become proficient in the language. Fascinated with engineering, the young Abrar assembled toy cars from automotive toy parts, designed models of houses with anti-burglary systems and automated entry systems while still in school.

After completing his Matriculation, Abrar wanted to pursue an engineering degree. However, his grades did not meet the requirements of his university of choice and he had to let go of that dream. He enrolled in a Bachelor's of Commerce program. Later, he joined a foundation course at ICMAP (Institute of Chartered and Management Association of Pakistan) but soon realized that the course did not interest him and started looking at other options. Inspired by the legendary entrepreneur, scholar and philanthropist, Hakeem Muhammad Said, Abrar applied for admission in the MBA course at Hamdard University, where he joined the first batch. "I used to read Hamdard Naunehal magazine as a child and its founder Hakeem Said was someone I admired greatly. I felt very privileged when I was granted admission in a university that he had set up."

While enrolled in the MBA program, Abrar's background in Urdu proved to be a hindrance. He faced several communication issues and had trouble grasping certain concepts. However, He overcame these obstacles and became one of the 32 students who graduated, out of a batch of 50.

Abrar's experience at Hamdard University strengthened his belief that studying in a prestigious institution shapes an individual's personality, revealing his/her strengths and weaknesses. While still at Hamdard University, he set several targets that he intended to achieve within a year.

At Hamdard, he met a mentor, Ahmed Raza, his statistics instructor. Ahmed Raza, who was a graduate of Cambridge University, believed in grooming his students. "He taught us life ethics more than he taught us statistics," recalls Abrar. Ahmed Raza taught him not to be afraid of failure, reminding Abrar that, "It is not the end of the world."

Talking about the impact his teacher-mentor had on his life, Abrar says: "…when your teachers say good and inspiring words about you, they become a sort of light guiding you through life."

And So, The Struggle Begins

After graduating in 2000, Abrar took six months to secure a job at an advertising agency where he worked as a client-services intern, at a monthly salary of PKR4,000. The next year proved to be a turning point in his life, as he joined the technical marketing team of Samtech, an e-commerce company that had just started operations in Pakistan. At Samtech, Abrar was soon leading a team of 20 employees. This experience in e- commerce, at a nascent stage in the industry, proved to be a great advantage. However, due to personal differences Abrar resigned from Samtech after a year and a half.

In 2002, with financing from a US-backed investor, Abrar and his friends started an e-commerce company called HerbsMD.com, a portal offering herbal medicines for online purchase. By 2005, HerbsMD.com sales revenue had grown to around US$3 million in the US. The team labored for 14 hours a day and their hard work was paying off. However, Abrar resigned as he felt that he was ready to take the plunge and start his own venture.

Bringing to Fruition

In 2006, Abrar decided to take start his own business. He founded of Webiz Media that provided web-based customized marketing solutions. He roped in his friend Babar Hafeez to take over its paid-advertisement division, and together they threw themselves into the uncharted territory of online advertising in Pakistan. Starting operations as an affiliate marketing company, Abrar and his team represented e-retailing stores based in the US. The goal was to generate enough revenue to finance the main project, Hamariweb.com. Webiz Media generated healthy revenues. Their hard work paid off when Webiz Media was ranked amongst the top 500 fastest growing companies in the MENA Region in 2012 by Arabia 500 Fast Growth Awards at a ceremony held at Dubai World Trade Centre.

On the side, Abrar Ahmed continued working on developing Urdu content for cyber space. He launched the info portal, Hamariweb.com on August 14, 2007, while the nation celebrated Pakistan's Independence Day. Abrar built a team of editors in his quest to provide a first-of-its-kind online Urdu dictionary. Hamariweb.com offered a platform for poets and writers. Over the years, some 12,000 writers have submitted hundreds of thousands of publications to the portal. Talking about the portal's growth, Abrar reveals that Hamariweb.com is the only official content partner for BBC Urdu in Pakistan. It now offers content on a variety of topics based on localized interest in both English and Urdu, lifestyle information, newspaper archives, first-ever Urdu voice dictionary (10,000 words voiced by Hamariweb in-house facility and more in progress), Cricket Dream Team (a type of fantasy sport popular in young cricket lovers), student corner and a career-counseling platform with other useful information.

They also introduced browser compatibility in Urdu and a popular web-based Urdu typing editor. Hamariweb.com also became the first to find a way to use high-quality Noori Nastaliq and other Urdu fonts on their portal. Initially, the fonts were large in size (storage-wise) and dramatically increased the megabytes of the page. This slowed down the loading speed and reduced the website's search ranking. However, Abrar and his team, including the existing Project Head, Rizwan Shaikh, always on the lookout for solutions, started running articles written in Urdu fonts on news aggregators and posted their snapshots on the webpages, significantly reducing the size of the webpage. They have also provided solutions to some of the leading news websites including Aaj TV and News Tribe. Hamariweb introduced the de facto standard for content-rich Urdu sites, which enabled quicker loading of the Urdu site.

The revenue model of the publishing portal is through online advertisements. Currently, Hamariweb is the premier partner of the region's leading Ad Networks (Google, Yahoo, Tribal Fusion and Taboola). Just seven years after its inception, in 2014 Hamariweb.com crossed US$1 million in annual revenues.

Raising The Bar

Today Abrar's brainchild receives an average of 18 million visits per month. According to Alexa Rank, in September 2016, HamariWeb.com ranked as the 13th most visited website in Pakistan, and is second on the list of top Urdu websites in the world. The portal is ranked amongst the top 1,300 websites of the world in terms of traffic.

Unlike info portals and affiliate marketing ventures where the need for resources is low, e-commerce business models require patience and long lead times to build readership. It is a lot more challenging and the risks are extremely high. However, there are numerous opportunities in the industry. A strong HR team and abundant financial resources can take an e-commerce project to soaring heights, while a single mistake can destroy all the hard work. "There is no room for mistakes in these business models," says Abrar.

His team has had to learn this the hard way. The Hamariweb.com team launched two e-commerce projects that lost out to fierce market competition. Abrar says that before 2014, the market was not mature for online shopping industry in Pakistan. On their third try, the team succeeded with ShopRex.com launched in late 2015. ShopRex.com generated remarkable revenue in the first year of its existence.

Speaking about market dynamics, Abrar says that women's clothing and mobile accessories are bestsellers, while men's products can be 'tricky' to sell. He is all praise for the role of 3G/4G internet penetration as well as social networking websites, in the e-commerce growth. He predicts a boom in the sector in Pakistan in the coming years.

An Express Tribune report 'The future of e-commerce in Pakistan' supports his prediction. Currently valued at over US$60 million, Pakistan's e-commerce sector has been doubling even multi-folding in size every year and the country's internet-enabled population, currently around 30 million, is expected to increase to 56 million by 2019, the report says. Industry analysts predict that this trend will continue for the next three to five years, and help the sector surpass the US$1 billion milestone in 2020. Promising ventures such as branchless banking and Inter-Bank Funds Transfer (IBFT) are expected to oil the wheels of the boom, as will fast expanding credit card systems.

Advice to Young Entrepreneurs

The Right Time: Abrar is against the prevalent practice of encouraging students to undergo entrepreneurship training right out of college. He believes that one should gain necessary experience and sound knowledge working in a professional environment, within the field one wants to set up a business in. He believes that successful entrepreneurs need to develop the required skills.

In contrast to popularly held opinion, Abrar maintains that investment should be the last thing one should worry about. He believes that the first three years of startup entrepreneurs are the most important for their ventures and only hardwork and patience can guarantee success and recognition. He recalls working 14-16 hours a day, and even sleeping at his office in the early days of Hamariweb.com. Abrar considers himself fortunate in being able to work in a field that he loves and earning from it too.

Nurturing An Effective Team: "Team building is the single biggest challenge an entrepreneur will face in Pakistan, especially if he or she is reluctant to share the sense of ownership or revenues," feels Abrar. He feels the CEOs should display strength of character by having the confidence to make sacrifices for their employees. At the Hamariweb.com office, Abrar ensures a relaxed work atmosphere. All new employees are immediately welcomed as part of the Hamariweb.com family. He believes that this is one of the main reasons Hamariweb.com enjoys a high rate of employee retention.

Industry Collaboration: Abrar advises that entrepreneurs should increase and strengthen their ties with relevant people in the industry. He also feels that one should not feel any shame in consulting experts regarding their weaker areas, as one person cannot be expected to oversee all aspects of running a business. He recommends registering a company in its early days, as soon as the entrepreneur has built a sustainable enterprise.

Future Education Trends: In future, Abrar foresees online education gaining importance in Pakistan. He is optimistic that this field will grow. According to him, quality online education will improve academic standards.

Abrar is critical of what he calls, 'the prevailing caste system' in education, based on inequality in the medium of education for both public and private sector. The private sector schools are further categorized into ordinary small schools and reputed grammar schools: this inequality in our education system is dividing our students into various segments, especially when they enter professional life, he feels.

He draws attention to the urgent need for the Pakistani government to invest heavily in improving the failing infrastructure of state-funded education.

Book 2: The Socialpreneurs
Social Catalysts for a Better Tomorrow

Dreaming of a Better Future
    The Dream Foundation Trust, Humaira Bachal 133

Connecting Women, Improving Health, Transforming Lives
    doctHERs, Dr Asher Hasan, Dr Sara Khurram and Dr Iffat Zafar Agha, ... 144

Opening Minds and Empowering Women
    Women's Digital League, Maria Umar 158

Effective Charity Systems
    PDX: Pakistan Development Exchange, Hassaan Shah, Sami Ahmed 171

Connect, Educate and Evolve
    Rabtt, Imran Sarwar.. 179

Reversing the Brain Drain
    Pakathon, Asad Badruddin, Zheela Qaiser......................... 191

Social Catalysts for A Better Tomorrow

As a nation, we are familiar with a number of private non-profit organizations working to fulfill a social need or correct a social ill. The Edhi Foundation runs the largest fleet of private ambulances in the world; Sindh Institute of Urology and Transplant (SIUT) and the Indus Hospital in the public health sector; and the Chhipa Welfare Association and Saylani Welfare handling social welfare projects are good examples of not-for-profit organizations that have made an impact in Pakistan. These organizations are effective at channelizing relief to disadvantaged communities. Until the turn of the century, social enterprises were largely dependent on donations and charity.

Socialpreneurs, social entrepreneurs or impact-preneurs, are relatively new terms for budding entrepreneurs whose organizations address social, cultural, economic and environmental issues. The organization may be a non-profit or a profit motivated one, but its focus remains on the social impact on the community it serves.

With the exponential growth of the internet, Pakistani youth have learnt about international social entrepreneurial models such as Acumen, the Skoll Foundation, and the Bill & Melinda Gates Foundation. As these social innovators develop new operational models for maximizing impact, young Pakistanis are also inspired to establish organizations that could solve tough problems such as poverty, health care, and environmental issues. As a result, aspiring social entrepreneurs have cropped up in society playing a positive role in its social, cultural and economic development.

This breed of social ventures is based on the model of sustainable social enterprises or hybrid models. Their key feature is reduced dependence on funding from founders, donors and sponsors while their focus remains on creating impact in their fields. Microfinance distribution models such as that of Akhuwat Foundation, the first non-profit microfinance entity to provide interest-free loans, now has a more than 99.87 percent recovery rate. Pharmagen clean water shops in low-income communities are also an effective distribution system. One of the stories featured in this book, doctHERs, is another example. While their setup cost of a clinic is donor-based, the operations are sustainable.

My personal journey of learning and association with philanthropy started at an early age at home and at my school, Habib Public School, where several of the kids were being fully sponsored by the Habib Foundation. However hands-on engagement or volunteering yourself for community service was learnt at the University of Houston-Clear Lake in the US. There I saw my professor, Dr. Robert McGlashan, riding a fire engine on the freeway. Later when I had a chance to ask him about it, he said he believed everyone, regardless of education or stature, must give a few hours to community service. This was a life-changing experience for me. After coming back to Pakistan, I joined Rotary International and that started my journey of 'service above the self' a motto that we Rotarians proudly and passionately live by.

To highlight the power of a social entrepreneur, I have shortlisted six relatively new organizations. My association with these organizations has been on a personal level. The initiatives have been established by young social entrepreneurs with passion and determination to change the society by contributing to bigger causes. Their work covers the gamut of social industries: from changing the status quo in education like The Dream Foundation and Rabtt; creating new livelihood solutions and job opportunities like Pakathon and Women's Digital League; providing affordable healthcare like doctHERs; pushing community development and initiatives as Pakistan Development Exchange and investing in other social enterprises like Pakathon.

Opportunities for Socialpreneurs

During my six years of working with both students and faculty in the academia, I have concentrated my energies on helping them focus on the immense opportunities available in serving local market needs, particularly serving the bottom-of-the-pyramid populace. This comprises

50-70 percent of the population, depending on the benchmark used to measure poverty in Pakistan. I see more and more students and research faculty opting to establish their startups to address this segment. The strategy has its advantages, some of which are as follows.

This segment does not require innovative technology. It requires low-cost solutions that lend themselves to mass production, or a quick scale-up as in the case of services.This results in relatively lower investment and funding. Since the need is largely unmet, scaling-up is guaranteed as long as one can manage expectations and take into account the purchasing power of this segment.
Replication is much easier and a product or service may be supplied at mass level without a large investment.

With a rapidly increasing population, Pakistan offers immense opportunities for social entrepreneurs to operate, grow and make their mark by serving the community. Persian poet Jalaluddin Rumi expresses this idea as follows:

Zindagi Aamad Bara'ay Bandagi,
Zindagi Be Bandagi Sharmindagi

This translates to "Life is for devotion, And without devotion, what is life, but a disgrace."

10
Dreaming of a Better Future

The Dream Foundation Trust
Humaira Bachal
Founder
Karachi
www.dreamfoundationtrust.org

"We make a living by what we get. We make a life by what we give." ~Winston S. Churchill, British statesman and prime minister

In a worl Born in a low-income, conservative community, Humaira Bachal dared to dream of a better life for herself and other girls like her. She now runs a multi-storey school for 1,200 students, an industrial home for women and a microfinance facility for 500 women in Moach Goth, a semi-urban settlement on the periphery of Pakistan's largest metropolis, Karachi.

Author's Note : I met young Humaira Bachal about twelve years ago. She was an angry young teenager infuriated by society's negligent attitude towards her community. My first meeting with her was at the PACC (Pakistan American Cultural Center) which Humaira attended for learning English. She burst out in the very beginning of our conversation, "How would you feel if people exploit you and take undue advantage of you, not paying you according to your services?" She was enraged about how shop owners of Karachi were underpaying women from her community. She had visited fashionable boutiques and seen the clothes marked up to 10 times the price that the home based workers in her village were getting for stitching them.

My reply had surprised her. I had said, "They have every right to do so." For a moment, she was stunned into silence. Then I explained to her that people who do not stand up for their rights, are always exploited. In the following year, I coached and mentored her and another young man, Sohail Rahi – two social workers who were working to set up the Dream Foundation. To be honest, though I never doubted this young girl's abilities or her mettle, her achievements in establishing a school, a microfinance initiative and others are truly beyond my expectations and put her in a class of her own. If the law and order situation in Karachi had been favorable, Humaira's initiatives would have grown exponentially.

A land where she was expected to limit her role to serving the home and family, Humaira Bachal dared to dream for more. She created a stir in her small conservative community at Moach Goth when she challenged social norms and urged people to send their daughters to school.

Humaira began the process of change in her community in 2001 while just 12 years old. She started a quality school in one of the poorest areas around Karachi and became a social entrepreneur. In 15 years, she has moved from a makeshift afternoon school operating out of her home into a three-storey, 1,500 sq. ft. purpose-built building with trained teachers and state-of-the-art facilities. Today, alongside the Dream School Foundation, Humaira runs a microfinancing scheme called Asan Rozgar and a clinic for the community.

Over 1,200 students study at the Dream Model Street School in four shifts.

Humaira has received numerous international awards and accolades, including theof Impact Award 2013, Coca Cola's Savvy and Success Award, the 2016 Trailblazer Award, the Chime for Change award, and the Asia Foundation's Asia 21 Young Leader award.

Humaira has been profiled in The Economist and Forbes.

She is married and has a daughter.

Every Disaster is An Opportunity

Humaira Bachal's story began in a community called Moach Goth situated on the western outskirts of Karachi. This is a small community with some 100,000 families of all ethnicities. Like many other lower class neighborhoods in the developing world, Moach Goth is a breeding ground for poverty, unemployment, disease, illiteracy and ethnic strife.

Born in Thatta in Sindh, Humaira moved to Moach Goth with her family after her village was destroyed in a flood. On moving there, her mother, a farsighted woman, enrolled Humaira and her sister in the neighborhood government school. They were one of the few girls in the locality who attended school.

As a child, Humaira loved to visit her ancestral village near Sukkur during summer vacations with her family. Once, during a visit to the village, one of her baby cousins died as his mother accidentally gave him some expired medicine. Humaira was shocked to learn that the baby had died because of his mother's inability to read the expiry date on the medicine bottle. She could not understand why a grown woman was not able to read.

"I couldn't understand why Guddo could not read the dates. Was she such a bad student? Then I found out that Guddo had never been to school. I had just given my Class 5 exams and I realized that I knew all the dates. Today's, tomorrow's, in fact I knew the dates of the entire next year too! That is when I decided that I would impart education, so that no Guddo unknowingly kills her Munna ever again," says Humaira. Munna's death was a turning point in Humaira's relationship with education. From being a reluctant student, Humaira now looked forward to going to school. She realized that it was vital for everyone to know how to read. She did not want any other baby to die because the mother could not read something as simple as dates.

Planting The Seeds of A Dream

This was how 12 years old Humaira, who was still in 6th grade, decided to set up a makeshift school and start educating her friends. Using paper torn out of her own notebooks, she assembled her friends and started a class in her house after school. Her teacher was furious when she found out that she was tearing out her notebook and young Humaira realized that she had to find a better solution for procuring notebooks and paper.

She begged her father for a small blackboard which he arranged, not aware that his home was about to turn into a burgeoning learning haven for the children of the community. By the time she started 9th grade, Humaira's normal routine had become going to school herself during the day and then taking evening classes for an hour at her house. She encouraged her friends to seek an education and persuade their parents to send their daughters to school.

Striving for Success

For 9th grade, Humaira had to move to a bigger government school. There she came across piles of old books to be discarded. Seeing the opportunity, Humaira set up a 'Book Box' next to every dustbin in the school and convinced her friends to 'discard' all their old books there. Every day after school, Humaira and her sister would put the books in a sack and head home. The women they met on the way home, tauntingly called them ragpickers and garbage collectors, but the girls were inspired with their mission and nothing could sap their spirits. Together with her students, Humaira would sort the notebooks, repair the torn ones and sort out the pencils and other stationery items.

That was the easy part. Convincing people from the community to send their girls to school was herculean in comparison. Many parents were reluctant to send their children, as they did not see the value of an education. Many believed that even if they received an education, their children would still not progress beyond working in garages and small factories, receiving the same meager wages. School seemed pointless.

Humaira focused on convincing the parents to send their children to her school, promising that she would take care of the rest. She felt that if she offered a subsidy to the parents in the form of free books and stationery items, they would be more willing to allow their daughters the gift of education. She recalls, "My sister, friends and I would go to the community every day to convince everyone to send their children to study and the parents would outright refuse to. Therefore, we concluded that receiving something for free might encourage them to enroll the children. We told them to just send the child as we wanted nothing more. We had no donor-driven project and no facilities. We did everything from scratch. We even saved our pocket money for days just to buy small supplies such as blackboard chalk."

A Growing School

By 2006, Humaira was using every room in her small house--the kitchen, the laundry and the bedrooms--as makeshift classrooms. Her brothers and their wives were fed up. She realized that the two-room house could not continue to accommodate her expanding family and her school, which now had over 110 students. Therefore, she and her sister started looking for rooms to rent.

In this quest for a bigger space, everyone she turned to, laughed at the then 16-year old Humaira. No one took her seriously. She convinced her mother to help them on this mission and finally found a kind-hearted *maulvi* (cleric) who agreed to rent out a room to them for PKR500 (US$5) a month. Humaira agreed to the deal not knowing where the next month's rent was to come from. When she realized that her family would not support her cause financially, she started working at a development organization, the Orangi Pilot Project, to pay for the school's growing expenses.

The Backlash

Around this time, Humaira was beginning to face severe backlash from her community. By starting the school, Humaira had upset the applecart in a community where most people were against educating girls. Not only was she imparting literacy through her school, she was also creating awareness of basic human rights of women and children. At the school, girls were made aware of their rights as women: They had the right to go to a hospital, they could use transportation at will and they too could control their lives.

This went against the rural traditions of the slum dwellers who began to shame her family mercilessly. Humaira's father was specifically targeted. He was invited to public meetings and ordered to put an end to the 'immorality' that his daughters were spreading. Humaira's community turned away from her and her father's family banished her from their village. The conservative folk sin the slums despised the change they were seeing in the girls of the area who were gaining confidence with education. There was even talk of kicking Humaira out of Moach Goth. There were protests against her in which people threw stones at her and at the school. There was even a threat to kidnap her. She was declared 'immoral'. The testing times reached a climax when even her own father turned against her and her brothers stopped speaking to her.

Despite these seemingly insurmountable obstacles, change was happening. Slowly and gradually, some people were beginning to pay attention to Humaira and trying to understand the importance of her cause. Her students' mothers were becoming aware of their rights, and learning the value of treating sons and daughters as equals. Humaira's teachings were slowly but steadily permeating the fabric of the community, especially amongst the women who could see a way to a better life. From just 10 students in 2001, the school had grown to 206 children in 2007.

A year later, the school was dealt a major blow when Humaira's landlord, the cleric, passed away. Humaira lost a staunch supporter of her cause. She rented another place but people from the community threatened the owner and turned him against her. He threw Humaira and the children out, but failed to weaken Humaira's resolve. She calmly continued lessons on the street outside the building. The school continued to function under the open sky for the next ten days.

A Ray of Hope

Shirkatgah is a Lahore based non-governmental organization (NGO) that works to empower women. Its representatives were visiting Moach Goth in 2008 to record women's views during the general elections. The NGO workers were astonished to see young Humaira and her equally young teaching staff hard at work on the street. Shirkatgah became instrumental in restoring Humaira's school in the building. Impressed with Humaira, the NGO decided to make a documentary about her and the school, which was functioning on the bare minimum, but was forging ahead fueled by Humaira's passion and devotion.

The Shirkatgah team was particularly impressed with the school's sessions on women's empowerment. Alongside the school and adult education, Humaira Bachal was also holding informative discussions about human rights in an informal setting. Each week she would choose a topic of discussion and ask the community members to share their opinions. They talked about marriage, women's rights and women's education. They also discussed how to talk to families about women's education and what to do in the face of opposition. Shirkatgah's documentary, "A Small Dream", was released in 2009. Humaira boarded a train for the first time to go to its launch in Lahore.

While watching the documentary in the hall, Humaira could not stop crying as the memories of all the hardships that she had faced over nine years--the pain, the agony, the misery and the joy--came rushing back to her. When her name was announced, it took her a good few minutes to realize that they were calling her to the stage. During her speech, she broke down in tears sharing her worries for her students and the need for some land for the school.

The screening of the documentary opened many doors for Humaira. Soon after, a Swiss foundation bought her a piece of land to build the school and the ball started rolling. She found mentors and professionals who guided her to create a bank account and set up her own trust. She also met willing allies and donors for her school who held charity drives.

In 2009, Humaira formed The Dream Foundation Trust. At age 19, she had done a lot for a community that still largely resented her. A number of organizations came forward to help her. The documentary was aired in the US, Thailand and Hong Kong and in local colleges and universities. Support started flooding in. Engro generously helped build a school for Humaira. Things were finally beginning to fall into place.

Humaira had a clear vision for her school that she named Dream Model Street School. She recounted to the Economist in 2013: "We want to have classes that go up to matric. We will have chemistry, physics and biology labs, a computer room, a library, an auditorium. We will have outdoor activities in the back yard, a staff room, principal's room, accounts room. In the back yard, we want to put fish and plants and birds. I don't want this to be a school, I want it to be a paradise for the children of Moach Goth."[1]

Humaira Bachal may have come from a slum, but she has strong entrepreneurial skills. She has a lot of insight and financial expertise into her projects and refuses to stop or stagnate. She aspires to have an organized and well-managed foundation and so The Dream Foundation has a formal financial policy and systems through which they receive funds, keep records and acknowledge donors. Progress is reported and shared quarterly with the donors to apprise them of the status of the foundation.

Global Recognition

When the Pakistani-Canadian filmmaker and Oscar award winner, Sharmeen Obaid Chinoy learnt of Humaira's dedication to the cause of education, health and women's empowerment, she decided to make two documentaries with her. One was an episode of Coke Studio's *'Ho Yaqeen'* series and the other was a short film titled 'Humaira: The Dream Catcher'. The documentaries were presented to audiences abroad by pop legend Madonna at the Chime for Change concert. **This helped raise PKR 5,700,000 (US$ 54,402) for the school from the audience at the concert. Madonna herself matched it with a donation of PKR 20,000,000 (US$190,088) the balance needed to complete the project.**

Speaking about the experience of filming with Humaira, Sharmeen says, "She is unstoppable. Clear about her goal and focused in its pursuit, she fought for her right to an education, and is now fighting for the rights of others. Her story gives me hope for Pakistan, and her courage and resilience bolsters and reminds me of the fact that there is still an insurmountable amount of good in this world, and it must be protected and celebrated."[2]

By May 2014, Humaira had a 15,000 sq.ft. purpose-built school building, just as she had imagined. It has a courtyard and labs, classes, computers and an auditorium. With a student-teacher ratio of 30:2, all her teachers are trained and from the community. Some 1,200 students are enrolled at the school in four shifts from morning to evening. At other times, the school runs adult-literacy classes, discussions and general awareness sessions. The students are encouraged to participate and are taught various skills. Class discussions include safety guidelines, socio-economic enhancement education, gender, social and civic responsibilities as well as minority rights. Both children and adults are offered appropriate counselling to create a child-friendly environment.

Asan Rozgar

With the help of the network that she had been building, Humaira wanted to do more for her community. Ever since she was a child, Humaira disliked how the wealthy would come to drop off wheat or sugar for the poor in the holy month of Ramadan and leave. She believed that if you truly want to help someone, you should help him or her set up his or her own business. She wanted the poor to be given adequate funding for starting their own microfinance schemes. Using her network, she soon set up the Asan Rozgar scheme.

She argued that a sack of wheat given by the rich could not feed a family forever, so it was more important to invest in the livelihood of the poor. She set up a system that collected zakat and funds and gave out microfinance loans. She coordinated with The Orangi Pilot Project and set up multiple trusts for this purpose. The motto of the trust was *'Zakat mat do, kaam do'* (translation: Do not give charity, give work).

Through these microloans, Asan Rozgar helps women living along the Hub coastline to earn a living while they wait for their fisher folk family members to return from the sea every six weeks. Asan Rozgar provides small loans to them to start small businesses. Simultaneously, The Dream Foundation offers skills development workshops to the women training them to embroider and sew. After receiving micro financing, these women are encouraged to start their own netting and basket-weaving businesses. Initially, loans are given for two months at a time while a team monitors the businesses.

Home-based workshops and community discussions have done wonders for this community. Many families have managed to raise themselves out of poverty because of education, skill development and microfinancing. Continuing her charitable efforts, Humaira has collaborated with the Sina Trust to build a clinic in Moach Goth providing basic healthcare.

Through social entrepreneurship, Humaira was able to bring major change in people's lives. She had to face numerous obstacles, but she persevered and made all of her dreams come true. For the community, it took one young woman utilizing her passion and dedication and today, the women of Moach Goth have different aspirations for themselves and their families with hopes for a better future.

Advice to Entrepreneurs

Finding the Right Supporters: Humaira's mother Zainab Bibi has always been her biggest supporter. Unfortunately, her father and brothers were influenced by the scornful villagers. For her daughter's sake, Zainab endured her husband's beatings, verbal abuse and torment. Yet she continued to motivate Humaira when things became tough. Once when Humaira was on the verge of giving up, her mother told her to get back up and fight. "When I saw my mother's bruised hands and felt the pain inflicted on her by my father and the people, I became disheartened and thought of giving up. But my mother backed me up and said, 'If I am not giving up on you, why are you? Go! I have your back.' My mother has always been my biggest support."

Managing Social Pressures: The community pressurized Humaira's father and brothers when they realized what Humaira was doing. As a result, her brothers turned against her. They were ashamed of her as the people of the community had branded her immoral and it took them years to realize that their sister was bringing great positive change in the community. For more than 11 years, Humaira's father detested her. Heavily influenced by the people of his village, he wanted Humaira to die or leave and never return.

Her father realized his mistake only after the episode of *'Ho Yaqeen'* premiered on TV in 2013. Having watched the episode, his boss at the Karachi Electric Supply Company (KE) embraced and congratulated him on his daughter's achievement. This made him realize her daughter's perseverance for a worthy cause. It was a bittersweet feeling for Humaira. She was happy that her father had finally seen the light, yet she was also sad that it took another man's opinion to convince him. She was heartbroken that she had been deprived of her father's love for 11 years, but happy that her father was now her biggest supporter.

Work-Life Balance: Humaira's husband Usman is the perfect match for her. He is loving and caring and shares equally in bringing up their lovely daughter Meher. After her marriage, Humaira realized that working while being married was different but not impossible, and that life balances out when you have a supportive partner and in-laws.

Law and Order Lapses in the Community: When gang wars broke out in the area, it dealt a major blow to the school. Shootouts occurred regularly. Children were orphaned and some also became victims of sectarian violence. That is when Humaira started using art and theatre as mediums to bring about harmony and peace. The message sank in slowly--first to the children, then to the mothers and then to the whole family. Open days and national occasions were used to spreadmessages of peace among all ethnicities.

Importance of Trust Within the Team: Humaira formed a team of young people to run the school. She held various trainings for them and soon realized that not everyone was capable of taking her cause forward. She had to part ways with some people who were giving her school a bad name and learnt to pick the dedicated ones who were in for the long haul.

---

[1] *From: Rahul Bhatacharya, "A Class of her Own", The Economist 1843, https://www.1843magazine.com/content/ideas/anonymous/class-her-own, September 5, 2013, Accessed July 2016*[2]

2 Jon Springer, Pakistan's Educator Madonna Wants You To Know, Forbes/Forbes Asia, http://www.forbes.com/sites/jonspringer/2014/11/25/pakistans-educator-madonna-wants-you-to-know/#651aaf4c3e9a, Nov 25, 2014, Accessed 2 July 2015

11

Connecting Women, Improving Health, Transforming Lives

doctHERS
Dr Asher Hasan,
Dr Sara Khurram
And Dr Iffat Zafar Agha
Karachi, KPK
http://www.doctHERs.com

"People have become educated, but have not become humans." ~ Abdul Sattar Edhi

Three passionate doctors founded doctHERs, which connects stay-at-home female doctors to the population in underprivileged areas through telehealth clinics. In eighteen months, they have set up eight facilities and treated over 100,000 patients, bringing quality healthcare to those who need it most.

Author's Note: The idea behind DoctHERs immediately touched my heart. It took me back to 2005 when I had established the first telemedicine network with the help of PASHA, Pak Army, Rawalpindi Medical College and the International Telecommunication Union. The 17 centers established in AJK and KP provided treatment to millions, saved lives and were a great example of emergency healthcare. I was able to guide them in the light of my own experience, expanding their vision from a few clinics to hundreds in the near future.

Numbers depict a strange reality in Pakistan's health system. According to the Pakistan Medical and Dental Council (PMDC), women make up 70 per cent of the 14,000 medical students who graduate every year in Pakistan. However, of all the women who graduate from medical school, only a small fraction pursue medicine as a career. The others stop practising due to social pressures and cultural expectations. In 2015, out of the 150,000 licensed doctors in Pakistan, 70,000 were women; yet only 9,700 (13 percent) women were registered as specialist physicians.

Pakistan has a burgeoning population of close to 195 million, 40 percent of whom live below the poverty line. Despite this situation, the total annual healthcare spending in Pakistan is just US$37 per capita (compared with the WHO recommended US$62). Public sector spending on health is a mere 0.45 percent of the GDP. Each doctor in Pakistan is serving a population of at least 1,038 people, which clearly pushes the limits of the healthcare system to breaking point.

Dr Asher Hasan, Dr Sara Khurram and Dr Iffat Zafar are three passionate doctors who care about delivering quality healthcare to the underprivileged. They founded doctHERs, an organization that connects stay-at-home women doctors to health consumers in need of quality healthcare through telemedicine.

In less than two years, doctHERs has established seven clinics in Karachi and Khyber Pukhtukhwa (KPK), and a tele-psychiatry clinic in Mansehra has provided inclusive employment to twenty female doctors, nurses and community mobilizers. The doctors consult from their homes in Chakwal, Quetta, Karachi and London has helped 22,000 patients through their telemedicine clinics and impacted more than 100,000 people through six medical camps and health campaigns.

"At its economic simplest, the doctHERs model is all about connecting the unmet demand for quality healthcare to the untapped supply of home-based female doctors," explains the co-founder, Dr Asher Hasan. "We use technology to address market failures and directly match supply to demand in a solution that is acceptable to the society in which we operate."

A Typical Urban Childhood

Dr Sara Khurram comes from a middle-class family and is the youngest of three children. Her father chose her profession for her even before she could crawl. He was in the police and had planned early on to have three children. He had also decided that he wanted one of his children to become a doctor, another to become an engineer and the third to become a banker. At her birth, her father announced that Sara was going to be the doctor.

As her father was in the Crimes Branch in the police force, Sara would sometimes accompany him to the courts. She dreamt of a life as a lawyer. Still, she worked hard towards becoming a doctor to fulfil her father's wish. As is typically expected of urban Pakistani girls, Sara finished school, went to medical college, completed her house job in May 2011 and was married by September 2011. "I had a traditional arranged marriage. I met my husband for exactly 11 minutes before we got married!" laughs Dr Sara.

After marriage, she continued to work and wanted to begin her specialization. However, in her new family, working after marriage-- particularly in the medical field that demands that doctors work at night-- was unacceptable. Sara managed to convince her husband and in laws to let her work during the day. This proved to be an immense limitation during her specialization, as a junior doctor is required to work nights under the supervision of senior doctors. She originally wanted to be a gynecologist, but was forced to take up Radiology as it did not require night duties.

Sara had enrolled in a two-year program. However, a year into the program she became pregnant and had to leave the training. While she waited to give birth, she spent a miserable time at home being unproductive. Some time later, she heard from a friend about the Naya Jeevan Foundation, a health insurance company founded by Dr Asher Hasan. Naya Jeevan is a social enterprise that works to rejuvenate lives by providing low-income families with affordable access to quality healthcare in the corporate, academic, industrial, NGO and SME sectors. Since Sara had already worked long hours at the hospital, a job like this sounded easier to Sara.

Docthers: Field-Testing The Prototype

In 2013, Dr Asher Hasan conceived doctHERs. The concept is simple: doctHERs provides quality healthcare by connecting home-based, remotely located doctors to consumers in need of quality health via nurse-assisted telemedicine. Using this approach, docHERs can potentially reintegrate tens of thousands of unemployed women doctors into the health workforce from their homes.

As part of her work with Naya Jeevan, Dr Sara participated in a USAID-funded community health project in Sultanabad in 2013-14 whose focus was to provide quality healthcare to individuals who previously lacked access. As Sara was living in Lahore at the time, she was asked by Dr. Asher to join as a co- founder and to provide clinical services to patients in collaboration with a physical doctor present in the community health center.

The community is typically conservative. Men work long hours as drivers or laborers, while the women and children stay at home. Most residents of Sultanabad come from traditional Pathan backgrounds, and their women do not step out of their houses, unless forced to. At risk for a host of conditions, they seek medical help only when the situation becomes unbearable and in many cases only when it is too late. It was an eye-opening experience for her. Majority of the people who walked into the clinic were poor and malnourished.

The Sultanabad clinic provided a mini pharmacy, lab referral services and tertiary care referral services, ultrasound specialist visits, monthly health awareness camps and a family planning unit. The clinic was equipped with a basic tele-health system through which the doctHERs team could communicate with the patients and the clinic nurse.

Over six months, the prototype catered to over 100 antenatal patients, with healthcare services delivered by Dr Sara via Skype. About 10 women were also referred to tertiary care centers for safe deliveries.

A Naya Jeevan For Iffat

In Dr Iffat Zafar's family, women did not pursue professional degrees. Her father himself was the first among the males in his family to pursue a professional degree. He studied engineering and went to work in the Middle East. Iffat spent her early childhood in Saudi Arabia.

Breaking with the family traditions, Iffat's father supported and encouraged her to pursue a professional career. "My father would refer to me as *mera beta* (my son). He had big dreams for my career that he transferred to me," Fascinated by hospitals and doctors from an early age, Iffat chose to pursue medicine as a career.

Disappointment came when she had graduated. "I had thought that once I graduate from medical college, I would have a line of jobs waiting for me. This didn't happen. I was barely able to recover my fuel money from the salary I received as a house officer. I needed to prove my worth to the world at the time. However, I found that personal growth in the medical profession was extremely slow."

"I worked for a bit in oncology and nephrology. I found that the journey to prove myself was going to be a long one if I pursued clinical medicine as a career. It would take at least a decade more of studying and toiling for long grueling hours. I became disheartened and thought of looking for something else."

Iffat eventually joined the multinational pharmaceutical company, Novartis. She also got married around the same time to a man supportive of her career. However, when she had a miscarriage at six months, she decided to quit and stay at home.

Staying at home became anticlimactic. She had initially thought that she would relax at home, in reality, she found herself miserable doing nothing of value. Soon, she became pregnant again and had a normal healthy delivery. When the baby was nine months old, Iffat had determined that she did not wish to stay miserable at home. When she heard of an opening at NAYA JEEVAN, she immediately applied for the job and was hired.

Breakthrough

Once the Sultanabad prototype was successful, the next step was to find a dedicated space where the telemedicine system could be deployed independently.

In March 2015, a mutual friend introduced the doctHERs team to Squadron Leader Captain Farhad S. Khan (R). A veteran of the 1971 war, he had spent his post-air force career in the corporate sector in the Middle East.

He moved back to Pakistan after his wife had passed away and was planning to set up a clinic. Sara and Iffat went to meet him and things just fell into place. Through Captain Farhad's generous donation of land, the doctHERs team launched their first clinic on May 11, 2015 in an urban slum in Model Colony, near Karachi's Jinnah International Airport.

The clinic includes a mini pharmacy, a family planning lab and a lab collection unit. To date, the center has seen over 3,600 patients (with over 1,200 video-consultation) who have visited the center for a range of medical issues. Patients also come to the Model Colony clinic seeking ultrasound and specialized treatments.

A Model Evolves

Between March 2015 and June 2015, the doctHERs team continued to refine and iterate the community-based model, carefully documenting Standard Operating Procedures (SOPs) to enable them rapid replication.

Each clinic has a nurse, two home-based doctors and a video-consultation system to facilitate doctor-patient interaction. In addition, a clinic assistant manages the medical tests and the pharmacy.

Female doctors connect remotely via internet to their assigned clinics. At each clinic, a nurse manages the tele-health system, takes the patient's vital signs, performs a general check-up and relays this information to the doctor. The doctor then conducts a consultation with the patient via an HD video call.

Nurses are recruited from the local community as trusted intermediaries. They are available to take patient histories, conduct physical examinations and communicate relevant details to the assigned female doctor who provides the patient with the required advice and treatment. The nurse carries out all procedures under the virtual supervision of a female doctor. The program also consists of peripheral diagnostic tools, so that the doctor can assess the patient's vital signs remotely.

Initially, patients were wary of the technology. They doubted whether the individual on the other side of the tele-screen was a real doctor. A nurse Abida Haroon recalls, "convincing the patients was very difficult initially. But after they had come and discussed their problems, many of their reservations were addressed and they gradually adapted to the system."

The clinic is dedicated to treating patients at a cost-effective price. It charges a minimum of PKR 100 (US$1) and a maximum of PKR 1,200 (US$12) per patient for a virtual clinic consultation. Forty percent (40%) of the revenue is paid to the doctor while the nurses and community health workers receive 20 percent of the receipts. Service delivery and operational costs are 25 percent of the revenue. This yields an average profit margin of almost 15 percent. In order to assist patients who cannot afford healthcare, the organization is also working on incorporating a Zakat and Welfare Model.

Fail Fast - Fail Forward

The secondclinic that was launched by doctHERs was in Hijrat Colony, a urban slum close to the Sultanabad area. While Model Colony was a multiethnic community, the inhabitants of Hijrat Colony were largely Pashhtun. The women in this area were deprived of access to affordable and quality healthcare especially in life threatening situations. To ensure it was a sustainable initiative with no external funding needs, doctHERs collaborated with a community-based organization to launch its second clinic on June 15, 2015.

This time, doctHERsempowered a local nurse in the community by upgrading and transforming her home into a telemedicine center. This was done so that she would be able to work within the cultural norms of the locality. The clinic served as a primary healthcare center offering OPD consultations, mini-pharmacy, primary clinical services, lab collection and referral to tertiary healthcare hospitals. In addition, health awareness workshops were held at the clinic every month to provide basic guidelines regarding preventive health strategies. A door-to-door mobilization campaign was also conducted to create awareness about the health services available nearby.

Despite this array of interventions, the Hijrat Colony clinic failed.

The doctHERs team learned about the numerous factors influencing the success of a community clinic. First, the Model Colony community was a multi-ethnic, middle-income community, while Hijrat Colony was an ultra-low income, single ethnic community. In addition to this, the nurse chosen to cater to this area was not convinced about the idea herself. Belonging to the same community herself, the nurse was still hesitant to go into the community and act as an influencer, activator or mobilizer. doctHERs had to close the clinic within four months.

Learning from this failure, doctHERs now evaluates new locations using multiple criteria: community dynamics, ethnic heterogeneity, the availability of high-speed internet service and on-grid electricity among others. The nurse's role, reputation and ability to adapt is crucial. The nurse should also be willing and capable of learningnew advances in digital health technology. Patient affordability and willingness to pay is also an important factor as doctHERs aims to operate as a self-sustaining social business. doctHERs analyzes existing healthcare services and fee structures in pharmacies and hospitals around the clinics, and prices according to the local market.

Testing The Rural Model

In 2016, a supporter of doctHERs, Riaz Kamlani of TCF and SINA Trust, found a clinic in KPK that needed revival -doctHERs launched its third full clinic in Mansehra on October 13, 2015 at KBDO (Kidney Blood Diseases Organization) in collaboration with HCP (an Abbottabad-based company that provides integrated business solutions) and Tech Valley Abbottabad (a tech community).

Built in the heart of the valley, the tehsil hospital lacked female doctors to care for thelarge number of women in the area. Qualified doctHERs from Karachi were linked to the people of Mansehra for nurse-assisted video consultation and women from the surrounding areas started visiting the clinic. The clinic provides affordable services, especially in cases that previously required women to travel long distances to a hospital in the maincity.

In this location also, one of the clinic's initial challenges was to convince patients to trust digital technology. However, with the passage of time, repeated exposure and the high quality of clinicalconsultations, patients are gradually embracing the system.

Through this network of telehealth clinics, doctHERs has demonstrated the technical feasibility of using technology to provide remote rural populations with access to quality healthcare.

Launching A Tele-Psychiatric Clinic

In 2016- Dr. Sara found a mental hospital in Dadar that required a psychiatrist to treat in-patients. The sanatorium in the Dadar area was established in 1939 and was once the biggest center for the treatment of tuberculosis in all of Asia. Some 13 years ago, the center became a mental and general hospital after the government had converted a mental hospital to establish the Hazara University in Dadar. The flash floods of 2001 and 2005 had left the facility in a shambles. Most of thebuildings were falling apart and abandoned and only three wards were in use.

The doctHERs team was appalled at the situation. The dire and unmet needs of patients in the area forced them to take on the project and test their model further. On April 1, 2016, doctHERs inaugurated the first-ever tele-psychiatry clinic of Pakistan.

Sara recalls, "At the inauguration, we made sure that the government officials responsible for rehabilitation were invited along with community leaders. We showed them the appalling conditions in which these poor, mentally challenged patients were living: Crumbling walls, barely functional equipment and severe shortage of staff with no doctors. The monitor in the tele-psychiatry clinics turned out to be the only one functioning in the facility."

Expansion Plans

DKT International is one of the largest private providers of family planning and reproductive health products and services in the developing world. It served 28 million couples in 2014, prevented 6.5 million unwanted pregnancies, 12,527 maternal deaths and 3.6 million abortions. DKT International launched its most recent program in Pakistan in 2012. The program is called Dhanak and addresses the problems of supply and demand that have kept Pakistan's contraceptive prevalence rate lower than its regional neighbors. DKT manufactures family planning products and has a nationwide network of 800 'Dhanak' clinics. The agency mobilizes midwives and community health workers.

By the end of 2015, DKT was collaborating with doctHERs in upgrading their Dhanak clinics to facilitate walk-in patient consultation for all primary-care diseases. The partnership will pilot five clinics, with a plan to scale up to 80 clinics over the coming year.

The partnership was activated on December 22, 2015, when doctHERs launched its fourth clinic in the Ilyas Goth slum in Karachi. Following this, an additional five doctHERs clinics have been launched in Karachi in collaboration with NAYA JEEVAN via the USAID Small Grant & Ambassador's Fund Program (SGAFP).

Within a span of 18 months, doctHERs has established seven primary care clinics and a tele-psychiatry specialty clinic. The core team consists of six people who work with doctHERs along with 20 doctors, nurses and community mobilizers. Since May 2015, doctHERs has conducted video consultations on 2000+ patients. The female doctors advise from their homes in places ranging from Quetta, Lahore, Islamabad and Karachi to Chakwal, Qatar and London.

Each clinic has a capacity to serve 600 patients a month, or 7,200 patients annually. The doctHERs team collaborates with partners to identify and recruit clinic locations. The average cost of setting up a clinic is US$5000 and the average annual cost of operating a clinic comes to US$15,000 per year or US$1,250 a month. These costs include purchase of medical equipment, machinery, setting up the clinic (furniture, medical supplies, etc.) and purchasing medical diagnostic instruments. The nurses are also trained to collect blood samples for basic lab tests, as well as dispense from a mini-pharmacy on prescription.

Initially incubated by NAYA JEEVAN, doctHERs became a legally independent entity in March 2015 and has developed several strategic corporate partnerships and sponsorships, expanding its footprint across Pakistan. The team has also been active on the startup competition circuit within Pakistan and abroad to gather support and funds for the model. Some of the competitions that doctHERs have successfully participated in are MITEFP Business Acceleration Plan 2015, The GIST I-Tech Competition, World SeedStars, Echoing Green, and HRH The Prince of Wales Young Sustainability Entrepreneur Prize. These competitions have given global visibility to inclusive employment for women in Pakistan and has helped drawn attention to the dire need to fix the healthcare sector in Pakistan through innovative solutions such as doctHERs.

"We are now working with many corporate clients that aspire to provide better healthcare to the communities they are operating in. They need a partner like us to activate clinics on the ground," says Dr Iffat. By 2020, the team plans to impact over 1.2 million lives through 500 clinics in Pakistan. They hope that the idea will be replicated in other developing countries to make healthcare accessible.

February 2017: The Pivot

By end of 2016, Sara, Iffat and Asher realized that the size of the market opportunity for the community clinic model was much larger than any of them had anticipated while it was clear that affordability and sustainability would remain formidable challenges. Given that the original vision for doctHERs was to be a sustainable, scalable business, the founding teamdecided to pivot and create a new company (Sehat Kahani) that would focus on the enhancing the social impact for marginalized communities while doctHERs would pivot towards the corporate sector and corporate value chains (suppliers, distributors, retailers and other informal workers).

So on February 2017, "Sehat Kahani" was legally registered by Dr. Sara Saeed Khurrum and Dr. Iffat Zafar, after a successful demerger of doctHERs. All clinical operations (comprising eight clinics in Sindh, KPK and Punjab), assets and partnerships along with the clinical and core team were transferred to Sehat Kahani. Sehat Kahani is a social impact initiative of Community Innovation Hub. It works on improving primary health care in communities through a spectrum of services focused on primary health care consultation, health awareness and health counseling. Sehat Kahani is a holistic health solution for healthcare delivery to rural and low-income urban communities. The venture will train female doctors and nurses in utilising ICT to deliver healthcare to the bottom 40% of the population. Common ICT technologies such as video conferencing, transmission of still images, e-health including patient portals, remote monitoring of vital signs, continuing medical education and consumer-focused wireless applications would form the basis of the health system at each of the clinics. The community clinic also aims to connect local and international medical experts for early detection and treatment of serious patients. Additionally, it plans to do capacity building of nurses to transform them into micro-entrepreneurs thus creating more jobs opportunities in the community.

Asher, whose first venture, NAYA JEEVAN, is already profitable and has been serving the corporate and corporate-affiliated BOP market since 2009, will be building a nationwide network of female doctors ('doctHERs') to serve the primary care needs of employees and dependents affiliated with corporations and corporate value chains. This includes DTC (Direct-to-Consumer) HD video-consultation-based services to corporate managers/executives as well as nurse-mediated services to factory workers, remote field offices, distribution centers, etc.

ADVICE TO ENTREPRENEURS

On Integrity & Authenticity: "One of the most important omissions made by business schools and incubator/accelerator programs in Pakistan is the lack of emphasis they place on honesty and integrity as necessary prerequisites to a sustainable business. " observes Dr. Asher. "Over the past decade, I've come across many bright entrepreneurs who unfortunately have embarked on their entrepreneurial careers in very unscrupulous, inauthentic ways. This is something the entrepreneurial ecosystem needs to pay close attention to, otherwise international investor confidence in this emerging sector will suffer and impact investments in Pakistan will be re-routed to other emerging markets."

On Team Work: "You have to discover your purpose instead of following the trends. It all comes down to your passion and total commitment about doing something. Do not think that you can do everything alone. It is not a one-person job. You have to have a team. Until you have a team and streamlined processes, you cannot be successful. I see people who say, 'I have the capability to do everything myself, I do not need a team'. They could not be more wrong," says Dr. Sara.

Dr. Sara emphasizes that being resilient is the most important thing when starting a company. There are many challenges and disappointments. "Sometimes you have to recognise a failure and rethink the process. There are multiple failures on several fronts. You need to accept those and move on. That is when you really grow," she says.

She feels that it is important to be selective about the people you work with. 'People try to fool you in ways unimaginable. That is why one needs to select partners and advisors very carefully,' she advises.

On Intellectual Property (IP): "It's critical for entrepreneurs to protect their IP before someone takes their idea and clones it" stresses Dr. Asher. "There are any number of unethical players in the Pakistani market who will pretend to be your donors or partners and then simply rip off your idea. The former head of HR of a well-known company who is now leading a major foundation here in Karachi is a recent example of someone who just recently did this to someone I know quite well. Entrepreneurs need to really protect themselves - both from predatory 'angel' investors as well as scam artists"

On Understanding Community Work: The communities in Pakistan are not homogenous. Therefore, it is very important to understand the makeup of the community. Though the patients have similar medical issues, their cultures are different.

Dr Iffat observes, "Verbal commitments are very important in KPK communities. If you promise something to them and do not deliver, they will never ever come back to you. In Karachi city, people are more understanding of human failings."

"Also in KPK, a social hierarchical system exists. Before we start any new clinics, we make sure to identify the elders and take them along. In contrast, the strategy for Karachi is different,' she shares.

On the Importance of Developing Systems: In a people-oriented business like healthcare, it is very important to build systems. Iffat recalls, "Initially we were only documenting and improving standard protocols. Then we found that the nurse and the location play a pivotal role in the success of the clinic. We also discovered that our systems helped us in understanding what can go wrong and we built continuous learning into the system also."

"This is why in the beginning, we were only able to open a clinic every three months. Presently, we can open a clinic every week," adds Sara.

On Working in a Social Startup: You have to know your purpose. It is not fun; it is a lot of hard work. Dr Sara says, "It is difficult to start a social business in Pakistan in the absence of any structured, social financing. Do it if you are committed and in it for your whole life. You also have to be a little crazy to take things through. There are limited avenues for funding and most of the time one has to be creative and extremely lean in clinical operations. There will be challenges, so expect them. Be prepared to fail and get up and start all over again."

Dr Iffat adds, "There will be a lot of criticism and setbacks but do not be disappointed. It is not always about the money, it is about the cause and the mission. Being in a social business means that people will have a hard time understanding your model because you are not a restaurant or a tangible product. But along the way, you will find people who will believe in you. It is important for the founders to stay positive and strong."

12

Opening Minds and Empowering Women

WOMEN'S DIGITAL LEAGUE
Maria Umar
Founder
South Waziristan Agency
www.womensdigitalleague.com

Maria Umar founded a social enterprise that mobilizes a home-based female workforce to earn digital livelihoods for economic empowerment. No matter where the women live, WDL ensures that they will always be able to find work, with just a computer and an internet connection.

Author's Note: Maria Umar is another young, aspiring social entrepreneur who is training women to secure their future through digital livelihood. After she was laid off on a flimsy reason, Maria took charge of her life and started work as a freelancer. A born leader, Maria was concerned about other women who were facing similar circumstances. This led to her conceiving and creating the Women's Digital League (WDL) recognized as a major player in women's development in Pakistan.

I have been associated with Maria for six years now and have thoroughly enjoyed assisting her with strategy, negotiations, program development and advising her in building this noble initiative. I am sure her inspiring story will help many young women follow similar paths by helping others to improve their livelihood.

"I have always maintained that no nation can ever be worthy of its existence that cannot take its women along with the men. No struggle can ever succeed without women participating side by side with men. There are two powers in the world; one is the sword and the other is the pen. There is a great competition and rivalry between the two. There is a third power stronger than both, that of the women." ~ Quaid-i-Azam, Mohammad Ali Jinnah, Founder of Pakistan.

Maria Umar is from South Waziristan, a conservative territory located in the mountainous region of northeastern Pakistan. She founded the Women's Digital League (WDL), a social enterprise that supports and trains educated women to work from home and create digital livelihood opportunities for themselves.

From struggling to find work for herself after a layoff in 2009, to setting up the WDL and participating in the Project Artemis/Goldman Sachs 10,000 Women Program, Maria's career has gone from strength to strength.

> *Today WDL has trained thousands who are part of a home-based female workforce on common platforms in KPK and Punjab to seek digital livelihoods and help them achieve economic empowerment.*
>
> *She was selected as a finalist in GIST's (Global Innovation through Science and Technology) "I Dare" business plan competition. Google Pakistan has also profiled WDL i its online campaign highlighting innovation in the use of technology.*
>
> *Maria was nominated as a Thought Leader by Ashoka Changemakers.*
>
> *She has featured in local and international media such as Mashable, Forbes, Virgin, Ashoka, CNN and Dawn.*
>
> *Maria is encouraging Pakistani women to explore and develop suitable avenues for work through partnerships*

with the World Bank, Enclude and others.

Maria Umar has trained thousands of women to find work and has mobilized common freelancing platforms for them. In a society where women are restricted from pursuing work opportunities outside home, Maria has stumbled on to a solution that succeeds in the cultural context of the Pakistani family. Women find employment from within the safety of their homes. As long as they have a computer and an internet connection, they will be able to find means of earning a livelihood.

Women in The Labor Force

According to the Pakistan Bureau of Statistics' Labour Force count for 2014-15, only 11.46 percent of all women living in the country were employed. Very few women reach higher education institutions, and 85 percent of those who do never work. Typically, Pakistani women are also constrained in their choice of careers. Those who step out for work usually teach or work as doctors. There are many cultural restrictions. This is especially true of a region such as Waziristan where women observe purdah (veil) and education opportunities are limited. In such regions, for a woman to work outside home is largely unthinkable.

Maria Umar was born in Bannu, in Khyber Pakhtunkhwa province, one of the most conservative areas of Pakistan where women seldom venture out of the house and households are highly patriarchal. Maria went to school in Dera Ismail Khan, Kohat and eventually Peshawar, the provincial capital. She recalls, "My biggest childhood dream was to live in a city where there were traffic lights. I was so happy when we moved to Peshawar."

She did her matriculation from PAF Degree College Peshawar and Masters in English Literature in 2003, becoming the first woman in her family to obtain a postgraduate degree. As per norms, Maria had an arranged marriage at the age of 21, while she was still at university. With her husband's support, she started working in a school after marriage. Again, she was the first woman in her family to work outside the house.

Fired

In 2008, Maria learnt that she was expecting her second baby. She was teaching at a private school in Rawalpindi at the time and the moment the school administration found this out, they let her go because they had no maternity leave policy. Maria was furious and frustrated by the lack of opportunities for respectable work in her situation.

Fortunately, she received an offer to work online through Rozee.pk, which was also posted by a woman incidentally. The job was to write content in English from home for a monthly salary of PKR15,000. This was an ideal job for her at the time. Maria says, "I was earning PKR8,000 per month for a full-time teaching job, and now I was getting double that to write from home in my own time. I thought it was great that I could work anywhere. I just needed an internet connection."

After a while, she did a little research and found that she could make more money if she worked directly with client platforms like oDesk and Elance. Hence in 2009, she started working as a virtual assistant on these platforms, learning how to bid for projects directly and how to get more work.

It was initially difficult. She had to convince her family that she was working to build a career and not merely following a hobby. And when she stepped out to promote her business to strangers mostly, her family pressured her to quit. It was some time before they understood her passion and started supporting Maria.

Spreading The Word

Writing an average of six articles per day was also a challenge. Seeing that the work was more than she could possibly handle by herself, she involved her family and friends to help her complete the assignments. An informal network of virtual freelancers evolved. After a while, it struck Maria that she could offer freelance opportunities through a Pakistan-wide network, "If my family, friends and I could generate work for ourselves while staying at home, why can't other women?" she wondered.

The idea was to engage educated women from remote and rural areas who are unable to work due to socio-cultural limitations. In these areas, girls are raised to be wives and mothers only. They are married off early with the primary responsibility of household duties. In many situations, even educated women in urban cities leave the workforce to look after their young ones. By the time their children grow up and these women are able to join the corporate world, they have lost their confidence to do a typical 9-to-5 job.

"I thought why not provide opportunities for those who could not work outside their homes? A network of women across the country could be formed to work on digital tasks. Little did I expect this idea to change things the way that it did!" Maria says.

"With time, girls are becoming more empowered and stressing for their right to education," Maria observes. "Unfortunately, not many actually utilize their education in the formal sector. So another gender gap exists because the current 9-to-5 work hours do not suit women."

Realizing the potential of the idea, Maria started hounding Pakistani techies through Facebook pages to find out how to do it. Initially, everyone was reserved and reluctant to help her put it together. Then someone challenged Maria, "If you think it is so important why don't you do this yourself?"

That is when Maria decided that she would be the one to do it. Maria laughs as she says, "The person's comment stuck in my mind like a personal challenge. And you know the saying, when something sticks in a Pathanmind, it stays stuck until it is done."

Freelancing in Pakistan

As of 2015, Pakistan's freelance community is estimated to have contributed close to US$850 million and is the second fastest growing market for freelancers. According to an International Data Group 2014 study, around 40 percent of all Pakistani IT professionals engage in some freelance work. This has helped Pakistan become one of the top 10 destinations for contracting online work.

The quality of output from Pakistani freelancers is quite high, so employers and contractors are willing to give repeat business or recommend them to others. Ironically, Pakistani women freelancers are paid more than men, whereas elsewhere they are at par.

With a global market that is rapidly expanding, and virtual work becoming the new norm, there are many opportunities, not only related to programming and design, but also in other areas including data entry, social media marketing, content writing, training and tutoring.

Women's Digital League

Maria launched Women's Digital League (WDL) in 2009. The aim of the social enterprise is to empower women by working online from the comfort of their homes.

Without a background in business, Maria's startup idea was just that--an idea. To her great surprise, a whole plethora of possibilities opened up before her eyes as she persevered. That is how Women's Digital League was born—from an idea, some encouragement and an initiative by some amazing women helping to empower other women.

Meanwhile, Maria was working harder in order to generate further work through oDesk and SamaSource, a not-for-profit based in Palo Alto, California, that specializes in outsourcing digital tasks to individuals in developing countries. She also continued to expand her network to include more women into WDL.

Maria's networking paid off when one day she connected to Azhar Rizvi who was at that time associated with MITEF Global Board. He sent Maria a message on Facebook, inviting her to participate in the GIST *'I Dare'* (Sponsored by Global Innovation of Science and Technology) competition scheduled for May 2012 in Dubai.

Maria says, "I couldn't even imagine myself applying to something so competitive involving people from around the Muslim World. Other contestants had entire teams that had already studied business and tech. Azhar encouraged me and because I didn't want to say no to him, I went ahead and applied despite being unsure."

Azhar helped coach and mentor her along the way, helped whet her application and provided feedback. They met again at an IT conference in Islamabad. Appreciating her work, Azhar gave her constructive advice on growing her business. Maria found this refreshing as others had shot her idea down.

Prior to GIST, Maria had not attended any conference, "I felt I would not fit in, I was just a small-time housewife doing some freelance work with my friends." Attending the conference required an immense amount of confidence and a big leap of faith on Maria's part. "What do you know! I was shortlisted by GIST for the semifinals of the 'I Dare' business plan competition. It seemed ridiculous! And not only that, I also made it to the finals with competitors from more than 40 Muslim countries!"

Ovidiu Bujurean, Senior Manager of GIST Initiative, commented on Maria's approach: "She is extremely passionate and persistent. She is also very committed to her mission of helping female entrepreneurs find job opportunities."

Even today, Maria relies on her local and international mentors to help shape her as an entrepreneur and as a person. In 2015, she included Azhar Rizvi as a board member in Women's Digital League. She says, "To an entrepreneur who is on a mission to find the pot of gold at the end of the rainbow, mentors like Azhar Rizvi are the North Star guiding in the right direction."

Maria also applied to the Women 2.0 Startup Competition out of curiosity. It had fascinated her--a bunch of women helping other women start their businesses with nothing more than an idea.

A line from a famous commercial goes, "An idea can change your life!" That is exactly what happened. She received an encouraging email from the judges at the competition, which said, "The idea is sound and, if it were to be marketed and executed properly, could compete with firms like Elance. With proper mentors and management assistance, this could fly."

Maria has treasured the email for it propelled her into action. "Here were people at the top of their game and potential investors. They were telling me my business model could compete with Elance! I told myself I would be a fool if I didn't pursue it."

Thunderbird

The next step for Maria was to join the three-week business management and leadership course jointly sponsored by the US State Department's Global Women's Initiative office and Goldman Sachs. Armed with confidence gained from the previous competitions, she immediately took up the offer this time. She graduated as both a participant of Project Artemis, where she was trained for two weeks at the Thunderbird School of Global Management, and as a participant of the Goldman Sachs 10,000 Women program.

"In the very first class at Thunderbird, the professor asked us if we knew what an 'Elevator Pitch' was. I was perhaps the only one who knew what it meant—that was my 30-second commercial! Three years ago, while filling forms for the Women 2.0 Startup Competition, I was not aware of it. But I had researched and worked on this since."

"My experience with Project Artemis has given me a bigger vision for Women's Digital League. I want to touch the lives of as many women as possible because I firmly believe that women can be potent catalysts of change. In a country traumatized by extremism, empowering a woman both financially and psychologically is to ensure a stable society for our future generations."

WDL Today: Big Idea, Big Vision

The WDL provides training and work for women in various fields such as content writing, transcription, medical billing, ghost writing, graphic design, data entry, voice-overs, website content writing and everything that can be done from home with a computer and the internet.

She has a full-time team in the Khyber Pakhtunkhwa region working on the Digital Livelihood Program. Another asset is a network of several hundred women who have been associated with WDL in one way or the other over the past few years. The women from all back grounds have been associated with WDL: Women from the remote northern areas of Pakistan working out of small IT Centers provided by local organizations; High school students; Expectant mothers who want to work during their maternity leave until they can rejoin their full time jobs; And housewives who can only invest a couple of hours on weekends, but need the extra income to pay off a loan or save for a rainy day.

WDL has trained women to operate computers and to find jobs online that match their interests and skill levels and are in demand outside. Women may work on Elance and Odesk, and they may also be trained to give Urdu or Quran lessons online via Skype.

More than a business, Women's Digital League is a social enterprise venture. Her goal was to spread the word about the possibility of women working online and open avenues for them to work flexible hours. Women from Pakistani cities, for instance, Peshawar, Karachi, Hunza, Gujranwala, Lahore, Islamabad and Rawalpindi have found work through WDL after responding to tasks put up as Facebook, Twitter and LinkedIn posts. Hash tags like #home based work, #writer needed, #job opportunities and #Pakistan are utilized on Twitter to advertise work opportunities. Maria's dream is to build a highly interactive Customer

Relationship Management (CRM)-based website to facilitate clients as well as make it easier to manage the remote team.

WDL conducts regular trainings and workshops in Punjab and KPK. These workshops have been held at Lahore College for Women University (LCWU) and the Alauddin Academy in Lahore. More trainings are being offered in KPK. The training schedule depends on the interest shown by institutes or organizations. If someone in a particular town requires a training and gathers enough people to attend, WDL conducts the workshop for them. Maria describes the experience, "The feedback I have received from women is fascinating. I get resumes nearly every day. It is the reason I have not given up on Women's Digital League despite the obvious challenges that I have faced – the biggest one financial. These women come to me and tell me, 'my father cannot earn', or 'we do not have male members in the family who can do it for us', or 'we are facing financial problems. So they really need the work, even a little bit to help generate enough income for the needs of their families."

Once they are able to start earning from the safety and the comfort of their homes, they go from being dependent on the breadwinner to becoming dependable contributors for the family."

This makes me more passionate, believe more in the idea and do my best to create this platform where I have enough work to give out to thousands of women, so no one stays home in a financial crunch and suffers just because they can't find online work."

"I have women in the remotest regions possible, like in the Hunza valley and the Gilgit-Baltistan region along the Silk Route, which is located about 5,000 to 6,000 meters above sea level. The women from those areas also reach out to me, saying they have received the necessary training at ICT centers. Now what is the next step for them? So, it is really opening up the world to women who do not go outside their homes because of cultural restrictions and spend their whole lives in their villages."

WDL works with them to develop realistic business models. So daughters have become content writers and mothers are teaching Quran and Urdu over Skype. Countless women have empowered themselves becoming data entry operators, medical transcribers, and others. "They are communicating with clients based in the US, the Middle East or

Germany. The kind of cultural interaction happening between them is mind-boggling and life changing," Maria observes.

KADO and KPK

Maria's success story has also touched Karimabad, the capital city of Hunza. The Karakoram Area Development Organization (KADO) in Karimabad was struggling to run an internet café and was close to shutting it down. Maria came to their aid with an idea that not only changed the business's fortune, but also helped the organization grow considerably.

"WDL experimented with the women there and started giving them IT work related to data entry and digitization. They did not knowabout digitization. They did not know how to utilize their resources back then, but now they have eight IT training centers flourishing in Karimabad. Even now, I am helping them with training and capacity building and guiding them towards commercial skills. This is a huge success story, where we ventured into an area which didn't even have internet, now they have the requisite equipment and computer power backup in the valley," says Maria.

Maria has become an expert in developing livelihoods for women harmoniously with the cultural norms of the country. Recently, she joined as a consultant for Enclude Ltd on a World Bank Project called WomenX Program. This program selected thirty women out of 80 applicants from the province, trained them in using digital tools for freelancing for a period of eight weeks, and later connected them to specific platforms to seek work. In another extremely successful project with the World Bank, Maria Umar and her WDL team have trained over 360 women in how to earn digital livelihood.

International Recognition

Maria has come a long way from being shy and unsure. She is grateful to the people who helped her get to where she is now. She is especially appreciative of Women 2.0 for believing in the innate strength of women and for providing them a platform to prove themselves.

Speaking about WDL, Alec Ross, the former Senior Advisor for Innovation to Secretary of State Hillary Clinton, said, "The idea of a woman coming from the remote areas of Waziristan, working on IT micro tasking is a very powerful affirmation of the platform."

Ross remembers being struck by Maria's dedication to helping other women find work. "I firmly believe that we need to empower women in the marketplace. There's so much insecurity brought on by men. This woman is empowering dozens of other women."

Maria plans to take the WDL platform to a level where women can be trained throughout Pakistan in both rural and urban settings. WDL is also developing an online platform where tasks are distributed following the UpWork model. However, the platform is very different from Up Work, as clients come to WDL with the aim of supporting the economic empowerment of Pakistani women. The clients do not go through the process of sifting through the talent and finding the right person for the job. WDL takes care of that internally. Tasks need to match with the requests that come in. For instance, unemployed doctors want to know how they can contribute online while sitting at home, and WDL guides them to explore the medical transcription field.

Maria was nominated as a Thought Leader by Ashoka Change makers--a global network of social entrepreneurs, innovators, business leaders, policy makers and activists. WDL also won the Early Stage Award in Change makers' 'Women Powering Work' competition.has featured in local and international media as an innovative leader. These publications include Mashable, Forbes, Virgin, Ashoka, and Dawn to name a few. She was also featured by CNBC in their Change Maker Series. As mentioned in the Mashable article, "She continues to break cement ceilings" as she expands her network and brings more women into the net she has cast.

Advice to Entrepreneurs

Being Patient and Taking It One Step at A Time: Maria belongs to a very conservative family from the tribal areas of Pakistan. Convincing her family to work outside home was not easy. She started slowly; teaching in a school at first, then working from home, then convincing them to let her go out and meet people, spread awareness and finally, take it to the next level where Maria was able to go to the US for a business program or to the UAE for a business fund competition. It was a huge challenge to break down that wall and convince everyone around her that this was a good idea.

Pros and cons of working from home: The advantages to women in working from homes are flexible timings, taking as much work on as they can manage and taking time off when they need it. This flexibility allows women to attend to their families and homes as well as plan travel and vacations according to their own schedule.

Although a big drawback is that one has to convince family and friends that working from home does not necessarily mean that one is always available. They need to realize that they have to respect the time and effort that the individual is putting in. Maria recalls that her family and friends had initially thought this was just a hobby. It was only with time that she was able to prove the credibility of work-at-home opportunities to her family.

13

PDX: Designing a Marketplace to Accelerate Development

PDX: Pakistan Development Exchange
Hassaan Shah, Sami Ahmad

Co-Founders
Pakistan, US
www.pdx.com.pk

"The poor themselves can create a poverty-free world. All we have to do is to free them from the chains that we have put around them!" ~ Muhammad Yunus. Nobel laureate, social entrepreneur and economist

Philanthropists Hassaan and Sami always wondered about the leakages in donation systems and the lack of transparency. They piloted an alternative charity match system through a social exchange bank, based on crowd funding, hyper-connectivity and community development. Attempting to shift the paradigm, Hassaan and Sami are proving to the world that it is possible to move a community out of the vicious cycle of poverty, one family at a time.

Author's Note: This story is about two young men, Sami Ahmad and Hassaan Shah, whom I consider my brothers and friends. Their idea is still a work in progress but it has all the makings of a major game changer for philanthropy. From the outset, I could see the potential of this model, which, if properly executed, would create new avenues to eradicate poverty and contribute to the economic development of the country. I helped them design it for global implementation, guided them to come up with their business vision and a strategy for implementation across country. I am still mentoring them on the execution and planning.

Hassaan Shah and Sami Ahmad have been part of the Pakistani diaspora and actively working for about a decade on ways to give back to Pakistan. Deeply influenced by Muhammad Yunus' book 'Creating a World Without Poverty', Sami Ahmad and his partner Hassaan Shah are now working on developing the first "Development Exchange" model in Pakistan. The model is based on a hyper-connected model of philanthropy and a crowd funding platform that focuses on developing one community at a time.

What makes this social venture different from others is that while other social entrepreneurs choose to solve one issue such as sanitation, illiteracy or low-quality healthcare, PDX adopts a multifaceted approach, under the term "crowd slumming". It works with social sector partners to develop a holistic solution for impoverished communities.

PDX's model entails linking Pakistani donors via mobile app to targeted communities through the mechanism of community resource centers--which operate robust poverty reduction program funded by the donors. Donors can conveniently and transparently engage and manage their giving in their adopted slums. In this manner, the poorest communities and households in Pakistan can gain access to basic services and an opportunity to quickly climb the ladder out of poverty.

This model has been running successfully in one locality in Lahore for the past year and the team is actively in the process of launch and scale up in the major cities of Pakistan.

Social Stock Exchange

In 2008, Sami Ahmad, a Pakistani-American entrepreneur hailing from Texas, met Dr. Muhammad Yunus, the founder of Grameen Bank and the recipient of the Nobel Peace Prize at an event staged at his alma mater Georgetown University. Dr. Yunus, one of the pioneers of microfinance, was presenting his latest book, 'Creating a World Without Poverty', in which there was a chapter on the concept of social stock exchanges. He had suggested a conceptual framework for such an exchange that would serve as a funding mechanism between social investors and social enterprises. Intrigued by the concept, Sami inquired with Dr. Yunus about real-world examples, and to his surprise, there were no such success stories to be found anywhere. It had remained a pipedream.

Managing a BPO business at the time between Pakistan and the US, Sami began to see mass poverty in Pakistan as the biggest opportunity around. It was with this realization that he decided to try his hand at developing a unique and innovative crowdfunding platform to solve the problems of Pakistan's donors, NGOs, and the impoverished in a sustainable and market-based manner.

Sami explains, "Because I had a financial markets background, I viewed the problem from a different lensaltogether. I saw it as an issue of intermediation. Demand and supply were unable to interact and transact efficiently, securely and transparently. Marketplaces are a natural phenomenon, but for some odd reason we never bothered to innovate one for the development sector. Where is the NASDAQ for social development? So, I saw it as purely a design issue. After envisioning the sheer and massive potential to unleash value in the lives of all stakeholders, especially the poor, I felt my philanthropic contribution in life would be to invest all my time, energy and ambition towards creating this new type of institution. It was my calling."

Troubled Stakeholders

True to the Teachings of the illustrious poet and intellectual force behind the founding of Pakistan, Muhammad Iqbal, Sami embarked on the journey and many believers in the same vision

joined the caravan. It took eight years of intense thinking, envisioning, networking, brainstorming, studying, immersive field trips and trial and error, before a definitive design emerged. Development was managed in sprints, while trying to balance the realities of everyday life-work, friends and family.

Sami realized that any efficient system would need to cater to three distinct stakeholders simultaneously. These were the poor who needed to break out of the endless poverty cycle; the donors who wanted the inner satisfaction of giving back to society for the betterment of mankind; and the nonprofit-that most often was focused on solving some aspect of the development equation and was usually short of funds to do so effectively. All stakeholders are constantly in search of each other in order to satisfy their respective needs. Donors are seeking deserving poor through effective NGOs, who are seeking more resources, to serve the poor who are always seeking help.

The Poor Would Think: "I hate begging, but there is no other way to cater to our needs. It breaks my heart to see my kids out of school selling newspapers or begging on traffic signals." Asima Naeem, a resident of Sultan Park, Lahore, is a patient of end-Stage renal disease (ESRD)-commonly known as kidney failure. Her husband, a security guard, does not earn enough to cover her medical needs. Previously, Asima used to collect small donations during Friday prayers to try to cover the exorbitant cost of her dialysis. Given their desperate economic condition, sending their children to school was out of question. They would often go to bed hungry. This is just another family out of the millions of people living below the poverty line in Pakistan. A relatively small amount of money can pull these people out of their miseries, and on the ladder of progress.

Typically, donor would rationalize: "I know I can pay one month's school fee of a child in Pakistan by skipping just one lunch, a Subway sandwich or Starbucks cappuccino." Mubeen, the owner of a software house in London, has never gotten used to the grievous tales of rampant poverty and unemployment in Pakistan. Even though his family had shifted abroad a long time ago, love for the homeland still burns bright inside his heart. Unable to find a way to contribute towards the betterment of the lower echelons of society but, he is yet another overseas Pakistani ready to give back to his homeland, by giving a helping hand to a deserving person. Whenever they give, they never know if it made a difference. He is like millions of fellow donors who are frustrated and distrustful.

The non-profit would be focused on meeting development goals: "We have a massive problem where over 25 million kids who should be in school, are not. We know how to tackle this issue, but without suitable resources, we cannot even make a dent in the problem." Kawish Welfare Trust is an NGO that has established a network of +300 informal schools catering to poor children from rural villages and urban slums. They are one of over 150,000 social organizations trying to bridge the gap in basic services to more than half of Pakistan's population-over 100 million poor. The most impactful NGOs in Pakistan are in dire need of support to enhance their own capacities, effectiveness and fundraising to expand their outreach.

Sami likes the current scenario to a financial sector that lacks a stock exchange. The business world would grind to halt the very next day. What would emerge would look very much like the development sector does today-a mess! In the absence of efficient marketplaces, there are inevitably high transaction costs as parties struggle to find each other to conduct value-adding transactions. Ultimately, there is market failure, which describes the prevailing development sector scenario in Pakistan, a country that is consistently ranked among the most generous in the world in terms of philanthropic giving and global remittances. Research shows there is more than enough giving and resources available to defeat extreme poverty affecting near 50 million poor. The problem revolves around a broken system.

Modelling a Better System

In 2009, Sami was back in Saudi Arabia working as a consultant for a large hotel chain. He had recently married and decided to settle down in the country. Around the same time that Sami was developing this concept, he met his future partner Hassaan Shah, a young entrepreneur from Lahore. Hailing from a political family that had extensive experience in grassroots community development, Hassaan became a natural partner. Sami would look after development of systems and strategies, while Hassaan focused on the backbreaking implementation of the model in slums and villages.

In 2013, Sami and Hassaan presented the concept of a "Development Exchange" to the President of the Islamic Development Bank (IDB)-a developmental financing agency with the purpose of fostering economic development in Muslim countries-a region that consists of 57 countries with approximately 1.6 billion people. Some of the richest countries are part of the Islamic bloc, like Middle Eastern states such as Qatar, Bahrain, the UAE, and Brunei as well as some of the poorest countries like Afghanistan and Somalia. The cumulative wealth of the Islamic bloc is estimated to be close to US$6.9 trillion.

The team presented the idea of crowdsourcing systems to address the need to effectively match the massive amounts of Muslim giving with the massive numbers of Muslim poor. The IDB president appreciated the idea immensely and stated that he would extend support to scale up the social venture across all 57 Muslim countries if Sami and Hassaan were willing to go and prove the concept through a pilot project in Pakistan.

Deep Dive

Buoyed by this encouraging response from one of the leaders of the global development sector, Sami and Hassaan decided to leave their businesses and lives of comfort, to move to the slums in Pakistan and pursue the beautiful goal. To the horror of their families, they took out all their savings to fund the idealistic experiment. A lot was at stake.

After two years of arduous product development, learning, research, and trial and error, the Pakistan Development Exchange (PDX) was finally born in 2016.

An innovative idea coined by PDX, "Crowdslumming" consists of connecting 'crowds' of donors to the respective recipients via the PDX resource centers situated in the slums. For example, a 3,000 household slum when paired with 3,000 donors giving $50 a month, can generate $150,000 a month towards development interventions across all domains, community projects, and cash support to the poorest. Over the course of a few years, this crowdslumming can transform the face of the slum, and the lives of its residents. At the same time, there is visible and data-backed impact that is shown to the donor to maximize their gratification.

The Needy: PDX sets up Resource Centers to provide basic services (including health, education, skills, microfinance, sanitation, etc.) at low-cost or free to the poor community, enabled to reduce poverty in an impactful and measurable way. One of the most important functions of these resource centers is identification and measurement of household development.

The Donors: PDX uses technology to "connect" donors to these Resource Centers, enabling them to experience the impact their much needed donations make in the lives of people and community. The key interface is a gamified mobile app that enables the donor to crowdsource the development of the entire slum.

The Ngos: Charged with delivering services, PDX funds partner NGOs, giving them free space from which to operate. It also produces short films to crowdfund their interventions and spread awareness among potential donors through the platform.

PDX's Goals: PDX aims to alleviate poverty for 50 million extreme poor, by establishing 5,000 specialized resource centers, in collaboration with the top 1,000 NGOs, sponsored by 500,000 donors, by the year 2030.

One concrete example of the solution in action is: Asima's family has been adopted by Mobeen, who learned of her plight after watching a video created by the PDX team and floated on social media. Now she receives her dialysis in a timely manner, and both of her kids go to a primary school in the branch in Sultan Park, where they not only get quality education but are also provided with a nutritious breakfast by another NGO named Rizq. Her family also now has access to a mobile health unit put up by E-Health in Sultan Park. Mobeen gets monthly updates on the situation via photos and videos by PDX's on-ground team. All parties are satisfied.

Launch

Over the two-year pre-launch period, PDX has worked with over 40 NGOs, served about 50 private donors as clients, and treated over two thousand cases of patients, students, micro-entrepreneurs, and many other victims of poverty. PDX has set up a resource center in each major city-Lahore, Karachi, Islamabad, and Peshawar and is looking to scale up in each city before moving on to the rural areas.

Sami and Hassaan want PDX to be a sustainable venture in the long-term. The team believes that many poor Pakistanis should start working since the country has a lot of potential and is suffering mainly because of a broken government system. Because of this, new models like PDX are born to fill in the gap.

The partnership duo of Sami and Hassaan has now swelled to over 15 team members-each contributing their core skill to develop the venture. Hassaan says, "the seeds of the movement have been sown, and in a decade we expect to number in the thousands, and will be serving millions, God willing". As of this writing (February 2017), PDX is priming itself for official launch to the public by mid of 2017.

The PDX team maintains that there are about 10 to 12 million Pakistanis in the diaspora and if even 500,000 (5%) of them can contribute US$50 a month, they can support 5,000 such resource centers, each of which can serve 10,000 people. This translates to 50 million individuals who can receive the services over the course of 10 to 15 years. It will make a huge difference in beating extreme poverty in Pakistan.

Advice for Social Entrepreneurs

Operate at Every Level: Social entrepreneurs should be willing to meet everyone who can help them take their work forward. From meeting heads of banks to 'getting their hands dirty' living in a low-income community to understand their problems, Hassaan and Sami are flexible enough to operate at every level.

Use Technology to Your Advantage: PDX uses technology to connect donors with the communities that they donate to, creating goodwill and trust in the process.

Human-Centered Design: When designing new products and services, it is best to use the HCD approach to build a prototype, and the lean approach to test and reiterate its design as you take feedback from users.

14

Connect, Educate and Evolve

RABTT
IMRAN SARWAR
CEO and Co-founder
Lahore
www.rabtt.org

"Education is not the learning of facts, but the training of the mind to think." ~ Albert Einstein

A vacation time interaction with students from underprivileged schools inspired Imran to start a summer program for children that would break down barriers of education, class and attitude, through critical thinking, connecting with others and identity development. Through Rabtt programs, doors open for children from all kinds of backgrounds as they undergo life-altering early experiences.

Author's Note: I met Imran about three years ago through another friend Aun Rehman, after he had came back to Pakistan after completing his MPA from Harvard Kennedy School of Government. He was inspired and charged with a dream to transform Pakistan's education system. Imran wanted to bring about change by adding new dimensions like critical thinking, empathy, creativity and self-confidence to an outdated educational system that centers on imparting information and rote learning. I helped him in broadening the vision from economically deprived schools to established middle class schools as I could see a clear need across the board for critical thinking. My role was to help him come up with strategy and vision

Imran Sarwar is a public policy graduate from Harvard University who wants to transform Pakistan's education sector. After a summer interaction with students of underprivileged schools, he decided that

he wanted to teach children in a style that would be challenging and engaging and would allow them to develop critical thinking skills, empathy, problem solving and leadership.

Imran and his colleague Aneeq Ahmed Cheema laid the foundation of Rabtt in 2011. Through this platform, volunteers and mentors interact with students from Lahore's schools. Rabtt works to make the educational experience more holistic for students of both government and private schools.

In a short span of time, Rabtt's programs have mentored more than 2,500 students in 20 schools in Lahore and Karachi and trained 300 teachers in Punjab. Motivated by the success of the idea, Imran plans to take Rabtt's programs to other cities in Pakistan.

Critical Thinking

Imran Sarwar received his early education from various Army Public Schools (APS) and Garrison Academy-a network of military schools spread over the country. After obtaining an A level certificate from a private school in Lahore, Imran started studying for a Bachelor's degree in Economics from the Lahore University of Management Sciences (LUMS) in 2006.

At LUMS, he developed an interest in the Social Sciences enjoying Philosophy, Sociology and Political Science. Finally, he decided to pursue Public Policy. After graduating in 2010, he earned a Fulbright Scholarship to study at Harvard.

Imran's school education emphasized memorizing facts and learning by rote. It was at LUMS that he realized that a student could question what was being taught. He could have his own perspective on the issues and subjects. "I started wondering why I had to wait for a good 12,13 years of education to come across this concept of critical thinking. And why couldn't it be incorporated into the education system earlier?" Imran remembers.

LUMS offers a National Outreach Program, which provides scholarships to students from low-income backgrounds to study at LUMS. In this program, LUMS' students teach a three-week summer course to prepare prospective students for the SAT entry test, a prerequisite for admission into LUMS. In his junior year, Imran participated in this program providing verbal English language training to prospective students.

It was a moving experience to see those students so charged to get into LUMS and Imran recognized the reason for their excitement to be the human interaction. The students had connected with the LUMS students on a deeper level and were thrilled to meet them. They would tell Imran: "We want to come here because you guys study here." This connection and interaction eventually led to the establishment of Rabtt.

After Imran graduated, he realized he would enjoy working in the development sector instead of the corporate world. He signed up as a research assistant at Lahore's Forman Christian College's Center for Public Policy and Governance where he met Aneeq Ahmed Cheema, Rabtt's eventual co-founder. They came up with the idea of Rabtt while working together.

Their experience of the National Outreach program and their observation of the differences between the students of private and public schools had convinced the two that the most important thing in life was to create connections. To them, the whole idea of education was to build a bond between individuals. Once a bond was forged, it was going to create a mutually powerful experience for both the student and the teacher.

They also realised that to change the mindset and attitude of the youth, it was important to create experiences that encourage discovery, problem solving and critical thinking instead of rote, repetition and reproduction. "We wanted to create Rabtt, which means 'connection' in Urdu," says Imran. "My idea was very simple. Rabtt will be an organization which will mentor the children of today and make them into the leaders of tomorrow."

Aneeq, on the other hand, had been a participant in the 'Seeds of Peace' summer camps. His final research thesis had been on the role curriculum plays in the education system. In December 2010, these dedicated men decided that they must develop this idea. Rabtt would work on introducing and developing critical thinking skills at school level. Imran and Aneeq also wanted to bring together students from different social backgrounds to break barriers and build a more inclusive and tolerant society.

Laying The Foundation

In January 2011, Imran and Aneeq started working at Akhuwat. It is an organization working to alleviate poverty by providing interest-free microfinance loans to economically marginalized families. Their experience at Akhuwat gave them a direction and they honed their plans for their social venture.

The goal was to develop a curriculum for intensive summer camps promote critical thinking and problem solving and polishes the students' leadership skills. The objective was to enable the students to develop empathy and participate in their learning instead of mere memorising.

When they presented the idea to Dr Amjad Saqib and Dr Kamran Shams, the co-founders of Akhuwat, they were supportive. Imran and Aneeq believe that if these two people had not supported their idea in the very beginning, they might not have gone ahead. Soon, Dr Kamran accompanied Imran and Aneeq to meet the head of the first school Rabtt had contacted.

They mentored 30 students in their first camp and it proved to be a transformational experience. Imran firmly believes that, "If you take that first step, if you take that leap of faith, there will be people to support you." They received support from their seniors and mentors from the start. In addition, they required 15-20 volunteers for the camps. They put up a Facebook page, spread the word and received around 60 applications for volunteers. Once again, it was a positive affirmation of the duo's belief that people want to reach out and help others.

Next, they created a framework for the team operations. They defined Rabtt's model and its core competencies, developed the modules and set the objectives of mentoring students in world history, art, drama, thinking skills, philosophy, English, mathematics and public speaking. The summer camp lasted for about three weeks and was a great success.

Keeping The Program Running

In August of 2011, Imran left to do his Master's in Public Policy from the Kennedy School at Harvard University, where he specialized in Political and Economic Development. While he was away, Aneeq and other members of the core team continued to work on developing Rabtt. During the summer vacations of 2012, Imran came home and helped Rabtt launch camps in two schools. Though Imran was unable to stay for the full length of the event, the team kept the programs running.

On his return from the US in 2013, Imran had to decide what he would be doing for the rest of his life. Working for the United Nations had always been a dream job for Imran. However, a summer internship at the International Labour Organisation (ILO) in Jakarta in 2012 had helped him realize that he did not want to work at the UN. He craved the connections that he had made with the students and volunteers at the grassroot level.

Imran met many mentors at the Kennedy School, including Aun Rehman who was there for his mid-career program. Aun became one of Rabtt's staunchest mentors.

Rabtt-Loud And Clear

During the last year of his Master's program, Imran decided to work full time at Rabtt. It was a tricky decision. They had started this venture on a pro bono basis and wanted to see how far they could take the idea. In contrast, working at the World Bank or the United Nations had the tempting prospects of job security and obviously a higher financial return.

Imran's family took months to adjust to his idea of self-employment. They continued to advise him to find a secure job at some NGO while working for Rabtt on the side. But Imran felt that it would be better to close down Rabtt than give it half-hearted attention.

"Rabtt was my baby, my idea. I didn't want to look back in five or 10 years and regret my decision of abandoning it," says Imran. He decided to give it a shot and set himself two years' time to make or break it. With time, his family realized that he was passionate about the venture and started to support him.

Meanwhile, Imran received a grant from Harvard's South Asia Institute. The grant was enough to fund Rabtt for three to four months.

They gradually started building a team. Rabtt started operations in June 2013 with Imran as its first full-time employee andseveral part-time volunteers. In November, the team began recruiting for Rabtt's programs for the first time. Salma, Rabtt's second full-time employee was responsible for recruitment.

Building Empathetic Learning Environments

Rabtt currently offers two core flagship programs: the Rabtt Scholars Program for high school students, and the Rabtt Fellows Program, a one-year program for university students who are trained to mentor high school students in different disciplines. The content of the programs is revised annually. By 2016, Rabtt had engaged about 200 students and 40 fellows in Karachi, and 600 students and 80 fellows in Lahore.

The organisation also has a program called the Change Agents, which unites Rabtt-trained public school students and high-end private school students of the same age group in an extensive learning environment for six weeks. "The fact that we bring together two different segments of society makes this program very close to my heart," says Imran. "Rabtt is a metaphor in a lot of ways because it represents the emphasis on developing human connections above all."

The organisation's goal is to build empathetic learning and working environments. Its vision is to create a society in which people listen to each other with respect and try to understand each other. Imran believes education is a vehicle towards accomplishing this.

It focuses on four basic matrices: Critical thinking, empathy, creativity and self-confidence. Everything in its modules is linked to these four matrices. Rabtt also offers different modules for different audiences with a few common threads. For instance, all the modules start with the discussion of 'Identity'-who you are and what your role is in society.Haider Shah, a student at Rabtt's summer camp in 2014, shared his experience, "I believe public speaking skills are very useful in my life. After participating in this program, my friends say that my personality has improved, my body language is better and I am more confident while talking to others."

Rabtt Fellows are a major success. They are encouraged to spread what they have been taught as much as they can. "We are very clear about the kind of society we want to build and we obviously cannot do it alone." Imran says it is difficult for them to reach everywhere, at least currently, therefore he wants people to take this model forward and this is achieved through Rabtt's Fellows. The Rabtt Fellows Program (RFP) is a year-long training focused entirely on their future plans. Rabtt has engaged over 200 fellows in the last three to four years, seven of whom have already started their own social enterprises, five of them in the education sector. The goal is to pass the torch on to the Fellows. Imran considers Rabtt's biggest achievement to be the nurturing of the youth's zest for giving back to society.

Take Off

The number of schools that Rabtt has worked with is steadily growing. In 2013, Rabtt was working with two schools that increased to seven in 2014 and 2015. By 2015, Rabtt had mentored over 1900 students. In 2016, Rabtt conducted sessions at five Karachi schools working with an average 35 to 40 students at each campus and as many as 80 Fellows were selected for the year. Rabtt initially planned to set up camps at 15 schools in Lahore last year, but the prevalent security crises in Punjab prevented the camps from happening. The 20 chosen institutions in Lahore and Karachi, are a mix of public and low-cost private schools charging less than PKR500 (US$5) per month in tuition fee.

Currently, Rabtt is almost entirely focused on depth. As Imran considers human interaction to be essential for the program, he feels that the program needs to reach out to more students and volunteers for building a sustainable network of people. While the programs currently in operation are extremely popular, Imran and Aneeq are hopeful about introducing more programs adding to Rabtt's breadth.

Rabtt's outreach comes through its teacher-training sessions. They recently conducted one such session for around 300 teachers in the rural areas around Faisalabad and Jhang districts in the Punjab province. "At a follow-up visit a month later, we found the teachers still energized and motivated. "These 300 teachers are conveying their learning to at least 12,000 more people," says Imran.

The team has faced problems at some institutions. At one school, they had to stop training in the middle of a camp once. The head of the all girls' school was objecting to having male volunteers at the camp, so female instructors had to be brought in instead. However, the headmistress later became so supportive of Rabtt's programs that she invited Salma to be on their School Committee.

Today, I Am Learning

Rabtt's Research Department focuses on impact evaluation and the team has planned the strategy for the coming years. Imran has planned a control group survey to make impact evaluation more rigorous. However, the anecdotal post-program data of three years has been extremely positive.

Many students who attended the Rabtt Scholars Program from 2011 to 2013, have joined it as Fellows. Six boys and girls are now mentoring junior students. Abdullah Nasir is one of them. He was a student at Rabtt's summer camps in 2013 and has been in touch with the team ever since. In 2016, he was the camp director at Yohannabad. He recounts his experience, "We had this boy in the summer camp who was shy at first, but soon began taking an interest and did his best to get involved. On the last day of the camp, he said to me, 'Sir Abdullah, you are my inspiration. Thank you for making me believe in myself.' These words mean the world to me. The best thing about being a Fellow at Rabtt is that I've figured out what happiness actually is. It lies in making others happy."

During the month of Ramadan in 2015, the team arranged an Iftar (the meal with which Muslims break their fast during the holy month) in every school to engage the parents. "The first question parents ask us is what magic do we have, as their children who hate going to school on regular days, are excited about going to the camp during the holidays," laughs Imran. "A lot of parents support us. A student's uncle told us that his nephew has become calmer than before and an active listener ever since he has enrolled in the Rabtt program."

Imran is satisfied with this progress. He remembers a student who used to stammer in his class of 20. At the end of the camp, the same student had confidently delivered a speech to around 200 people. Another shy student who came to him and said, *"Ab tak mein yaad kar raha tha, aaj maine seekha hai.* (I was memorizing until now. Today I have learnt.)" left Imran beaming with pride.

Taking Rabtt Forward

Rabtt has stepped into a phase of rapid growth. Until 2015, the team had not even thought about going to other cities. Nevertheless, the opportunity to start operations in Karachi came up and they grabbed it. In 2016, Engro supported Rabtt's entire program in Karachi. Imran describes this as their growth model. They will gradually be rolling out the same model in different cities. Next, they will introduce the Fellowship and Scholar programs in new cities. After that, they will build the capacity of local teams in different cities so that teachers' and corporate trainings can be performed locally. Ideally, all these hubs will be self-sustainable.

A major achievement for the Rabtt team is that other organizations are now approaching Rabtt to conduct trainings in-house. Five years down the road, Imran expects that the challenge for the team will be to structure and institutionalize Rabtt.

Meanwhile, out of the three core team members who have been working for Rabtt for the last two years, two have received Fulbright Scholarships to the US and another will soon be leaving on a Chevening Scholarship to the UK. "This is a huge achievement for us," says Imran.

Another challenge for Rabtt is to take the organizational ethos forward when scaling up. The team will be getting their heads together to devise a strategy for structured progress.

Business Development in The Corporate Sector

In the corporate sector, the Rabtt team conducts a needs-assessment for each client. They consider this a very important part of the program and find no point in generic training sessions. The client organizations value this because they believe that a tailored program will address their needs better.

Traditionally, trainings in the corporate sector are skill-based. However, Rabtt tackles attitudinal and behavioral changes and effects employee's productivity and attitude. These are not regular corporate skills issues. At one of their clients' company, Imran felt that the employees lacked the feeling of ownership in the enterprise. To cultivate ownership, a person needs to feel like he is part of a bigger system and engaged in something productive. "We find meaning when we think of ourselves as part of something bigger. That's what our religion gives us; that is what our community, our society gives us, and that's how we develop feelings of ownership," he explains."That is the kind of thing that we work on and this is where systematic thinking comes in."

Rabtt has around nine to 10 training modules tailored according to the needs of audience. These cover areas such as identity, communication skills, story-telling, systems thinking, adaptive leadership, leadership presence, team building. Leadership and authority are the other aspects that Rabtt targets in corporate trainings.

Need for Government Support for Scaling

Imran believes that the government has an immense role to play which cannot be ignored. Being a public policy major, Imran's contention with the current system is the top-down policymaking, with individuals from the development sector sitting in Islamabad in air-conditioned rooms, making strategies for deprived cities like Khairpur, Khanpur and Rahim Yar Khan. At Akhuwat, Imran had learnt that a bottom-up policymaking structure is more conducive for empowering the grassroots. This means taking certain measures and actions, figuring out if they are working or not, improving them, scaling them and then evaluating their impact on society.

The market itself rejects whatever is not working. "You have to prove that the concept you are working on really has what it takes to be successful. Each pilot translates into market acceptance to scale to the next level and every measure that fails indicates that there is a need to correct a strategy direction," says Imran.

He further explains, "Let me give an example of the limited perspective of policy makers with the top-down approach. In each of the government schools that we work in, the head needs a permission letter from the Secretary Education to allow an external team to come and conduct the program. Once, a permission letter was delayed. The head barred the Rabtt team from entering the classrooms. The team spoke to the guard who gave them access to the school grounds. For two days, Rabtt ran their program in the school ground, until the classrooms were opened for them upon receipt of the permission letter. "You have to make this connection; you have to build this trust all across the spectrum, with the Secretary Education to the security guard of each school."

The team hopes that once the program matures, the public sector will take it forward. They have started negotiating with the government because they cannot continue to operate without the approval of public institutions. The Punjab government has recently outsourced the training of around 5,000 schools that have become Rabtt's biggest clients.

The team recently met KPK government officials who are willing to fund the programs. The Directorate of Staff Development (DSD), responsible for training teachers and other staff at government institutions, is currently outsourcing some of their trainings and the team will be pitching for that.

Evolving The Model

Since 2015, Rabtt's focus has been on self-sustainability. Until 2013, the organization was not self-sustaining, as the team was building the program back then. In 2014, Rabtt started conducting training sessions with private schools, but they were only able to generate less than one percent of the required funds. In 2015, they began conducting trainings with LUMS and the rate jumped to almost nine percent. In 2016, the team also started training sessions for corporate professionals. This enabled them to raise more funds. Today, they generate 25 percent of what they require. The team covers all the administrative expenses (salaries, utilities and rent) themselves through these sessions, making it possible for Rabtt to utilize 100 percent of the grants and the donated money for its programs.

Financial challenges still exist, and as Imran elaborates, it is hard to predict the money trail for more than two months as Rabtt is still dependent on donors. "We require solid funding for the next three to four years because sponsorships for a few months become very stressful and we are at a stage where we need funding for the long run now," says Imran.

Until now, the team has shied away from approaching private

schools for trainings, and is instead focusing more on teachers' and corporate trainings. For political reasons, especially in Punjab, private schools have been having problems with the provincial government for the past few years. First, they were barred from increasing the tuition fees. Then terrorism threats forced them to beef up their security. As a result, what private schools can afford keeps fluctuating. "We've realized that private schools are a very volatile market. It is very uncertain working with them and they're not willing to pay," he shares.

Imran believes that even if Rabtt is taken to private schools, it will not be the institutions that pay for it and the cost will inevitably be passed on to the parents. The best way forward for them is to engage students and parents directly, a model that is followed by tuition centers all over the country. However, for that a separate place is required at a great cost and more time and effort.

The biggest bottleneck right now is the security situation in Punjab. Summer schools were discontinued on instructions from the Home Department. If a school opens in summer (even for a summer camp), it is fined heavily. Rabtt is taking this up in Lahore and the team has had meetings at the Secretariat level. They are still figuring out the strategy for the summer programs.

Opportunities from the corporate sector have been the best thing that has happened to Rabtt. Using the same matrices and core competencies, Rabtt aims to increase employee job satisfaction and communication within departments. The feedback has been extremely positive and the team has realized that returns are higher. The sector is more responsive and the impact is immediately visible with fewer issues.

Rabtt is approaching its partners, The History Project, who have tapped into the private school market and have asked for their input. Despite the limited resources, Rabtt model for public schools and low-cost private schools is flourishing, as are their teachers' and corporate training programs.

15

Reversing the Brain Drain

Pakathon
Asad Badruddin,
Zheela Qaiser
Co-founders
Boston
www.pakathon.org

"Take the first step in faith. You don't have to see the whole staircase, just take the first step." ~ Martin Luther King, Jr

Asad and Zheela started a civic hackathon to brainstorm solutions that would help the Pakistani diaspora connect back home and develop products and solutions to Pakistan's most pressing problems. What started as a small hackathon has created a multiplier effect that has mobilized 45 universities in Pakistan, many universities abroad, students in five countries, 15 cities, five host countries and 1,000+ global participants.

Author's Note: Pakathon is Asad and Zheela's story. I regard these two as my own children. I met them in 2013 in Silicon Valley at OPEN Charter Members Retreat. They were pitching for funding at a three-day hackathon for Harvard, MIT, Boston University and Tuft students in Boston. I could clearly see the merit of their ambitious initiative, provided it got Pakistani students and academics involved. The two hijacked me against my will to join them in the fantastic idea of mobilizing the diaspora to create social ventures.

Pakathon is building a platform to address social issues in Pakistan by engaging the diaspora and local talent. It is an effort to reverse the brain drain and get Pakistani youth around the world engaged in solving local issues and help build a great country. Working with them and watching

Pakathon grow has been a great journey of over three years. Currently the fourth Pakathon is in process.

Because of the time zone differences , Asad and Zheela in USA and me in Pakistan, they usually call me after midnight, and never apologize. They consider it their right, which I have now accepted. As a cofounder of Pakathon, I request you all to visit our website and join us in any capacity you can, as a trainer, expert, advisor, donor, or even design a role for yourself. We welcome everyone who may be willing to contribute to our movement and help build Pakistan.

An estimated eight million Pakistanis live overseas and approximately 10,000 students leave Pakistan each year to study abroad. These people create immense value and respect for Pakistan globally, both as part of the diaspora and when they return to their homeland. However, despite this contribution, a number of these people are torn between serving their adopted country and yearning to fix the problems of their native country.

Asad, Zheela and Azhar Rizvi started an organization to reverse the brain drain from Pakistan. In a short period of three years since Pakathon's inception, the network has grown manifold. A small organization has created a multiplier effect mobilizing more than 45 universities in Pakistan, several universities abroad, numerous students in five countries, 15 cities, five host countries and 1,000+ global participants. Many of the contestants have since started work on their social ventures. The chapters themselves have hosted hundreds of events to connect, motivate and mobilize participants into creating the Pakistan of their dreams.

A Chance Encounter

A chance meeting can lead to great things. Asad Badruddin first met Zheela Qaiser through a mutual friend in Karachi. Having attended the same high school, both discovered common links in the US and in Pakistan. Asad remembers, "I was surprised by her words, because urban, cosmopolitan Pakistanis are usually apathetic about the issues facing the country."

A year later in 2013, Asad had another chance meeting with Zheela- this time at the train station in Cambridge, Massachusetts. Both were at crossroads in their lives at the time. She had just dropped out of architecture school at MIT and was trying to figure out what to do next. Asad was working at a startup called Blue Fin Labs, which had been acquired by Twitter just before its initial public offering. This time they discovered that they had many things in common in addition to friends.

While talking, they agreed that Pakistanis in Boston felt uncomfortable and disconnected with their homeland. They decided to do something about it. At that time, Twitter was organizing a programming hackathon. The fast-paced format brought together people from different backgrounds to collaborate in a limited time. Asad and Zheela decided to put together an event that was based on the same format, but instead of tech solutions, the teams would have to come up with solutions to social issues in Pakistan. They came up with a unique and catchy name for the event and the organization: Pakathon.

They piloted a workshop in Boston, inviting teams from the Pakistani diaspora in Toronto and Seattle. The teams worked together to brainstorm solutions that would help average Pakistanis meet their basic needs. At the end of the workshop, the teams left energized and believing that this was a winning cause that could potentially create a movement of Pakistanis motivated to fix the broken parts of their country. At that point, the idea of building Pakathon seemed truly magical.

Pitching The Idea

The duo pitched the idea to a number of investors, including once at an OPEN (Organization of Pakistani Entrepreneurs Network) retreat.

There they met another supporter.

Azhar Rizvi, co-founder of OPEN in Pakistan and co-founder of MITEFP, was at the retreat when the Pakathon team was pitching its idea. Azhar be came a keen supporter of the idea and strongly recommended that it should be funded. He had launched a Business Acceleration Program from the MIT Enterprise Forum of Pakistan in 2007 and two of the main business plan competitions from NUST and IBA. He could sense an ideal synergy between his efforts in Pakistan and Pakathon. Azhar told the two, "I will arrange for funding on one condition: You also include Pakistani universities in the competition."

Initially, Asad and Zheela were not sure about how many Pakistanis would actually be interested in launching a social enterprise. Instead, they focused on virtually connecting participants in the US with participants in Pakistan in the hopes that they would team up and work together.

Once all three were on the same page, Azhar Rizvi managed to convince the Rector of NUST, Lt. Gen Muhammad Asghar, and, vice chancellor LUMS, Sohail Naqvi to join the competition. Both contributed US$5,000 each to run the event. This was the beginning of a partnership between the three team members.

The First Pakathon Competition

The first Pakathon was organized over a three-day weekend in September 2013 in Boston. The universities that participated from Boston were MIT, Harvard, Tufts and Boston University. From Pakistan, NUST and LUMS joined via Skype and contestants from Toronto and Seattle flew in.

Author and former LUMS vice chancellor Adil Najam; the blackjack player and hacker turned angel investor Semyon Dukach; and chairperson and Entrepreneurship Ventures Inc. CEO Ken Morse, were there to motivate and share their experiences. The 28 teams were given an orientation and then asked to develop ideas and pitches. Over the weekend, the teams conceptualized, researched and designed solutions. Some of the great industry leaders and professors were available to mentor them.

In the final round, each of the shortlisted teams presented a three-minute video that judges, including professors at MIT and Harvard and Pakistani leaders, watched and rated.

The winning idea from Boston was Agripak-anSMS-alert platform that gives daily updates on farm conditions and alerts farmers to emergencies, based on the analysis of satellite imagery. Another team presented AsliGoli (renamed ProCheck), anSMS-based system to deal with the issue of counterfeit medicine by scanning the barcode. Since then, this team has gone on to launch its idea as a full-fledged business being piloted with partners in Pakistan. Other winners from Pakistan were Lookout 360 and i-Track. Lookout 360 is a smartphone application that enables people to report a criminal incident through a simple text message. The second winner was i-Track: an eye movement-operated mouse for physically challenged individuals using computers.

The participants were extremely happy with the quality of interaction and energized enough to carry forward their ideas to implementation. Beyond winning, all the teams gained some invaluable mentorship and incubation opportunities.

The feedback was very positive. "The kind of people we met at the event... getting that kind of access is super rare at any hackathon, period," said a participant. Another student quipped, "You can go to school for years and not meet this kind of people; the concentration of contacts and talents was pretty profound."

Financial support for Pakathon came from passionate believers of the cause, who pitched in via online donations, as well as generous sponsors who helped through food and transportation. "It was great to work with and meet so many young people who were so switched on and who have not given up on Pakistan just yet," said another attendee.

Rapid Growth

The following year, the Pakathon team recruited eight more volunteer chapters in Washington DC, New York, San Francisco, Chicago, Atlanta and Toronto in North America. There were volunteers from the Middle East, Melbourne in Australia and Karachi in Pakistan and 11 city teams including the three original ones: Boston, Lahore and Islamabad. The volunteer teams worked throughout the year and held mini events to gather participants, get them to think about the issues, and mobilize them for the main event in Boston.

Through Azhar Rizvi's previous work relationships with Discover and Invent, the Pakathon team had representation from eight universities to host the events. Unfortunately, an unstable political situation, floods and bad weather made it difficult for more teams to participate and the event remained a low-key affair. In addition, due to management changes in the Higher Education Commission of Pakistan, traction was slow and public universities could not be notified in time to put together teams for Pakathon.

Toronto also joined that year and hosted the Final Demo Day, which was live-streamed to all other chapters. The teams participating from Pakistan sent videos that were shown to the audience in the US.

The Pakathon event format was changed and the teams received additional credit for connecting to global teams. To facilitate this, Pakathon invested time and effort into developing an online forum for participants to team up and collaborate. Unfortunately, due to time constraints and hesitation to use technology, less than 5 percent of the 1,500 participants in the events used this forum. Of the teams that did communicate through the forum, an even smaller percentage connected via Skype and had face-to-face conversations. The Pakathon team learned that technology systems must be made stronger and that the individual chapters would need to work on developing online collaboration capability for the next hackathon.

Facing the challenges that year, the University of Georgia won the first position. The University of Pennsylvania, the University of Waterloo stood third and fourth. The team that secured second position surprised everyone. It was a team from the University of Malakand in Waziristan, which had pitched an idea for an educational app portal.

Building A Sustainable Model

Asad and Zheela continued to work at their jobs and pitched Pakathon in their free time. In the meantime, Azhar Rizvi was working with them from Pakistan, helping them refine the model, rope in the mentors, train the competitors and bring the Pakistani universities on board.

The Pakathon team also started studying about how to finance the initiative. The young team studied about venture capital, venture philanthropy and impact investing. They recognized the importance of finance in making change happen. Asad realized that if they wanted to help, Pakathon must be able to raise money and invest in its entrepreneurs.

Asad recalls, "I knew the potential but wasn't sure where we were going with it. Some people told us to become an event management company. Others told us to become an outsourcing company. However, these opportunities all seemed too safe, and were examples of what had already been done. These ideas did not capture the magic of what we were trying to do."

"We had built a lot of momentum. But we didn't know how to push it forward and make it sustainable in the long run," says Asad. In the meantime, cash reserves were low and Asad felt that he needed to bootstrap, so he started working at a marketing company to makes ends meet.

The other setback was that Zheela had to move to London for personal reasons. She had been an integral part of the operational and marketing team in Boston. Her experiences with TechStars and her own startup were important for Pakathon.

With Asad working and Zheela moving, a temporary void was created in the top management and new volunteers were required to fill it. In addition, managing a team that was dispersed around the globe was an extraordinary challenge. All the chapter heads were volunteer students and were responsible for raising their own funds and managing their events.

At that time, Asad had a job that required him to put in 60 hours a week. So, he gave the city leads the independence to run their chapters. Asad and Zheela were not able to check-in with these co-leads regularly. However, they trusted that the process was going well.

Three weeks before the annual hackathon, Asad got a call from one of the chapter leads saying that their teams werenot performing well enough and that they were worried about the status of the hackathon. The person who had been assigned to look for the location by the leads lacked the network or the necessary skills. Asad realized that he had made the mistake of not identifying problems and mentoring the leads. They managed to salvage the situation by having a lighter brainstorming session, instead of a full-blown hackathon that time.

The Secret Sauce

In 2015, the Pakathon team took the competition to a new level. Different tracks were introduced in healthcare, energy, gaming, women entrepreneurship and education. Now participants could focus their efforts on solving one or more problems. The chapters were also given implementation manuals and KPIs (Key Process Indicators). Each chapter was responsible for holding two or three mini events focused on meetings with mentors, investors or entrepreneurs. This led to an orientation session in each chapter in the run-up to the finals. In the last quarter of the year, a three-day hackathon was held on a weekend, after which finalists from each team were chosen. The finalists then went on to participate in the Global Finals and win the prize money. In addition, partner incubators and seed investors watched the finals on the lookout for their next investable venture, thus making this a fantastic networking ground.

In the next year of operations, in 2015, the Pakathon team finally signed a partnership agreement with the Higher Education Commission (HEC), a body that oversees all public universities in Pakistan. The partnership would allow Pakathon's events in all 50 universities in Pakistan. The teams were excited because their reach and the scale of the event was increased dramatically. They could now work with up to 10,000 students across Pakistan. The HEC would allocate US$200,000 from its budget for universities, to implement this program in Pakistan.

The 2015 final was a star-studded event at the Aga Khan Museum in Toronto. Many people, entrepreneurs, innovators, researchers, industry leaders, academia and students attended the event. Actor Ali Kazmi was the master of ceremonies. The winner was a startup called Ammi ('mother' in Urdu) that was developing automated voice messages for expectant mothers, disseminating useful health information to prevent neonatal and maternal deaths.

It occurred to Asad that the companies that performed really well would be poised to become successful ventures. Investing in these ventures would give Pakathon returns on its investment, which would in turn make them sustainable. With this revenue model in mind, Asad was now sure that he had enough information to take the leap and focus on Pakathon fulltime. The Pakathon team also saw that their earlier participants such, as Saim, Ahmed and Hira had been quite successful.

Saim Siddiqui of AsliGoli had moved back to Pakistan in 2015 and realized his pitch idea by launching his own startup, ProCheck. In November 2015, he collaborated with Ferozsons Labs, a leading manufacturer of pharmaceuticals in Pakistan, to serialize 35 million units of medicine using ProCheck's track and trace solution. As a result, more than 50,000 patients across the country will be able to distinguish between genuine and counterfeit medicines.

Another participant that made a lot of progress is Ahmed Tariq Khan. Ahmed had come to a hackathon in Boston. Since then he has moved back to Pakistan where he continued to work in the area of education and has recently launched a teachers' training company in Karachi.

Hira Batool Rizvi was a Georgia Tech student who had attended the Atlanta Pakathon 2014 and worked on an idea for women's transport in Pakistan. After completing her degree, she moved to Pakistan and launched She'Kab, a company that provides reliable transport for women. By 2015, she had launched her model in two cities and had 800 clients. Hira credits a Pakathon event for sowing the initial seeds for her venture.

The Pakathon team started analyzing its large data set. When Asad looked for patterns of success and failure, an interesting trend emerged. One of the biggest patterns was that a social venture was successful when it was launched by a student who had come to North America to work or study and had then moved back to Pakistan. Other factors like having the most polished presentation at the workshop or using the forum did not emerge as important indicators of success. Intrigued, Asad began doing more research on the "returnees" and found that about 5,000 persons return to Pakistan every year from the US, the UK and Canada after their visas expire.

The team spoke to Saim and other returnees and found that they faced several challenges when they moved back to launch a social venture. There was no seed funding available to them. Upon return, it could take them up to three years to rebuild their network. Even conversations with parents to explain their career moves was tough for this demographic.

Full Steam Ahead

By the end of December 2015, Asad had made his decision. He finally decided to concentrate full time on Pakathon. Mid-January 2016, Asad gave a two-week notice to the marketing company and joined Pakathon full time. He was going to make this dream come true. More members were added and a strong board of advisors was engaged.

Asad believed that Pakathon must focus on the "returners"-students who were going back to Pakistan on completion of their studies. Pakathon's workshops already helped these people by giving them business planning and prototyping tools. However, to complete the cycle, these budding entrepreneurs also needed seed investment and valuable mentoring connections.

Making this decision was daunting. Previously, they had scale and could survive even if many universities did not participate and the chances of them failing were lower. With a smaller footprint, they made themselves more accountable and increased the quality of their work. Their new mission also gave clarity and motivated the volunteer team.

During the last three years, Asad has faced many challenges: Volunteers backing out of commitments at the last minute, partners not delivering and segments of the Pakistani community being lukewarm or discouraging of their efforts. Instead of giving up in the face of these challenges, Asad and his team have become more resilient and optimistic.

In mid-2016, Pakathon had a small, but significant win in terms of funding. The South Asia Institute at Harvard signed on as an official partner committing grants worth US$10,000 per annum as well as providing mentoring support to Pakistani students who move back to launch businesses in the social sector. This is a one-year pilot partnership. If it is successful, it will be extended for five years. Work is also underway to set up a seed fund specifically for a non-profit, to be used by a Pakistani expat social entrepreneur.

In giving a voice to the young enthusiastic diaspora that wishes to work for the betterment of Pakistan, Pakathon has grown. The concept that started as a drawing-room discussion is now a reality of the best kind. It is registered in the US, Pakistan and Canada. Hundreds of mini events and many hackathons are held in 15 cities during the course of a year with 100+ volunteers running the events in three continents-North America, Asia and Australia. The participants work together to solve some of the most pressing problems facing Pakistan today. The movement has now developed its own seed fund; has a pool of excellent mentors and supporters, and regularly engages with the Pakistani diaspora in social entrepreneurship workshops. The selected participants are presented on a global stage and connected to domain experts.

Advice to Entrepreneurs

Guerrilla Marketing: The Pakathon team used guerrilla-marketing techniques to create a strong yet effective recruitment plan. During Ramadan, the holy month of fasting, Muslim organizations would host free iftars where the community would come to break their fast. They decided to hold their weekly meetings during these iftars. This gave those fasting, the opportunity to eat and attracted a lot of interest in Pakathon from Pakistanis and others attending the iftar. They were able to get four recruits through the power of location.

They also grasped the importance of having the people in the group get to know one another. Asad used his promising cooking skills and had everyone over for iftar. During the Eid-ul-Fitr holiday the first summer in 2013, he offered to cook the traditional Pakistani dish of nihari and all the team members contributed to cooking amazing food. Creating a sense of community is one of the most important things he learned to do as a volunteer leader.

Problems of Running a Volunteer-Led Organization: The

learning was that team members must be carefully chosen and vetted and their passion for their ideas should be gauged. In particular, if a team member is not experienced enough, following up frequently is very important. If you are working with someone who has a history of delivering and accomplishing his or her tasks, then you can reward this volunteer with more autonomy. Inexperienced leaders needed follow-ups, mentorship and yes, micromanagement, especially at the early stages of their enrollment. It is also important to note that it is trickier to follow up in a volunteer organization since people have limited time for additional meetings and documenting steps.

Understanding human psychology is also very important. Some people enjoy accomplishing tasks and checking things off. Others thrive on starting tasks and being creative. Some volunteers are people-focused, while others are goal or achievement-focused. It is important to understand the personality type, and communicate and follow up accordingly.

Book 3: The Silverpreneurs

Silver And Savvy
  Secure Tech Consultancy (Pvt) Ltd, Brigadier (R)
  Saleem Ahmed Moeen 207

From Lab to Market
  Center for Advanced Studies in Engineering (CASE),
  Dr Shafaat Bazaz 220

Clinic on The Cloud
  Infogistic, Sajjad Kirmani 231

Cracking the Reinvention Code
  EGS, Abid Hussain 240

Entrepreneurs Who Leveraged Experience And Made Impressive Comebacks

In my years of training, mentoring and coaching, it has been a great pleasure working with silverpreneurs-the people who have had a previous career and are now moving towards an entrepreneurial engagement, post-retirement or after midlife.

There are many reasons why silverpreneurs want to startup: Medical advancements have increased lifespans and improved the quality of life for seniors. A person retiring at 60 years of age can easily expect to live to his late 70s or 80s, with his faculties intact. In order to function fully and fruitfully, he or she may seek engagement and adventure.

Financially, we see that recent economic downtrends, inflation, market crashes and financial bubbles during the previous decades have also made big dents in individual savings as well as state funding towards retirement pensions and benefits. This creates added pressure on seniors to continue working to manage their cost of living comfortably.

Silverpreneurs start with a distinct set of circumstances bringing a different set of skills, discipline and leadership style to the table. Often they have spent decades learning about their industry and honing their craft. Now they are in the game to make a difference. At their age, they also have a wide network of people with whom they have worked as colleagues or as customers or vendors. They are able to ramp up these networks to engage in collaborative work faster.

I like working with this group because they are extremely focused and keen to learn. After they go back from a session, they are able to implement the concepts they have learned to perfection, as they have a strong sense of discipline and a good work ethic. Given the right set of circumstances, silverpreneurs can quickly ramp up because of the doors that are already open to them. They demonstrate that anyone with the right vision, passion and commitment can establish and manage successful ventures and can become a serial entrepreneur.

As a sample of their power and strength, we have chosen four such entrepreneurs-Brigadier Saleem Moeen of Secure Tech, Dr Shafaat A Bazaz from CASE University, Sajjad Kirmani of Infogistic and Abid Hussain of EGS. Their stories are inspirations for anyone looking for a mid-career or late-second-career start.

Opportunities for Silverpreneurs

Until the turn of the century, retirement was cherished as a time when one hung up the gloves and enjoyed a slow-paced life. However, for multiple reasons the mindset of this generation has changed. An estimated 20 percent of the Pakistani population will retire by the year 2025. At the same time a significant proportion of the population will be under 25 years of age. Pakistan's economic managers will, therefore, be facing pressure to not only ensure retirement benefits, but also to create and train young people for jobs.

At 70 years, Pakistan is a young country. The silverpreneurs come from the first generation of Pakistanis who were born in Pakistan. They are a veritable goldmine of experience and knowledge. They have the industry knowledge that young people struggle to earn. First-time entrepreneurs in their late forties and beyond, also have a distinct advantage of understanding industry cycles and dynamics. When these entrepreneurs start their new ventures, they not only extend their careers, creating job opportunities and economic growth for the country, but they also have good chances of success through leveraging their existing networks, knowledge and skills.

Self-employment is the new trend. In some economies, it is responsible for 80 to 90 percent of new job creation. Telecommuting and freelancing is a great option for flexi-work and well suited to a semi-retired workplace. Seniors can create their work engagement based on their age limitations or health considerations, and instead of retiring completely; they can pare down the workload.

Advances in technology and the emergence of digital economy have created a completely new paradigm for silverpreneurs, with all sorts of business and career opportunities. They are now opening online stores, offering tutorials and online tuitions, starting their consulting businesses, setting up travel and tour services and creating cooking shows. They are competing in almost all the areas of business as a second career or as a side business, to augment revenues or simply to keep themselves busy.

Those who are not ready to go solo again after a long professional marathon, are finding it more feasible to help new startups, by joining as board members, partners, advisors or investors. Having an experienced board member brings a voice of sanity to the venture, helps improve the performance of startups and reduces chances of failures. Senior board members also leverage their expertise and strong networks to quickly open doors and seek investment.

At the turn of the century, the famous first prime minister of Singapore, Lee Kwan Yew, was asked what his focus would be during the 21st century. His was a simple two-word answer: "Human Resources." He explained that technological developments have created a global level playing field. Nations that will develop their workforce to appreciate the available tools and use these most effectively to compete will have the edge over other nations.

If our labor strategy focuses this way, Pakistan can surely turn the tide in its favor by harnessing the capabilities of the workforce at both ends of the spectrum.

16

Silver and Savvy

Secure Tech Consultancy (Pvt) Ltd
Brigadier (R) Saleem Ahmed Moeen,
Sitara-i-Imtiaz

Founder
Islamabad
www.securetech-consultancy.com

"Discipline is the defining fire by which talent becomes ability."
~Roy Smith, author.

A massive cardiac arrest changed Brigadier Saleem Moeen's career track. He retired from the armed forces, to serve as Chairman of NADRA. Following this, he came out of retirement a second time to set up his own firm Secure Tech. He took advantage of the lessons he had learnt in his previous careers and ramped up operations to grow a firm with annual revenues of US$10 million and approximate valuation of US$35 million in just six years.

Author's Note: Secure Tech was established by Brigadier(R) Saleem Moeen, who retired after completing a successful career with the army-engineering core. Later he was hired as Chairman NADRA. His professional competence and commitment established NADRA as one of the most successful government ventures in Pakistan, for which he has been awarded the Sitara-e-Imtiaz. The team he left behind is making valuable contributions to the nation. Another important development is that NADRA has become an international player in its domain and has been instrumental in establishing similar ventures in other countries, generating valuable foreign exchange and laurels for the country.

Anyone with a set of successful careers would have called it a day, and opted for a comfortable retirement. However, Brigadier Saleem continued to work hard and established a software firm. I first met him in 2012, when he came with his team to participate in an acceleration program organized by us. During the program, they were always eager to discuss new ideas, operational issues, market potential and almost all aspects of running a successful business. We helped him give a global approach to his strategy. This interaction provided him and his team a fresh perspective on running the business and enhancing the organization. The results were amazing. From revenues of US$ 2.0 million in December 2012, his firm closed at US$ 10 million in December 2014. That is an almost 500% growth. The journey has not stopped here. Secure Tech continues to grow, creating more jobs and adding to the economic growth of the country.

An engineer by qualification, Brigadier Saleem Ahmed Moeen started his entrepreneurial career after he retired from high profile jobs in the army and allied government services

He founded IDEAS (The International Defence Exhibition and Seminar) and spearheaded the establishment of the National Database and Registration Authority (NADRA). He built NADRA from scratch and became its first Chairman in 2001. He has been awarded the Sitara-i-Imtiaz for his contribution to the country in building an organization of national importance.

His knowledge, skills, disciplined approach and experience of large-scale projects played a crucial role in setting up a technology-consulting firm, serving the global security technology market. As a Silverpreneur, he took advantage of the lessons he had learnt in his previous careers and filled a gap in the very specific vertical market of identification technologies. Today, in a short span of time beginning in 2009, his firm Secure Tech is boasting revenues of US$10 million and has a valuation of US$30 million.

Brigadier Saleem Moeen has had his share of failures along the way. He had a massive cardiac arrest while serving in the army and lost his beloved wife to cancer while setting up the firm. However, nothing deterred him in his mission to establish an exceptional international firm. He remains a great model for both retired servicemen and civilian professionals to follow.

Becoming A Soldier

Brigadier Saleem Moeen was born before the partition of the Subcontinent in 1947, in Bangalore, which is now India. His father was a civil engineer and mother a homemaker. In 1947, the family migrated to Pakistan, where they lived in Chittagong, Rawalpindi, and Quetta before finally settling down in Lahore.

In Lahore, Saleem Moeen studied at St Anthony's High School and Government College Lahore and graduated from the University of Engineering and Technology, Lahore (UET) in 1969 in Electrical Engineering with a concentration in Communication. Saleem joined the Pakistan Army in 1970 and served there for 30 years, of which he spent eleven years in education and training.

"Whatever little I know today is because of my association with the army. The first things I learnt there were discipline and organization," recalls Saleem. "The discipline, training, education and management skills that you receive in the army are unmatched and provide an individual with the qualities required to meet the challenges that come his way."

A Second Lease on Life

In 1997, Saleem was attending the National Defence University (NDU) for a Master's in Strategic Studies prior to heading a team working on a challenging project. Certain external sources were opposing this particular project. To counter the pressure, Saleem and his team worked hard under tremendous stress. Two weeks after joining NDU, he complained of chest pains while sitting in the classroom at the university and collapsed due to a heart attack. On his way to the hospital's emergency room, he flat-lined for a short while. Fortunately, the emergency team managed to revive him. "I am grateful to Allah who gave me a second lease on life. Within two months, I was back at work, and was given special permission to complete my course." says Saleem.

However, he realized that after the heart attack, he would receive a lower medical rating in the army. "I had my best time in the Army, but I knew it was nearing an end."

Ideas 2000

In 1998, Military ruler General Pervez Musharraf had just assumed power as Pakistan's 'Chief Executive Officer' and the country was becoming increasingly isolated in the wake of the nuclear tests (Chagai 1 and 2), the Kargil war and the martial law.

General Musharraf requested Brigadier Saleem to help organize a defence exhibition with the intent of inviting the chiefs of staff of all Muslim countries. The aim of the exhibition was to show the world that Pakistan was not isolated. At that time, Pakistan was the largest contributor of troops to the United Nations (UN) peace-keeping forces. Saleem and his team used this fact to have a conference clubbed with the exhibition and named it 'Arms for Peace'. They also requested the UN to send a representative to speak in the conference. The UN agreed to support the venture and the first-ever defence exhibition in Pakistan called 'IDEAS 2000-Arms for Peace' was held."It was a new experience for me in the field of event management and a huge success for Pakistan," says Brigadier Saleem.

The exhibition continues to be held biannually and is one of the largest defence exhibitions held in the world.

A Gargantuan Task

At the turn of the century (year 2000), Pakistan's National Identity Card system needed streamlining in order to develop a National Registry System for nationals of Pakistani origin. Since 1973, the government had been unable to produce a complete statistical data base as the entire system depended upon paper-based record keeping. The Musharraf government decided to tackle the problem with a vision: "To create and maintain a secure, authentic and dynamic database that comprehensively covers the demographic, geographic, social and statistical aspects of the citizens of Pakistan and provide to our own and foreign governments effective homeland security solutions and assistance in good governance."

In 1998, the National Database Organization (NDO) was under the Ministry of Interior. By March 10, 2000, NDO and the Directorate General of Registration (DGR) were merged to form the National Database and Registration Authority (NADRA), a corporate body with the requisite autonomy to operate and facilitate good governance. It had the authority to re-register 150 million citizens using the latest multi-biometric technologies. The National Identity Card project was developed in accordance with international practices for issuance of security documentation in the year 2000 to replace the paper-based Personal Identity System of Pakistan that had been in use.

A consortium called Net21 led by the Hashoo Group was given the combined task of designing the cards and setting up a card-printing factory in association with the Fauji Foundation. The project fell through despite best efforts of all the parties. The Fauji Foundation decided to give Brigadier Saleem the responsibility of setting up the factory. Though his family was preparing to move to Karachi as his daughter was studying there, the managing director of the Fauji Foundation gave this task to Brigadier Saleem, with full authority to buy all the machines and acquire or develop the software to enable a state-of-the-art printing facility. The cards were to be manufactured and then certified by a foreign laboratory as per ISO standards. His first assignment was to survey the systems already operational in the world and correspond with global manufacturers to purchase the required equipment.

"I was in the process of negotiations with a couple of vendors and the solution cost between US$1 million to US$2 million. Quotations gathered already by a predecessor were far above the amount that I was negotiating. A decision was made and steps were taken to set up the card printing factory in-house," Saleem recalls.

A Foolproof System

The factory started operations, however once the cards were printed, numerous mistakes in the printed information were discovered. For instance, a male's card would carry a female's photograph or the name and the given data would not match. The team found out that the problem was occurring at the data-entry stage.

During one of his rounds, Brigadier Saleem caught ten people putting their thumbprints on a stack of forms to complete them. When he inquired, the officer explained, "Sir, there are over 200,000 NADRA forms without thumb impressions. This team is merely completing the forms."

The Brigadier became furious, "This must be stopped immediately!"

The officer asked, "What about these incomplete forms?"

Brigadier Saleem answered, "I do not have an answer to that question. We will decide that later. But for now this has to be stopped."

A worker spoke up, "Sir, even we are tired of putting thumbprints on these forms. There are another 29 million forms that need attention."

That was when Brigadier Saleem realized that the paper-form based system did not work. Just before this, the census data had been digitized and had been a total failure as the data entry was faulty. Additionally, Optical Character Recognition (OCR), the identification of printed characters using photoelectric devices and computer software, did not work well in Urdu.

There was another problem: Erroneous forms were coming from two main categories of customers. The first group was that of literate individuals, who had delegated the responsibility of filling out the forms to their assistants, who had made the errors. The other group comprised the large population of illiterate citizens, who were hiring professional form fillers for a fee of about PKR10. These professional form fillers served a large number of individuals at a time and made mistakes in entering data. Saleem resolved that the ID card must be a zero-error document and the process of identification needed to be foolproof.

When he had first joined NADRA, the organization was outsourcing most of the work because of lack of expertise within. This made the organization dependent on external contractors and caused control problems. Changes in the system would often be difficult to communicate and delays happened. Brigadier Saleem decided that NADRA would build its own centers. The center would have data-entry operators so that the entire form could be finalized at NADRA-designated locations.

"We hired dedicated, technically qualified individuals for the team. The data entry system was designed in Urdu nastaliq with the help of a local vendor who had already completed the Urdu characters in Unicode. The first NADRA center opened in Satellite Town, Rawalpindi and once this format was successful, two more centers were built in Karachi and

Lahore. The first center was inaugurated by Lieutenant General (Retd) Moinuddin Haider, then Interior Minister, who was instrumental in supporting NADRA and getting the necessary approvals from the Cabinet," Saleem shares.

More than 300 Swift Centers and mobile centers were designed and spread throughout the country to enable rapid data entry process. Around 300 mobile vans were also deployed to cater to the country's urban and rural areas.

Developing A Failsafe National Center

There were several areas of concern: The main database was sourced to NCR and there was general unease about such sensitive data being accessible by a foreign company. When modifications were required, the backend system had to be changed and there was often a mismatch. The software changed rapidly. Brigadier Saleem's vision was to make NADRA a learning organization, based on customer feedback. When he left NADRA after seven years, the software was already in its 30th version. A Technology and Development Department was created in order to migrate all technology operations from NCR to in-house within NADRA.

At the time, NADRA had already run up liabilities of PKR2.2 billion (US$20,980,000 approx.). The organization had spent from a loan of PKR4 billion (US$38,158,000 approx.) from a consortium of 12 banks. "I remember it was the end of 2001 when I promised the cabinet NADRA will become self-sustaining by 2004. We received an amount of PKR 500 million (US$4,769,000 approx.) to continue NADRA Operations. As a result we were able to pay back the bank loans of PKR2.2 billion (US$20,980,000 approx.) by February-March 2002, including PKR153 million (US$1,459,000 approx.) interest that had accumulated."

By 2004, NADRA became a self-sustaining organization. "At that time the National Assembly asked 'Why does NADRA not have any budget allocations?' I replied, 'This is because we do not require any budget allocation," says Brigadier Saleem beaming with pride.

From ID Cards to Passports to Facial Recognition

In 2004, NADRA bid for and secured the Pakistani passport project. The team wanted to ensure that the document changed to a digital-first system. Brigadier Saleem contacted most of the renowned firms to digitize the paper-based finger print procedure into an automatic fingerprint identification system (AFIS) was the optimal solution and required installation of optical scanners. This time, NADRA had the funds available and the decision was easy to make. With the help of optical scanners, around five million fingerprints were digitized. The team went on to integrate some of the most sophisticated systems in the world in the NADRA and Passport projects.

NADRA was the first to install the Facial Recognition System in the world. It was purchased for US$300,000 whereas just four months later, USA's Homeland Security paid US$7.50 million for the same system from the same company. Since NADRA was their first client, the negotiations were in their favor.

Hat Trick

Brigadier Saleem resigned from NADRA after seven years and enjoyed his retirement for a mere four months performing Hajj and playing golf. When he told a friend he had no plans to work, the friend pressed him suggesting a business in partnership with him. Even though Saleem hesitated at first, the idea was appealing. Secure-Tech was born.

In the meantime, seeing his success with NADRA, other governments had started calling on him for consultancy assignments. The Government of Sudan contacted him to take on a consultancy assignment. They already had a German consulting company on board for their passports and ID cards system, but the government required another individual to oversee the project. Saleem also secured a project of the Kenya Electric Supply Corporation. Only three companies were shortlisted for the Kenya Electric Supply Corporation: a Swiss one, a German company and Secure Tech. The tender selection criterion was based on a technical to financial ratio of 70:30. "We quoted US$150,000, significantly lower than the competitors' quotes. We secured this project and proposed a three year US$30 million plan which was accepted," remembers Brigadier Saleem.

With these two consultancy assignments in hand, and a third one in the pipeline, Brigadier Saleem formed Secure Tech Consultancy with three other partners.

Unfortunately, during that time Brigadier Saleem's wife became critically ill. This put him in a dilemma. He did not want to work more, due to obvious reasons. When Secure Tech received another project to design and implement the Pakistan Army ID cards, Saleem declined, "I told them that I'm very busy for now, I'm going to London for her treatment."

Saleem's wife knew about the army's open-ended offer. A few days before her death, she told him, "Continue to work. What will you do staying at home?" With his wife's last advice in mind, Brigadier Saleem came back to Pakistan and took on the project after winning it through open bidding.

From there, the group went from one success to another. Secure Tech Consultancy (Pvt.) Ltd specialized in enterprise-level, identity and security management systems, which included integrating the latest biometric, cryptographic and RFID technologies. They did many projects in ID cards, e-Governance Systems, Secure Access Control Systems, Interactive Data Acquisition Solutions, Biometric Verification System, Biometric Enrollment System IT Consultancy, Online Biometric Time and Attendance System, Biometrics/Smart Cards/RFIDs/Registration, Project Management, Advisory Services and Computer Services/IT.

"At that point, someone guided us to the MIT Enterprise Forum Pakistan's Business Plan Competition," recalls Saleem. While Secure Tech was already doing quite well earning a couple of million in revenue in its first year, the competition helped its founders consolidate their business and develop a strategy to go forward. "It gave us a proactive perspective: If you do things like this, the result would be like that, and vice versa. We set a target that we achieved the very same year. Secure Tech won this competition and then others as well. We established ourselves as one of the Top 50 suppliers in the global auto ID industry, according to the ID World International Congress 2010, 2011, 2012 and 2014," he recalls.

Leading The Market Locally And Abroad

For some time, Brigadier Saleem had anticipated that a cell phone SIM-verification system would soon be required in Pakistan. The growing menace of terrorism and criminal activities necessitated deployment of such a system to help identify as well as locate persons. Secure Tech started working on solving the hardware problems.

At the time, an Android tablet was worth PKR 12,000, much cheaper than other tablets. Brigadier Saleem asked a programmer to study how the finger-recognition system worked on the android mobile phone and create a local one, using android technology. When the government issued a tender, Secure Tech was the only one with an optimal solution, leaving behind big companies who had participated.

The company's Chief Commercial Officer (CCO), Umer Moeen, visited China to find the best source for an android point of sale machine (PoS) that could contain a fingerprint scanner. Eventually, a new product was developed for biometric verification by NADRA, directly through their operators. By 2017, Secure Tech is one of the market leaders of this industry, even though the biometric verification terminal entered the market just three years ago.

The success of this product can be gauged from the fact that Secure Tech's competition also uses their hardware. Due to its effectiveness and success, Secure Tech was able to finance the project. The product is now mature and ready to be launched internationally.

Secure Tech has made its mark internationally. Iraqi war victims, pensioners and nationals had money in banks, but could not withdraw it due to a lack of documentation. Secure Tech was able to streamline the process through an integrated system and solved the problem. It enabled two government banks to restart operation after the war in Iraq. This way the Iraqi officials could manage to import and export documentation and other processes, using the complete document managing system that Secure Tech had created. They personalized the card and individuals were biometrically certified through a multi-model system for fingerprints, facial and IRIS recognition and analysis. The project was implemented four years ago and currently Secure Tech is helping to integrate their credit card system.

Brimming with Ideas

Today, Secure Tech has revenues of US$10 million and close to a US$30 million valuation. Having tasted success, Brigadier Saleem's vision for Secure Tech is for it to continue working in the high-tech sector. However, he also wants to contribute to agriculture-based information technology systems by creating a better environment through smart energy solutions. Saleem Moeen envisions a system that would attach sensors to the tractors and connect them to smart phones through an application. The tractor could provide data regarding the soil and its humidity level, which can assist in making informed decisions about the kind of fertilizer required.

Brigadier Saleem has a similar idea regarding transforming ID cards into de facto debit cards for every individual. He had initiated work on this at NADRA, which has very rich data. In Brigadier Saleem's opinion, an organization could hire an expert and pilot analytics projects and provide value-added services of their own product.

Talking about entrepreneurship, Brigadier Saleem says, "The bottom line is that a person can contribute in more ways than one, even after retirement. Perhaps by then, he is well placed to become a founder of an enterprise."

Key Advice for Entrepreneurs

Taking Risk: Brigadier Saleem says, "One should not be afraid. Take risks and have faith in God for He has brought you to this point and will make the endeavor a success." He pauses before adding "or else you will learn the necessary lesson. Every time that I thought 'This is the end of the road for me', I was pushed in the right direction by someone or the other."

Fear of Failure: Do not be afraid of failure. There will be some failures. It is important to turn them into your strengths by learning from them.

Faith in God: Have faith in God and do the best you can with honesty. "At NADRA where I served for seven years, the team was able to implement the project with God's help and our motivation. With every center, new equipment and new transformers were installed. The team worked without any governmental interference, because updates were given to authorities every six months."

Team And Teamwork: You have to build a good team to work with. At one time, NADRA had around 8,000 staffers. Brigadier Saleem was the only one who was above 60, with 28 years being the average age of the team. NADRA also inherited 4,500 employees from the registration department, whose assignment was to fill the manual cards. These would have no place in a high-tech computerized environment. It was a challenge to manage the organizational change and inculcate the culture of merit. Eventually 4,000 people had to be retrenched, and in their place, young computer literate people were recruited.

Talking about that time, Brigadier Saleem says, "In every area that we created a center, we would place a vacancy advertisement and hire educated locals who belonged to that area. Everyone from the assistant managers up wards was either a Master's in IT or a Bachelor's in Computer Science. Everyone else was computer literate. The 8,000 to 9,000 employees who came on board were selected on merit via an online test designed by the professors of Allama Iqbal University. The test consisted of a randomized sample from a database of around 1000 questions, related to either computer literacy or social aspects. We feel NADRA's success was not only due to its strength in technology, but its ability to solve the techno-social matrix."

17

From Lab to Market

Center for Advanced Studies in Engineering (CASE)
Dr Shafaat Bazaz
Dean Academic and COO, CASE
Islamabad
www.case.edu.pk; www.biomisa.org

"There's a way to do it better-find it." ~Thomas A. Edison

A research team took on the challenge of transforming a PhD thesis and an eye disease diagnostic product from a mere blueprint to a commercial product installed in premium eye-care hospitals across the country. This story demonstrates the mutual benefits of industry-academia collaborations, saving millions for the industry and in the process creating two PhDs, 10 MScs, 12 research papers and many jobs for students and an MOU of US$3 million to build a state of the art HMIS for Al Shifa hospitals Islamabad.

Author's Note: Dr Shafaat is a leading researcher in Pakistan's IT sector. After completing his PhD from the University of Toronto, he worked with the Government of Canada for 10 years. He then returned to Pakistan and joined Ghulam Ishaq Khan Institute of Technology and Sciences (GIKI) as the chair of the IT department, before joining CASE in Islamabad where he is now serving as COO. I met him in 2012 during a four-day workshop on commercializing research that I was conducting for National ICT R&D Fund. He was among the 60 participants – all senior academics and researchers from leading Pakistani universities. They all had projects that were funded by ICTR&DF at the time.

My relationship with Shafaat continued after the program had ended. Working on business plans is not a new domain for him, as his job in Canada required multi-million dollars BP implementation. However, in

Pakistan, circumstances needed more fine-tuning to local norms, procedures and mindsets. This is where my role with him began. Shafaat has demonstrated that one can derive results and commercialize research at any stage in life, all one needs is to follow a solid business planning process.

Dr Shafaat Bazaz returned to Pakistan in 2006 after a long stint abroad. Today he is Dean and Chief Operating Officer at the Centre for Advanced Studies in Engineering (CASE) where he has helped develop a strong research and commercialization process. The center has developed Health Management products and services, including Al Basr, an eye care management, diagnostics and information system.

Their Health Information Management System (HIMS) is now deployed in seven leading hospitals and has a US$2 million Expression of Interest (EOI) by another leading hospital to build a state-of-the-art HIMS.

The project has also produced a PhD, 10 Master's in Computer Science and more than 15 research papers in leading journals.

Every student engaged in the development, deployment and operations of the product has found employment.

DrBazaz and his team seized the challenge of taking a thesis project and the blueprint of an eye disease diagnostic product to the research lab and ultimately to the customer. This product is able to compete internationally, is a classic case of end-to-end, research to commercialization success and a role model for others researchers to follow.

Groundbreaking Research

In 2012, Usman Akram, a PhD student at CASE, completed his research work on eye disease diagnostics for diabetic retinopathy (DR) under the supervision of Dr Shoab Ahmed Khan, CEO, CASE. DR is an eye disease caused by high levels of insulin in blood that eventually leads to complete loss of vision. Pakistan has a very large population of diabetics, many of whom lack knowledge of the effects of diabetes on their retina and vision. There is a pressing need to create awareness about (DR). It is a progressive disease that requires regular monitoring and screening, which is costly and time consuming for ophthalmologists. Diabetics need to regularly test for DR symptoms in order to save their vision.

Before Dr Usman Akram's groundbreaking research, the process of diagnosis involved asking the patient to observe points which the ophthalmologist noted on a graph. Eventually the doctor drew a line through the plotted points and identified the positions of the weak muscles in the eye. The process was tedious and took at least 30 minutes.

As part of his thesis, Dr Usman Akram designed a system that programmed the camera to automatically capture images of the eye during examination, which are then processed to identify different phases of the disease. The project thesis and experiment were highly successful with great lab outcomes.

The groundbreaking nature of Dr Akram's research becomes especially significant when you consider that an estimated 12,000 Pakistanis are diagnosed with diabetic retinopathy each year. At 7.1 million patients, Pakistan has one of the highest numbers of diabetics in the world. Therefore, immense scope exists for a machine that drastically cuts down diagnosis time and provides more accuracy.

Excited by the potential of this machine, Dr Akram's supervisor, Dr Shoab asked his colleague Dr Bazaz to carry the research forward to the commercialization stage so that ophthalmologists would be able to use this research tool for precise diagnosis.

Testing The Waters

After Dr Akram graduated, a project team began the process of commercializing the system, under the supervision of Dr Bazaz as Principal Investigator.

A company called BIOMISA (BIO metrics, Medical Image and Signal Analysis) was set up for this purpose. A team consisting of Dr Bazaz, Dr Akram, Dr Shoab Ahmed Khan and M.Sc. students belonging to College of Electrical and Mechanical Engineering at NUST (EME College) and CASE was formed. Team members were assigned various projects in the area of biomedical engineering. The idea was to concentrate research efforts to develop devices and systems (both hardware and software) indigenously for the healthcare community in Pakistan. This would not just lower medical costs for Pakistanis, but would also create job opportunities for engineers and computer scientists.

In the meantime, Dr Shoab's MSc research student Abu Bakr Amin had a breakthrough in the area of eye-care diagnostics. Abu Bakr automated an important diagnostic technique known as the HESS Chart. Eye specialists have used this technique to measure paralytic strabismus for decades. Patients with strabismus complain of double vision and their eyes are not aligned properly. An eye specialist manually implements the traditional HESS Chart technique in more than 30 minutes. In contrast, an eye technician on the computer could perform Abu Bakr's software solution in just seven to ten minutes.

"We have an acute shortage of eye specialists in Pakistan. Our HESS Chart software solution allows the doctor to spend more time caring for patients. A patient's wait time also decreases, reducing the load on the hospital," Dr Bazaz observes. To date, the testing system remains one of BIOMISA's most successful products.

The team conducted trials for over a year and approximately 160 patients underwent this procedure. The next challenge was to convert this software tool for use in the hospital environment and make it convenient, robust and cost effective at the same time.

The Green Light

Motivated by the success of the research-based systems Dr Bazaz, Dr Shoab, Dr Akram and the team applied for a grant from the government's National ICT R&D Fund to further develop this system. CASE received a grant of PKR14 million in 2012.

However, the grant came with a condition. Dr Bazaz explained, "The National ICT & RD Fund told us that to obtain this grant, we had to develop the system in such a way that an ordinary doctor could use it."

"When we started work on the grant project, we found that the system works well under lab conditions and the algorithms quite perfectly in MATLAB, but the real challenge was to integrate it into Hospital Information and Management System. So we decided to work very closely with researchers, software developers and the doctors."

The team chose two hospitals as their implementation partners. One was a private hospital chain, Al Shifa Eye Hospital, and the other was the Armed Forces Institute of Ophthalmology (AFIO) in Rawalpindi.

Customer Insight

The team built a stellar, fancy user-interface and then confidently demonstrated the system to doctors at the AFIO. The doctors' feedback was reserved. They liked the possibilities, but did not understand the operation.

"We showed them the tool that worked on the eye, and they said that it was a very good tool, but how do we use it?" remembers Dr Bazaz. "This was very different from the plug and play systems the doctors were already using. The doctors' time is too valuable to spend time in preparing the system for use, even if the camera diagnosis was accurate."

The AFIO doctors continued to guide the research team patiently about the trends in other countries. They listed all the software currently in use and asked the BIOMISA team to study those diagnostic products carefully.

Al-Basr-A Medical Records And Diagnostic System

The logical solution for the CASE research team turned out to be Hospital Information Management System (HIMS). Through constant interaction, the CASE team built a HIMS, but with additional capabilities such as diagnostics for diabetic retinopathy and the HESS Chart. The system AL-BASR, which means vision or eyesight in Arabic, is an Electronic Patient Health Record System that allows access to a patient's entire medical history.

Another team of software developers was put together for developing the HIMS and the biomedical product was integrated within it. This team worked alongside Dr Akram's existing team, which was developing the technical biomedical diagnostic system.

"We decided that the HIMS system should be super-easy for doctors to use, so we consulted them every step of the way," explains Dr Bazaz. "The doctors would test the features and give us feedback. We would improve and then approach them again to verify the changes."

Many a times, the development team came back disheartened, because they had worked hard to build a format, but discovered that doctors found it difficult and that training them was just not feasible. Dr Bazaz explains "Doctors trained in Pakistan do not learn to use such software tools in their university courses. They go by the traditional method of writing with their hands. They still do not know about keyboarding and storing data. So we had to sit with the doctors and see what they were comfortable with."

The Ordinary Man, The Customer And The Patient

It took about two years to test the product, at times scrapping everything and starting all over again. The researchers at CASE learned the hard way that the path from research to commercialization was any thing but straight. Like other researchers in Pakistan, the CASE researchers also used to complain that no one funds or uses their research, making the research paper only a means to get promotion. They did not realize that people do not use their research because it is neither customized to their needs nor validated by consumers or industry.

Dr Bazaz says, "I think the main thing we learnt was the need to change our mindsets. The problem that I have seen with researches, even those that I have been a part of, is that we are very rigid about them. We feel satisfied that we have seen a foreign research, and published a paper on the same lines and leave it at that. That often happens to the PhD and Master's researches here.

"Through this experience, the whole team has gained a new perspective on what research should be like. A research can actually translate into a business opportunity. We can contribute our expertise towards solving a problem. If the project is researched with the end customer in mind and validated by the people who can benefit from it, then you will have a product along with your research," shares Dr Bazaz.

Dr Bazaz strongly believes that a research will not translate into a commercial project, unless the team is attached to the customer from day one. He reiterates: "It is only through continual customer feedback that the product can be tailored to the market needs. Only then will it sell."

CASE has granted 10 Master's, one PhD and 15 publications through this single project.

Having No Money is An Opportunity

During the project, they ran out of funds due to time slips. Dr Bazaz recalls, "To counter this, at one point we added more human resource and created another team, but we had nothing to pay the software developers."

Dr Bazaz decided that the programmers could moonlight as faculty members, teaching and researching simultaneously, so they could retain their salaries. That worked well for CASE and this strategy paid off in many ways. The programmers passed on their learning from the project to the students with real life examples.

Another interesting benefit of this sharing of knowledge in real-time was that the students became more involved in the project. Earlier, students doing their Final-year projects would work on separate unrelated ideas. Now CASE was able to help them choose from a range of related subprojects of Al Basr. CASE also helped students apply for grants from the National ICT R&D Fund. Thus, CASE developed substantial components of the system through its students.

Installed And Running

In 2015, Al Basr and the eye imaging system went live at the Armed Forces Institute of Ophthalmology. The system serves 150 to 200 eye patients with about 20 specialists using it every day.

At AFIO today, more than 200 patients have been diagnosed through the HESS chart. In addition, the HIMS stores patient records along with images from various cameras in a centralized database.

Dr Bazaz elaborates, "A picture taken through a fundus camera, the OCT camera, the Slit Lamp and other types of cameras is stored in one server. The doctor has all the images in front of him while diagnosing. This consolidation of data means that we are now able to track all of the patient's records, through a singular point system from anywhere within the hospital."

Eyeing Revenues

Dr Bazaz refers to the HESS Chart system as "…our most successful product so far. It comprises the HESS chart screen, the computer, the printer and the software and costs just PKR175,000 (US$1670). We can install this in both government and private hospitals."

The first installation at the AFIO was free of cost, because the hospital was a partner in the research. The second HESS chart system has been installed at the Mayo Hospital Lahore as a donation from Dr Duraiz, an ophthalmologist practicing at the King Abdul Aziz University, Saudi Arabia. Dr Duraiz also plans to donate the complete software system to Al Shifa Eye Trust, Rawalpindi.

Dr Bazaz and his team are developing the next version of the system that will be more generic. This will include data from the ophthalmology department, radiology (X-rays, ultrasound), dermatology and dentistry and will be worth approximately US$4 million.

Dr Bazaz says, "This is a big project for us, as Al Shifa Eye Trust has hospitals at multiple locations in Rawalpindi, Sukkur and Muzaffarabad."

In future, Dr Bazaz and his team are planning to integrate different eye clinics through telemedicine centers. "We are helping to develop telemedicine centers. About eight doctors already work at remote clinics. They handle data collection and upload it to the centralized lab. The next challenge is to train more doctors in this process and enable them to move past the lack of trust in telemedicine centers. We are jointly exploring telemedicine and improving the level of expectation of what we can and cannot do through it. This is more productive, but an uphill task."

Key Advice for Researchers Going into Commercialization

Strategies for Commercialization: Research always looks good in the laboratory, but its application will require the customer's feedback. Dr Bazaz believes that research and development can go hand in hand. "I do not agree with people who say research should be separate from development because that confines all great research to paper. All the great inventions and constructions such as bullet trains, buildings, planes and ships would not happen if that were the case. Research should be something that solves a problem for society. If a student cannot find a solution to a problem in his field, then he is of no use to society."

Customer Validation: This case study shows that customer validation should start as early as possible. If a university or company wants to have a shorter lead-time to commercialization, the research team should involve customers at the earliest. The idea is to create what the customer wants, based on their needs and not on mere assumptions of the researcher. The researcher's and the innovator's knowledge should be used to satisfy the customer's needs.

Involving Students in Research: Students in universities are a valuable yet untapped human resource. Not only can they help in developing a product, their participation in a project also teaches them to build from an entrepreneurial point of view. This process changes the mindset of students from hunting jobs, to thinking in terms of commercializing a project and turning it into a business. Dr Bazaz quotes an example, "We included students in our HIMS project from time to time. A student team sat with the doctors, looked at all the different ways reporting was being done and came up with a customized solution that was incorporated."

Dr Bazaz believes that students should be involved in product development process so that they learn to create something from scratch. He points out another advantage that it exposes them firsthand to state-of-the-art technology. "So when a student works on such a product, his job prospects increase dramatically. All students who worked with us found jobs easily."

Team Diversity: The CASE team has involved BBA students in order to sell the products. Dr Bazaz explains, "It took us about one and a half years to learn that teams need to include people with diverse skill sets. Earlier, whenever I sent a technical person to sell, all our technical work fell behind. We are getting MBA and BBA students to do marketing for us now. We believe that they know their work and with perseverance, they will succeed. The developer at the backend should be left alone to do his work."

University Collaborations: Dr Bazaz is a big proponent of inter-university collaborations since they often do not possess ample resources separately. He says, "We are a big country with small universities, so the researchers in Pakistan are relatively few and scattered. Because we cannot hire everyone we would like to, we encourage inter-university research teams so we can pool our best resources."

However, he cautions that when institutions collaborate, they should make a concerted effort to cultivate an atmosphere of trust and protect everyone's intellectual property rights. He strongly advocates recognizing and crediting your collaborator's contributions at every step.

"In Pakistan, the problem is that every university conceals its work from others, which is wrong when it comes to knowledge and research. They have to realize that collaboration is essential to grow as institutions."

Faculty Papers: Dr Bazaz encourages teachers and professors to work beyond immediate monetary considerations. He believes that if they are able to develop a good product, they can earn much more than what they are earning at their university. "The researchers who have written papers should try to make use of them now. If you need to write 10 to 12 papers for your promotion, please do that, but afterwards do take those to the market. The researchers will have to work very hard, but this hard work is much better than publishing papers that have no utility in society. Our average researcher is not aware of this potential."

18

Clinic on the Cloud

Infogistic
Sajjad Kirmani

Founder
Lahore
www.infogistic.com
www.cloudclinik.com

"Don't judge each day by the harvest you reap but by the seed you plant." ~Robert Louis Stevenson, Scottish novelist, poet, essayist

Respected IT industry leader Sajjad Kirmani's early experience in the corporate sector and as part of Netsol Technologies' core team helped him gain market knowledge. Post-retirement, Sajjad set up Cloud Clinik, a SAS-based electronic management record system, to transform the Middle Eastern mid-size healthcare market. Cloud Clinik has captured close to a 50 percent market share in Qatar.

Author's Note: Sajjad Kirmani established a new firm Infogistic after an illustrious career in IT. He was one of the leading architects behind Netsol Technologies. However, just when Sajjad hit early retirement, he decided to embrace yet another challenge. He established a venture in 2012 and selected Qatar as the test market, developing a SAAS-based cloud solution for the healthcare industry.

I have seen many risk takers and several risks being taken, however, Sajjad's venture impressed me because he and his team scored a hat trick. All their key decisions were correct and it became an instant success. This was only possible because of his knowledge and the professional equity that he had built for himself over the years. Sajjad and his team worked incredibly hard with the Qatar-based clinic hospital, to develop a solution customized to their specifications and implemented it successfully. As a result, in a short span of four years, he was offering one of the most successful cloud-based health care solutions, with a leading share of Qatar's healthcare sector. Now Infogistic is expanding to other Middle Eastern countries, and has already started its pilot launch in Lahore. Sajjad and his young team have clearly demonstrated that there is absolutely no dearth of talent in Pakistan. Marry talent with the experience that a professional Silverpreneur brings, and the chances of establishing an excellent product are much brighter with fewer chances of failure.

Sajjad Kirmani's story tells of a typical IT career path, until his early retirement. He had started out aspiring to be a banker, but a chance internship at an IT company changed the trajectory of his career and his aspirations. After completing his education, he continued to be associated with the IT industry in key positions in Systems (Pvt.) Limited, Oman International Bank and the Coca Cola Company-South West Asia Region. In 1998, when NetSol Technologies was just a startup, he chose to join as Director Operations, giving up stable and lucrative options in the corporate sector. The risk paid off as NetSol became one of the largest software companies in Pakistan, and a global business services and enterprise application solutions provider to the asset finance and leasing industry.

In 2011, Sajjad Kirmani-then in his early 50s retired early after almost 25 years of service. However, a few months later, he decided to put his hat on once again and set up his own firm Infogistic. In a short span of three years, Infogistic has evolved as a major player in IT solutions and services, specializing in Information Security, Governance Risk and Compliance and Information Management in Pakistan and the Middle East.

The fascinating thing was that Sajjad chose to take a measured risk in a new product area he had identified, after being exposed to startups as a mentor. In 2014, he spun out CloudClinik, an e-health solution for medium-sized health practitioners and healthcare facilities, based on the SaaS Model. His experience was valuable in helping him strike big and Infogistic CloudClinik is the fastest growing EMR (Electronic Medical Records) System in Qatar with close to 150,000 patients and 200 leading doctors.

Background

Sajjad Kirmani was born and brought up in Lahore. He did his Matriculation from a government school and went on to do his Intermediate and graduation from Government College, Lahore. After graduation, he enrolled in Punjab University's Institute of Business Administration.

Sajjad's entry into the field of Information Technology was accidental. Talking about the years when he was doing his MBA, Sajjad says, "I think it is interesting how I got into IT. After Government College, when I enrolled into the MBA program at IBA, there was no concept of IT and I had no clue what it was. However, before you finish your MBA, you have to do an internship and a project in which you write a report on some business organization." Rather reluctantly, Sajjad did his report on Systems Limited, after failing to find any organization in his preferred sectors. "At the time I was quite disappointed that I could not get an internship at a pharmaceutical company or anywhere else."

Systems Limited is headquartered in Lahore at the Lahore Chamber of Commerce and Industry office. Established in 1977 with investment from Syed Babar Ali (Chairman, Packages Ltd), Systems Limited was the first proper software company in Pakistan. As the oldest software house in the country, it became a training ground for people like Sajjad who eventually went on to form their own companies.

A Fascinating New World

Sajjad had a captivating first impression of Systems (Pvt.) Limited. He recalls, "The moment I entered the building, I saw a fascinating sight. Big rooms housed rows of mainframes with blinking screens and people working on those machines. It was a neat, clean and absolutely immaculate environment."

He was introduced to the firm's Managing Director, Aezaz Hussain, who mapped out a plan for the young Sajjad. He asked Sajjad to spend two-and-a-half months learning the then popular programming languages FORTRAN and COBOL, then write the report. During this time, he worked on the IBM mainframe computer laying his hands on WASA's

(Water and Sanitation Agency) billing project.

"This was one of the biggest mainframe systems in Pakistan, doing data processing for many large organizations, including Packages and WASA. When I completed my internship, I went back to the business school and got my degree. But the internship experience was so powerful that after completing my MBA in 1982, I went back to Systems Limited to join their one-year apprenticeship program instead of joining the banking sector or a business house."

Since there was no formal IT education at that time, the firm trained apprentices in programming and IT concepts before hiring. Ten individuals from diverse educational backgrounds were chosen for the apprenticeship program in Business Analysis and Design.

Sajjad worked at Systems Limited for six years during which he studied for his Master's degree in Computer Science from the University of London, through the British Council. After obtaining his Master's degree, Sajjad was offered a job in a bank in Oman in 1987 during the Gulf War. He worked in an online environment at one of the fastest growing banks that had adopted online banking and multi-currency ATMs, an innovation in the banking industry back then. In 1992, Sajjad returned to Pakistan for personal reasons and joined the Coca Cola Company as their head of IT for South West Asia Region.

Taking The Plunge

After spending a good 15 years in the corporate sector, he joined NetSol Technologies (Network Solutions) in 1998, a startup founded by legendary IT entrepreneur Salim Ghauri. Sajjad remembers that he had a few good offers at the time. However, after he met Salim Ghauri, it took Sajjad a mere fifteen minutes to decide that he wanted to take the plunge and join a startup.

Sajjad recalls,"...there was space for doing something in Pakistan. Therefore, I took a big pay cut and jumped in. I did not look back." He joined NetSol Technologies as Director Operations and worked on products and services mainly in the financial market.

From 1998 to 2004, the company faced typical teething troubles. He remembers a time when cash was short. The top management, consisting of Salim Ghauri, Sajjad Kirmani, Tahir Malik, and others, borrowed money on their personal credit cards and contributed to the payroll, to pay the salaries of the rest of the team for the next three months. Sajjad feels they built NetSol "a day at a time, brick by brick."

Eventually, the same team made NetSol Technologies one of Pakistan's largest software houses, working across a broad spectrum of software development and IT services portfolio, as well as human capital management, network operations and quality engineering.

Remembering NetSol's success, Sajjad believes that customer-centric companies that develop products based on their needs and requirements are the most successful. In order to fulfill customer's requirements, companies need not focus on big projects, because products evolve over time. He believes that customer feedback is crucial for the development and improvement of products. For B2B enterprise products, Sajjad believes it takes time to develop and mature the product before it can be taken to the next level. NetSol Technologies became the largest IT company in Pakistan, employing about 1,200 people, with listing on the NASDAQ in the US and the Karachi Stock Exchange and with offices in China, Australia, the US and the Far East.

"I think it was probably the finest phase in my career working with the dynamic Salim Ghauri. There were of course many ups and downs. Twice or thrice, we felt that perhaps we would not survive, tomorrow may not come and the company may shut down. Nevertheless, we kept believing in ourselves. Our sole focus was to organize a team that could create products people in Pakistan would appreciate."

Sajjad worked with NetSol Technologies for 14 years. He played a vital role in expanding NetSol Technologies to the US, the UK, China, Thailand and Australia. He also spearheaded the efforts that led to NetSol Technologies becoming the first company to obtain CMMI ML 5, ISO 27001 and ISO 20000 certifications.

His contributions to Information Technology in Pakistan earned him the title of "CIO (Chief Information Officer) of the Year" in 2010 by Teradata.

Infogistic

In 2011, Sajjad decided to take early retirement. He had spent close to thirty years of grueling service and felt that he had had enough of the corporate grind. He took time off and stayed at home to relax and rediscovered his passion for gardening and socializing, something he had not been able to do for years. The inner perfectionist that he was, he developed an award-winning garden.

However, for Sajjad, who was used to working so hard, it was not easy to enjoy retired life for too long. He started seeking new challenges. For that, he enrolled in the Lean Startup Machine program where he met individuals from different startups. He found it energizing to meet the young entrepreneurs and was able to learn about new things. The mentoring experience was mutually beneficial for himself as a mentor and the mentee team.

In 2012, Sajjad launched Infogistic, a company that would provide services in the cyber securities and information security domain.

The E-Health Management System: Cloudclinik

Having mentored startups in the past, Sajjad craved to experience the excitement typical of a startup meet. The LUMS startup weekend in 2012 was a natural next step. Within three days of participating, the Infogistic team came up with an idea for an e-health management system. CloudClinik would target small to medium-size practitioners, clinics and healthcare facilities. The system would run without any IT infrastructure and it would be simple to use or clickable. Users would be able to connect to it via mobile phones, as well as through one's workplace.

The team developed a cloud-based EMR (Electronic Management Records) system. CloudClinik provides e-health solutions based on a Software as a Service (SaaS) model. SaaS is a software licensing and delivery model in which software is licensed on a subscription basis and is centrally hosted.

Sajjad was the only one aged over 50, amongst the group of 20 to 25 year old students at the startup weekend. However, he feels it was a great learning experience for him, during which he picked up ideas working with other teams. Sajjad's e-health idea was rated as one of the top three at the weekend.

Sajjad's first business plan did not materialize. Then the team funneled revenue from a services project in Saudi Arabia into product development and spent two years developing CloudClinik. Through prior experience, Sajjad knew that customer's feedback is important, especially in the early stages of development, to modify the product according to the needs. Therefore, they requested six doctor friends to provide feedback on the medical and clinical aspects.

Once the product was complete, Sajjad met with Dr. Yousef Kayyali, Clinical Director of a reputed medical center in Qatar, who was looking for medical software. Dr. Yousef liked the demo of the product and was willing to invest in the project. He requested Sajjad and his team to deploy the system and train all his doctors, nurses and staff members to use CloudClinik. After three months, he would evaluate the product implementation based on the feedback from his staff. The team started working swiftly on the product, integrating the feedback received from doctors and nurses into the system. Sajjad presented the product to a group of 20 doctors and 10 nurses and received positive feedback.

Dr. Yousef and Kayyali Medical Center became a great reference for further deployment of CloudClinik in Qatar. During the early days in Qatar, CloudClinik signed a strategic go-to-market partnership with Ooredoo, a leading telecom company. CloudClinik became the fastest growing EMR (Electronic Medical Record) System, with 150,000 registered patients and data on 200 doctors. Doctors are using the system in medical centers, dental clinics and multi specialized clinics. The system is hosted in Qatar at Ooredoo's most secure data center. The key qualities of the product are its simplicity and efficient customer support.

After deploying the system in Qatar, Infogistic intends to replicate the e-health product in Pakistani clinics nationwide. The greatest challenge that Infogistic has faced in Qatar is that potential users were not ready to accept cloud-based computing for security reasons. Secondly, individuals are ready to pay only once for the deployment of the product, but not on Software as a Service model. In addition, as the system was developed for Pakistani market, it required tremendous amount of tweaking to fit the requirements of the Qatar market.

For Pakistan, Infogistic further developed a services portfolio that expands on their previous experience of governance and cyber security. Infogistic has a large number of bluechip customers in Pakistan as well as in the Gulf Cooperation Council countries (GCC Countries) in the cyber security portfolio.

In 2016, the team has also developed another product, this time in the security domain, named PhishRod a cloud-based phishing simulation and user-behavior management service. The product has already been deployed with a few customers. The development team is now preparing PhishRod for mass marketing and deployment.

Advice for Entrepreneurs

Team and Yourself: Believe in yourself. Even if you are crying inside, you have to get ready, come to the office and face your team to encourage them and build their confidence. Never leave the company when you are failing. The most important asset you have is your team. They should be fully empowered to drive the business. When people make mistakes, accept them. Mistakes are often good for the company as learning.

Product Development: The ideal product is the one that is sold before it is developed.

Finance: One of the key focus areas for a startup is financial management. Unfortunately, there is a lack of awareness amongst technology entrepreneurs of business and financial management tools readily available.

Technology: Most tech startups focus on technology first and think of the business model and commercial aspects later. While technology has its place, the latter two are equally important, if not more.

Perseverance: If you have a plan for one year, you should multiply it by two. "We worked with a lot of perseverance as it was not always smooth sailing. How much belief you have in yourself, and how much patience, decides your fate," says Sajjad.

Mid-Career Changes: "If I had done something 15 years ago, I would have done it carelessly. Now, my family commitments have limited my risk appetite. If you have an idea, and a strong belief, go for it otherwise you will end up regretting it all your life."

On Organizations: There is no perfect organization in this world. Give the company the opportunity to understand you and for you to understand them. You have to be patient and give time to build your career. Quickly hopping from one job to another spoils your career.

Customer Relationship Management: Whether your product is average or good, how you manage your customers, how you talk to them, how you take care of them and respond to them, plays a pivotal role. Continue giving good service to the customer, improve the quality of your service and understand their requirements so that your customers become your sales representatives.

19

Cracking the Reinvention Code

EGS
Abid Hussain
CEO
Islamabad
www.egs.net.pk

"A wise man adapts himself to circumstances, as water shapes itself to the vessel that contains it." ~ Chinese Proverb

Abid Hussain of EGS reinvented a pioneering IT services company to compete at a time when many national and international ventures went bust. Not only did EGS survive, it continued to grow through rapid industry changes. This story demonstrates the unique challenges of an established company that responds to the vagrant business cycles to manage growth for the last 35 years.

Author's Note: Abid Hussain and his firm EGS is one of the oldest and the most respected IT firms in Pakistan. Operating for almost 35 years now, it has made a great impact on several industries through its cutting edge IT implementation projects. However, like any other IT firm, EGS has had its share of ups and downs. Many local and international firms that were set up in the past thirty years have ceased to exist or have been acquired by other firms. However, Abid and his team have shown remarkable adaptability and resilience. They have been continuously trying new approaches, technologies, industries, and partnerships to stay current and on the scene.

Abid Hussain came to us during the training for the MIT-EFP Business Plan Competition in 2015. Working with a person of his caliber and his team was a tough call, as teams with such experience always come with a significant amount of baggage. However, to our surprise, we found them to be extremely open-minded and receptive throughout the five-month course. Our mentoring sessions with him were actually brainstorming sessions, where we were learning from each other. At that time, EGS had a wide range of business areas and product lines. We suggested that they streamline the business and focus on key areas of strength. We worked out plans and strategies to develop business focus, and tested them to see their effectiveness. The suggestions were appreciated and in a period of six months, they have been able to turn around their revenues and pare down costs. This was a great demonstration that you can learn and adjust according to requirement, at any stage in life; all you need is an open mind and the willingness to accept change.

The Information Technology sector has seen many high and lows since the 1980s. The 1980s and 1990s were the peak period with high growth, proprietary hardware and solutions, and high margins on sales and profits. However, by the mid 1990s, the IT sector had moved towards open systems. Cheaper systems came about due to Microsoft and Intel. The industry landscape changed. There was competition from a wide array of newer firms. In the late 1990s and early 2000s, the dotcom era characterized new opportunities and new business models, for old and new players. Those who took advantage of the time enjoyed the windfall. However, there was a market correction in 2000 with a severe dotcom crash and trillions of dollars were lost on the stock market. The industry was revived, but many giants fell because they could not keep up with the times in this volatile industry. Digital, Compaq, AST, Gateway, 3Com and Informix, were either merged, acquired, or worst, shut down. Others such as IBM, NCR, UNISYS needed to learn the cost of reinventing themselves the hard way.

EGS began operations in Islamabad in the early 1980s. One of the first local IT firms in Pakistan, EGS was a pioneering company that remains among the leading IT companies even now. Considering the volatile nature of the industry, EGS has demonstrated extreme resilience in its journey of over 40+ years.

EGS is currently in another cycle of reorganization based on current marketing needs. This is undoubtedly a tough decision for organizations with a long list of customers and relationships, but EGS and Abid Hussain have demonstrated that the viability and growth of your firm depends on your ability to read market signals and adapt to them. This is the story of the unique challenges that an existing company faces when it is looking to keep itself relevant and with the times. It is a lesson for all entrepreneurs to understand a company's growth from a long-term perspective.

Background

Abid Hussain was born into a military family. His father was an instructor at Staff College and later became General Pervez Musharraf's Military Secretary. His family lived in different cities because of his father's frequent postings.

Abid remembers that everything in his childhood was influenced by the military-lifestyle, activities and friendships. "Our life was about the Armed Forces and the people associated with it-nothing else. In the Army cantonment, we would step out of the cantonment, perhaps a couple of times a week. We wondered about people who were not in uniform. We used to wonder 'What do they do with their lives?' The social life of an army family revolved around the cantonment and the same was instilled in us at school." Abid was an automobile enthusiast. As a young boy, he would always check out the newest cars.

After the 1965 war, Abid transferred to the Aitchison College boarding school from where he completed his O levels and Intermediate. He wanted to become an automobile engineer, while his father wanted him to join the Pakistan Air Force. He secretly went for a test at the British Council. "One day, I announced to my father that I had got admission in the Chelsea College of Aeronautical and Automobile Engineering," recalls Abid.

His father shot down the idea and Abid was forced to apply to the Pakistan Air Force. He passed all the tests. However, the air force rejected him because of a temporary medical issue, though he still could qualify for the army.

By then, Abid had become stubborn. He decided to spurn a career in the army too if he could not choose automobile engineering as a career. In protest, he enrolled for a BA in Economics, and left for the UK for further studies. There he completed his foundation courses in accounting, clearing articles and passing all the relevant exams. However, passing the stringent requirements of the exams was frustratingly difficult. Abid decided that he had passed too many exams and had passed every exam at least once-so he gave up and came back home.

Working Life

Within a month of coming back, Abid found a job in a new LPG company Lifeline as a Finance Manager. This was the first step in his accounting and finance career. He realized that in spite of the challenges, he liked working in the field, and the field of finance and accounting became his new passion. Abid recalls that at one point, he was working 18 hours a day. Concurrently with Lifeline, he was also consulting at DHL and TCS (the courier companies). This gave him good exposure of meeting bankers and insurance companies, and negotiating finances for these companies. It was a lot of fun, alongside pressure and tough work.

Two Hats

Around that time, Hasan Akram had established EGS in 1983 as a sole proprietorship. Hasan was the first and the only engineer in Islamabad who was selling medical equipment such as CAT scanners. PIMS (Pakistan Institute of Medical Sciences) was his customer. In 1986, EGS became a private limited company when Abdul Shakoor Amjad (ex-Schlumberger) joined Hasan as a partner. Around the same time, Fida Raja, a serial entrepreneur with large businesses, was marketing Apple Computers through a company called International Business Computers. Realizing that the computers would need annual maintenance services, Fida saw EGS as an ally with technical support and maintenance staff and offered to join hands with them. Soon he was a partner in EGS and heading it as the MD.

In 1986, while Abid was working for Lifeline he became very keen to implement financial computerization at the company. Lifeline was amongst the first in the LPG industry to be substantially computerized. The computerization project went very well and through their working relationship, the EGS team and Abid developed mutual respect for each other. After the project ended, Abid joined EGS as Director Finance in 1989.

In the first three months of joining, Abid was able to secure projects from the Peshawar Development Authority and the Supreme Court on complete turnkey basis. Seeing his skills in the area, the company gave him the additional responsibility of software business development. "This was a time of exponential growth for EGS. We were developing bespoke software for big organizations. We were in a period of massive growth complete with the excitement and adrenalin rush you experience while making a deal."

In hindsight, he realizes that wearing the business and the finance hats simultaneously was not prudent. Abid elaborates, "The finance function is about being prudent and balancing risk. On the other hand, business development is expansive. There is a compulsion to say, *"Yeh deal karni hai"* (we must cut this deal). We'll manage and cut costs from somewhere else."

"So, while the finance and accounting was continuing, my eye and priority had shifted to getting the project, and having developed the business, to executing the project successfully," says Abid explaining his predicament at that point. "With focus on business development, everything else takes a back seat. One cannot do that in such a cash intensive business," says a wiser Abid.

Expansive Growth

Despite this, EGS was growing rapidly. The industry was expanding and EGS was stepping in to get projects. They had some great system development projects under their belt, such as Lifeline, the Supreme Court, the Peshawar Development Authority, sugar mills and many others. Consequently, they were also making a lot of money-growing revenues, increasing headcount and adding branch offices. Yet, in the growth phase, the team did not think about conserving or investing for a bad business cycle. All the directors were in their early or mid-thirties. They were spending on training and going beyond working capital.

EGS also had many annual contracts for hardware maintenance. The money from this stream was a good percentage of the company's revenue. The company would receive the full year's payment at the beginning of the year. However, rather than treating the incoming cash as a liability to be amortized over the year, the team ended up using the cash for growth.

"We had grown to a 427-man company and had a turnover of US$120 million over six branches in those days. In accounting, we talk about over-draining when we spend over the company's capacity in the same way that creditors' stretch out with cash flows. That is what we were doing without realizing it," remembers Abid.

"In the IT industry, especially software services, one can never be sure when money will come through. Usually any project that has a six-month cycle often has delays of a couple of months. The expected revenues for six months, often arrive a few months later. However, the costs and salaries still have to be paid. A technology company, specially, a software services company, has to be really smart with cash flows."

EGS had run-up bank liabilities. All EGS employees went through a lean period, when they had to retire this liability. The strength of the model was that they managed to survive. "In those days, there were only a handful of local medium- or large-sized companies. There was Dadi Associates, CMC, BCI and there was us. Then there was IBM, NCR and Jaffer Brothers, and the rest were mid-size and small companies. Many of these companies have since shut down or shrunk operations," recollects Abid.

Retrospectively, Abid realizes that they were able to keep EGS afloat because they had four partners. The partners had very strong ties and met very frequently to strategize a way forward. Abid elaborates, "We were a private limited company and we would have regular board meetings to thrash out all areas of concern. This made us responsive to market conditions,"

"Nevertheless, it is never easy for a company to manage shrinkage and consolidation," says Abid. "It is perhaps the most difficult job to close a branch, fire employees, inform the banker that you will not be able to meet commitments, or tell customers that the company will not be able to deliver in time, not for any other reason, but because the business is under some kind of strain. These are extremely tough decisions. These decisions become even more difficult as company grows."

Abid talks about the partners' commitment to EGS, "It is difficult for an individual to deal with these people alone. Our strength as a group was that we were able to come together and act as one. I feel we were able to recognize both the positives and the negatives and that is basically how we survived the tough times."

Air Force Project-A Breakthrough for EGS

Finally, at the end of this period, EGS had a major breakthrough. The team focused on a key project that the directors decided that they must do. Amjad, the technical expert of the EGS team, had discovered a Pakistan Air Force (PAF) project. The PAF was designing a Radar Warning Receiver (RWR), which is an anti-radar radar that goes into the F7PD aircraft. This particular piece of highly sophisticated electronic equipment was being developed as part of a Pakistan-China program agreement.

EGS went all out and tried to convince the PAF to give opportunity to the private sector. They cited the example of India's defense industry that has private sector companies as its backbone. The PAF Chief of Staff heard them out and finally agreed, but with a caveat: EGS would have to compete with KRL and SUPARCO.

EGS won the contract. In order to proceed with the project, the directors put their houses on mortgage, and got bank financing. EGS delivered that project successfully. "Since then, the product has gone from strength to strength," says Abid with pride. EGS spun out the RWR radar project into a separate entity and Abdul Shakoor Amjad took charge of it.

Taking Different Directions

The partners saw that they had developed different areas of focus and mutually agreed to work towards spinning off some projects in new areas. Shakoor Amjad went on to head RWR.

This left Fida, Hassan and Abid on the EGS board. Then, Fida saw an opportunity in the food business. His wife Nadia made excellent cheesecakes. One day in a semi-formal meeting, Fida said that he wanted to develop this idea. "That was a great decision for him, as Kitchen Cuisine is now doing fantastically," says Abid.

Hassan Akram felt he wanted to do another Master's in Petroleum Engineering at Imperial College. At age 46, he went back to school selling his assets and his house. He was hired by Schlumberger later.

EGS was 13 years old when the partners left to pursue other interest. While they remained partners on the books for some time, Abid became the main working partner who was steering EGS in 1996. Abid was getting a clean slate as Hasan offered to pay off some of the debt. Hasan and Amjad transferred their shares to him.

Captain of The Ship

Abid was not happy with this development, because he was used to the partners as a sounding board and advisors. "This is all very well, but you are leaving me alone! Who will help me?" Abid complained to his partners.

He was going to take over as MD when he requested Hassan to review the strategy together and make some key decisions.

One thing was clear. There was no possibility of family succession. The directors decided to bring in managers and offer them equity in the company. They had tried a similar experiment previously at the Lahore Branch too. While the experiment seemed successful initially, it eventually failed as problems arose when EGS's business values and the managers' work ethic was not aligned.

EGS had a very strong culture of commitment. For example, if the implementation timeline for a project was two weeks, it would not be changed. As a company, they did not take an extension and had a policy of transparent communication with their customers. Therefore, it did not work out when managers started taking liberty with deadlines and did not manage them responsibly.

At the time in 1996, they had six branches including one in Quetta. Initially, the branches were not responsible for profitability, which was something that Abid and Hasan wanted to change.

Abid drew up monthly balance sheets for each of the branches. They tracked the revenue and maintenance to figure out the bread and butter lines of normal operations in the company and identified the mismatch in each branch.

Then Hasan and Abid jointly asked each branch manager to review his operations and give suggestions about how to turn the cost center into a profit center. With each of the managers, Hasan built upon the idea of revenues, costs and shortfall, keeping in mind the strategy of concentrating on the strength of the company and particularly the branch.

"Every manager was given the challenge and the responsibility of turning around their branch."

Initially, the branch managers focused on expansion programs. Their plans suggested increasing sales by adding marketing people and advertising programs. However, having been burnt before, both the partners emphasized that they focus on the strength of their coverage of the market. Instead, they suggested focusing on costs by rebuilding the program and increasing revenues through the same customer base, by rebuilding programs.

The last thing that the branch managers wanted was to lose customers. Therefore, each manager was given the responsibility of scaling down the headcount and find better opportunities for those who were let go. This eventually gave ownership of profitability of the branch to the manager.

Eventually, a compensation structure based on performance was devised so that the team was rewarded according to its results. This proved to be great, because the managers realized that they could have a take home, even larger than the MD's. They found that they could earn up to 70 percent more than their basic pay.

Injecting New Blood

Arif Kundi was the General Manager of Business Development at the time. Arif was good at presentations and great at identifying, pursuing business opportunities, and developing proposals. He was technically strong and capable of business development in these terms. However, he needed stronger skills to close deals.

At that time, Arif had taken on a young junior marketing manager, Ali Khan. He had roped Ali in to look after the Peshawar market. However, Ali was not very happy in this branch because business opportunities seemed limited. Ali was transferred to the Islamabad branch. Here under the top management's watchful eye, Ali Khan blossomed. He was given the responsibility of Business Development. Ali Khan took up this challenge. He would come up with long lists of companies to target and make twelve or even fourteen cold calls every day at NGOs and banks. He was very organized and very good at pursuing leads with a focus.

Initially, he was frustrated that all the running around was not translating into money. Abid recalls, "We liked his enthusiasm. He was making the calls and dropping the proposals. However, the proposals would not materialize into contracts for EGS. I could see that he was getting frustrated. One day, we sat him down and explained that a proposal has a typical gestation period. One should wait for it to materialize as it takes time. This motivated him to stay on track. We had faith in him. This trust in Ali paid off. EGS had a major revival and turnaround because of Ali Khan."

Eventually, Ali was offered the position of Director Operations and looked after maintenance projects, client relations, networking, hardware and software opportunities. He remains the main person who pushes the team in the right direction when an opportunity comes up.

At the time, Fida Ali had 40 percent of the shares and Abid had the rest. Hasan and Amjad had already divested their shares to Abid. Fida, wanted to offload his shares from EGS, because he was not able to give EGS much time. They evaluated Ali and when they felt that he would be a good fit, they offered him the board position with 40 percent shares, which he holds today.

After Ali took on the responsibility of business development and marketing, Abid found that he was able to concentrate on other areas. "I was able to look at the GBS, our financial ERP and improve it. Now, we are better able to look at new business opportunities with a long-term perspective," says Abid. He also says that it is easy to grab any opportunity without considering the risks. However, one must balance risks and synergies and see if it makes sense to do a project in the end.

EGS rebuilds

EGS currently looks into IT solutions covering hardware sales, networking solutions, maintenance contracts, software development, data management and software implementation. The company has a very long history of serving the Pakistan market. EGS has served a variety of segments such as manufacturing, the service industry, discrete manufacturing and the process industry. They have also worked with many medium- and large-sized businesses, excluding the banking sector and the core telecom industries in terms of core business solutions.

Currently, Abid says that EGS is not being selective in terms of implementation. Because of the number of projects that they have done, they are uniquely positioned to move fluidly in many areas.

However, EGS is pursuing some new areas aggressively. There is an opportunity to move into Hospital Management Systems in the next three to five years.

In terms of growth, EGS strongly believe in partnerships, alliances and even divestment. They have recently spun off a financial product, the GBPS into a separate company. EGS now only does business development for them. Similarly, EGS has built alliances for campus management solutions (CMS), and hospital management system (HMS). They have strategic collaborations with these partners. EGS will not develop an HMS or CMS; nor will the alliance partners develop an ERP.

On the technical side, EGS is moving their systems to become cloud ready. Software as a Service (SaaS) infrastructure has also opened up as a side opportunity.

Another thing that has worked for EGS is nurturing implementation partners. Building a software is one thing, its implementation and support is another. EGS focuses on establishing alliances with companies that can work as implementing partners.

"EGS-GBMS is growing on what we call certified implementing partners. The model is very simple. The product is licensed out, and then EGS provides whatever technical support is required. EGS gets very little revenue from the product itself. It is perhaps 20 percent of what we will get for the whole lifecycle of the implementation. Eighty percent of the revenue come from after sales support. The company is happy, because it gives us the turnovers in terms of number of sales," Abid explains."SAP has certified implementing partners, so has Oracle, then why can't we do it?" questions Abid, "You are sharing part of the process but the multiplier effect is tremendous."

Abid advises that if a company wants to look into a new opportunity in a domain that it is already operating, they should expect to need an additional 30 percent of the company resources. However, whilst entering a new area or domain, it requires 90 percent of one's efforts-especially that of the top management. Therefore, Abid says that they encourage the team to come up with ideas. If someone is excited about a particular area, he or she should take ownership. In this scenario, having a mid-tier level employee team operating in isolation does not work; one also needs top to bottom organizational buy-in.

Abid feels that the BAP (Business Acceleration Plan) training helped them a lot. Now EGS develops business plans at all levels for all their business lines and revisits them every year, if not half yearly. Talking about the business plan, Abid says it forces EGS to step back and look at the business, which is the one thing that one can over look when a business is running.

Where EGS is Headed

EGS now has a team of 75 employees in three branches: Peshawar, Lahore and Islamabad. It is a solid asset-based company. They no longer have financial liabilities. Their principles and clients are very forthcoming, based on their history. Talking about another kind of asset, Abid says, "The testimonials of our past clients are our best asset off our balance sheets. We do not do delays; we deliver on time and deliver what we promise."

Today EGS is in a very healthy financial position. The backbone remains very service-oriented. The orientation to deliver requires a very fast response time. That is why clients such as National Bank of Pakistan have been their customers for the past 27 years.

Hasan is now on his last assignment at Schlumberger Pakistan after which he is retiring. Abid Husain says, "Hasan is now looking at retirement soon-and dreading it. I have invited him back to join us at EGS. I said to him, "It was you who started this terrible thing (laughs) called EGS. Come back to it. Spend some time and perhaps you will get new ideas."

He hopes that his group of silver-haired men will be contributing positively to EGS!

Advice to Entrepreneurs

To Expand into A New Line of Business: For IT, domain knowledge is important. Whether a company has a product for a vertical that cuts across like Financial ERP or a focused product that is unique to a large industry or sector, like the telcos, a company with domain knowledge is in a strong position. Generalist software houses do not work anymore. One must specialize in one or another area. One must have strong domain knowledge in one or the other industries.

Developing A Product: The GBMS-ERP was initially developed as a byproduct of a PSEB project. Someone else had designed it and we implemented it. The sixth version is currently being implemented on the cloud. While the product is now highly configurable, the team anticipates that the final quality assurance and testing is done at the site of the first implementation. This is when they do the final packaging of the product. The team looks at it as an opportunity to make the product better. "One should not be defensive if there are bugs in the system, but use it as an opportunity to improve the product and ensure customer satisfaction," says Abid.

Startup After Graduation and Getting Industry Experience: It all depends on one's experience and what he or she does in school. There are students who end up making great apps. However, they need to plan an exit in at least two or three years.

Measured Growth: Growth must be measured and sustainable. As they say 'Getting up is easy, maintaining it is very difficult,' Abid advises that one should be very clear of the next step after growth. This is imperative; otherwise, a retraction hurts a company more. He elaborates that if word gets around in the market that a company is shutting branches or an office, it affects the company, the morale of the employees, as well as the customers. Meanwhile, keep a close eye on your finances and have good financial advisors, as opposed to an accountant or tax consultant. The company should have tax advisor, auditor and accountant, who do the basic accounting of balance sheets and cash flow statements, etc. It is imperative to have a trustworthy financial advisor.

Hiring And Retaining the Right Person: "To retain the brightest will always be difficult, unless they see an opportunity linked to equity," says Abid. "They will not stay in one place if there is a brighter future out there, and no one can grudge them that."

Talking about who one should recruit, encourage and retain, Abid says that certain employees may not be the brightest of the lot, but are hardworking and will stay with you. He advises grooming them, giving them opportunities and encouraging them to prove themselves. A company needs to focus on retaining these people by encouraging, motivating and training them.

Trust is of prime importance, and one should make sure that a person is given enough time to learn and grow. Abid cites an example, "It is tricky hiring a marketing person especially in a field like ours where lead times go into years. If a boss starts looking at the cost of the resource in three or four months, he is setting his system up for failure. Instead, Abid recommends tracking intermediary indicators. Have a chart and remind them of all the things they can be doing, PR, networking, keeping track weekly and daily. Make them understand that this is so that you can add value to their work, rather than micromanaging.

Partners: Managing partnerships is no different from a marriage. You spend more time with your business partners than you do at home. "Make sure that you treat partnership as a sacred trust. Understanding between the partners should be very clear. A root cause of the failure of many partnerships is differing value sets, which eventually cause a rift amongst the partners. The other thing is that partners should have complementary skill sets. If one partner is great at finances then the other should have another competency," says Abid revealing the secret behind EGS's successful partnerships.

Offering Equity vs Commission Rewards System: Not everyone wants to be an equity shareholder, because equity partnerships come with exposure to liabilities. If individuals do not take the option of being shareholders and prefer not to take on the risk of being partners, then a commission-based reward system is a good alternative. "We have sales managers who have a three-unit salary, however they are earning up to seven times more in commissions. As long as the incentive system encourages growth, even to the extent that your subordinate may be earning more than the CEO, then sky is the limit," explains Abid.

The Sources of Capital: Bring in money not because you need it, but because you know exactly what you are going to do with it, to make it grow. There is a huge distinction in these two concepts. "The venture capitalist has seen the product and reviewed the business plan. He will monitor you and the company. Banks are not the best lenders. According to Abid, collateral-based lending is the bane of the young industry, which one has to be very cautious of using. If a bank loan is required for a particular transaction, return it as soon as possible" recommends Abid. He believes that loans should be taken as a mere transaction, for low risk funding only. Banks will entice the owner to keep the loan as a working capital. However, one has to be wary. In that sense, Islamic Banking is very clear in terms of murakaba, musharaba and mudaraba and these can be utilized efficiently.

Importance of Leisure in Life: Abid advocates that entrepreneurs take time off for leisure. "Leisure time is very important. Discipline your life in a way that you do not take the morning hours easy. Work during the morning and afternoon hours and do not leave anything for the end of the day." Abid advises the youngsters to stick to the 9 AM to 5 PM timings. "Do not compromise friends and family. It is not worth it."

BOOK 4:
The FUTUREPRENEURS

The Rickshaw Kings
    Travly, Shahmir Khan, Talaal Burny, Mehmood Ali,
    Faizan Khan, Mohammad Zohaib 260

Harvesting an Agricultural Vision
    Zaraei Ootaque, Umair Malik, Abdul Samad Sahito 273

No Speed Limits
    XGear, Muhammad Ahmad Khalid 282

The Need for Speed
    Omni Motorsports, Dr Syed Ovais Mashood Naqvi 293

The Bazaar of the Story Tellers
    Emperor's Bazaar, Muhammad Ahmad Ibraheem,
    Usman Khan, Haroon Baig 302

Cancer Killing Virus
    ASAB NUST, Tahira Khan 314

Embracing Indigenous Knowledge
    NanoSmart, Faria Khan 322

Running Towards my Dream
    Stanford University, Maha Yusuf..................... 331

Future Innovators and Entrepreneurs

Students and researchers are the backbone of academia and imperative for industrial and economic development. The long-term growth of a nation is dependent on its ability to channelize its young to become inventors, innovators and entrepreneurs and fuel new venture creation. These are futurepreneurs-the bright minds of today who will build the nation of tomorrow.

We started working with academia in 2010 when Cambridge Advisors Network, our consulting arm, launched the Invent Business Plan Competition in collaboration with the IBA, Karachi. Dr Zahir Syed and I worked with IBA to design a semester-long program comprising training workshops, mentoring sessions, one-to-one coaching by industry experts, three stages of elimination and a final competition. Finalists were also awarded prize money. Unfortunately, very few universities had incubation centers then. So for the first two years, the winners only received the prize money and only one or two got the incubation opportunity. In 2012, we invited 15 universities from across the country. Slowly the number exceeded 65 with training programs in eight to ten universities each year. A similar program was initiated in northern Pakistan in collaboration with NUST, Islamabad. Through the two programs, our team was able to induct and train close to 10,000 students from these universities by 2015.

The young recruits were extremely enthusiastic to have a platform to test out their ideas. However, faculty participation was inadequate. Traditionally focused on academics, the teachers feared that these activities would influence students' classroom performance negatively. However, soon our students started participating in international competitions like GIST (Global Innovation for Science and Technology), Startup Weekend, Jumpstart, Lean Startup, and winning them against students from some of the leading nations, getting both local and international recognition. Others learned from these competitions and were able to start their own small ventures. This created a ripple effect and the entrepreneurs started being noticed on their campuses. By 2012, the faculty was largely convinced about the effectiveness of entrepreneurial education and its positive impact on students' academic performance.

In our experience, we came across two kinds of teams that benefitted most from our programs: studentpreneurs and researchpreneurs.

Studentpreneurs

Studentpreneurs are those who germinate their ideas during college and go on to start their ventures soon after, perhaps because of a burning passion or compelling financial needs. For the most part, these students would have financed their ventures through bootstrapping or through customer acquisition. Five ventures whose founders' stories are narrated here are Zaraei Ootaque, Travly, XGear, Omni Motorsports and Emperor's Bazaar.

Smart student teams often have great ideas. Some also have an inkling of how to take it forward. What they usually lack is market understanding, bootstrapping or team-building, amongst others things. Frequently, this lack of "street smartness" causes their failure rather than any technical shortcoming.

Through our training programs and competitions, we give these students business plan training-market needs assessment, competitor analysis, marketing, product development, financial planning, operations and pitching. After this, we pair them for a few months with experienced industry mentors for one-to-one discussions. Through this intervention, we are able to teach the students to think and act like entrepreneurs. The process polishes their perspective. The brighter competitors are usually able to start their own ventures within a couple of years.

The heartening thing is that even if the student participants ultimately opt for a corporate job, their bosses find these people to be quick on their feet and, therefore, good hires.

Researchpreneurs

The second set of students we observed in our interactions with universities, was those more inclined towards pure or applied research. These students possess tremendous passion, skills and knowledge about their field and require a future pathway to commercialization of their research. Given a clear vision, these students find that their path to commercial fame and fortune will take longer; yet, they are also high-return entrepreneurs who need long-term nurturing.

The stories this section are representative of typical researchpreneurs-incidentally all passionate young women, working on current issues and looking to solve them through scientific innovation. Tahira Khan is developing a virotherapy for liver cancer using a local string of chicken virus; Faria Khan is evolving an antibacterial coating process using nanoparticles; and Maha Yusuf has landed in Stanford University researching hydrogen fuels at the Jamirillo Research Labs.

Though in the early stages of their ventures, these young women demonstrate extraordinary perseverance and serve as role models for their compatriots.

20

The Rickshaw Kings

Travly
Shahmir Khan, Talaal Burny, Mehmood Ali, Faizan Khan and Mohammad Zohaib

Co-founders
Lahore
www.Travly.io

"Don't find fault, find a remedy; anybody can complain."~Henry Ford, Founder of the Ford Motor Company

When a group of students found public transportation unnavigable, they decided to create a rickshaw app that allows customers to connect to rickshaw drivers through their phones. Four years ago when they came up with this idea in a business plan competition, they were taken as young, overambitious, aspiring entrepreneurs. Today, the same concept is a vibrant industry with major players such as Careem and Uber operating on the similar model.

Author's Note: This team has launched an Uber-like rickshaw service in Lahore. Rickshaw is Lahore's preferred vehicle for commuting. The Travly team was a group of young boys who came up with the idea of starting a web and mobile application for booking a rickshaw. They are now gradually consolidating in other cities. The Travly story is great example of value addition when major customer buy-in can be brought about through improvements in the logistics of small tech-based interventions. I met these boys in a business plan competition NUST-Discover. The five and a half month program took them through rigorous mentoring and coaching for business planning. In the process, they became among the top contenders. It was a new concept and much before its time in Pakistan. I could see the value these kids could bring into the transport sector through telecom and mobile tech. As a mentor, it was a pleasure training them and today it is evident that major platforms like Uber and Careem are using the same idea though on a much larger scale.

Five classmates at the Beaconhouse National University (BNU), Lahore decided to make a bus route app that would make life easier for commuters by connecting them to public transport.

In 2013, they took time off their last year of college to pilot this idea at Plan9. However, they soon realized that bus commuters were not a viable market from a commercialization standpoint. They turned the project around and, in rethinking the model, developed an app that connects commuters to rickshaws registered with them. Not only do their rickshaws have more customers, but also the rickshaw commuter market has proven to be more lucrative in terms of purchasing power and market size. Travly has more than 500 registered rickshaws in Lahore and are now expanding their services to other cities.

Travly demonstrates to young entrepreneurs that an idea is only as great as the market it serves. If the venture has market value, the product will have better chances of success. The entrance of the global ride-share apps and Uber and Careem for Rickshaws are a big endorsement for the Travly team and they gain to benefit from the first mover advantages.

An Idea is Born

Shahmir, Talaal Burny and Mehmood Ali were school friends who did their O and A levels from the Beaconhouse School System (BSS) and the Lahore Grammar School. They then joined Beaconhouse National University (BNU), Lahore to pursue B.Sc. (Hons.) in Software Engineering. Here, they met Faizan Khan and Zohaib. Faizan originally attended the Beaconhouse, then KIMS and finally BNU. Mohammad Zohaib is a graduate of Divisional Public School, Foreman Christian College and BNU.

The idea for Travly was Shahmir's brainchild. It was born when he was compelled to use public transport and faced the problems of daily commuters. One day, Shahmir decided to take a bus to the university. He walked to the bus stand closest to his house and waited over 40 minutes for the bus to arrive. While waiting for the bus, he inquired about bus timings and routes from the other waiting commuters, but the information he was able to glean was confusing.

Running late, he hailed a rickshaw to get to college. The ride cost him PKR250 (US$2.38 approx.). It was a lot of money for a student to spend every day for a one-way commute. Shahmir started mulling over this problem. He had spotted the need for an app that could organize information about public transport and make it easily accessible. A software engineer could easily devise such an app that would benefit the countless commuters using public transport.

Shahmir discussed the idea with Faizan who himself was a frequent bus commuter. Together, they took the idea to their teacher Huda Sarfaraz, who was supportive. She pointed out, "There is great potential for such a platform, especially since Google Maps has not extended its support to Lahore due to the lack of a proper public transportation infrastructure."

Shahmir and Faizan handpicked a team from among their classmates. They did the initial working in their Human Computer Interaction classes, and built a small prototype of a bus arrival app, which would give the estimated time of arrival and different routes to a particular destination.

PLAN9 and PLANX

In their eighth semester, the team applied to Plan9-a Pakistani tech incubator-to pitch Travly and were incubated. It was 2013 and the five partners simultaneously dropped out of college to pursue their entrepreneurial passion. A year later, they resumed their studies and ended up completing their Bachelor's in five years.

"While we were developing the bus route app, Plan9 was reaching out to different universities to incubate companies in their third incubation cycle. The team was offered incubation for six months with salaries, state-of-the-art facilities and free office space. The idea of incubating at Plan9 excited us. All of us decided to freeze our eighth semester for six months to try to turn this into a viable business," explains Shahmir.

Shahmir, Talaal, Faizan, Mehmood and Zohaib attended Plan9's three-day Launchpad after which they applied. Travly was one of the 60 startups that were selected out of 1,800 applicants for the next round. Only 20 startups made it to the final round. They were the fourth team to be selected for incubation.

Of December 9, 2013-their first day at Plan9-Talaal recalls, "We were very naïve, very raw. We didn't know anything." The initial two months consisted of rigorous training sessions. The Plan9 trainers showed them how to lay down the foundations of a company. The aspiring entrepreneurs learned about incorporating, legal entities, private entities, partnerships and private limited companies. The team also worked on developing their business models and devising a go-to-market strategy.

After the training, the Travly team started working on the product. By then, they also had a better sense of where their startup was headed. They knew they had to build a smart route planner, which would be able to guide the users about the fleet, the routes available to reach their destination, and estimated bus arrival times.

To enrich Travly's content, information of all the bus stops and routes had to be integrated in the app. To the young team, it seemed that the natural next step was to present the startup idea to the Lahore Transport Company (LTC) so that they could help Travly to map the routes. The LTC officials shooed the boys away and the team returned depressed.

Faizan stood up to reassure his team and raise their morale. He told them, "Do not worry; I will document the entire city myself. I will travel on all the bus routes and map them out one by one." That is exactly what he did over the course of the next two months.

Shahmir and Mehmood started working together on the app, while Talaal created the social media campaign and worked on the marketing. Zohaib took care of the day-to-day operations. By the time, the app was complete and the entire city was digitized, the Travly team had mapped around 1,500 bus stops and over 18 routes.

They released Travly on Facebook and on Google Play Store as an android app. The initial response was overwhelming. People loved it. The app was a godsend for a burgeoning city of almost 10 million people. The team took their app to the LTC again. This time, the LTC showed interest and signed an MOU.

The six months at Plan9 were ending and the Travly team was due to graduate in June 2014. At around the same time, the government announced the PlanX accelerator program. Travly was among the five startups chosen for the program. Although, due for launch later in October, Travly's team decided to take up space in the PlanX setup. Meanwhile Travly was meeting its planned milestones on schedule.

Funding Challenges

From March to October 2014, the team faced difficulties in creating a business model and financing the project as the funds from Plan9 had stopped in January. In order to raise money, the team started participating in competitions and went on to win I2I (Invest 2 Innovate) sponsored ChallengeX, Mobilink's Discover-NUST Business Plan Competition and others. It was a desperate attempt at survival. The team worked on weekends to develop apps and websites in order to ensure cash inflow to operate Travly.

The team was also invited to pitch at an Indian competition called Challenge Cup, but did not get visas. The organizers, a global incubator called 1776 based out of Washington, DC, fast-tracked Travly to the global finals, held in the US in May 2015. Though they did not win, Shahmir's exposure to the experts became a turning point in their quest. He met the representatives of Ride Scout (a trip planning app) and Uber (the online transportation network company) who said to Shahmir, "You are missing a very important part of your story. You are ignoring it actually. When you could not hitch a ride on a bus, you took a rickshaw to get to your destination. So, that is the more reliable form of transport. You should think about doing something in the rickshaw space."

The company entered into serious talks with two investors for the bus app but the deal did not go through. As the team was nearing graduation from university, the pressure to deliver revenues had begun to build up. The team started to rethink its model. Talaal recalls, "We started noticing rickshaws everywhere. There were more rickshaws than buses. Whenever we went out for lunch, all we ever saw were rickshaws. So we began to think, could this be our model?"

Meanwhile, a serial entrepreneur, angel investor and industry expert, Faisal Sherjan, approached Travly team. He advised them to explore and penetrate the rickshaw space as it seemed more promising. He pledged to support the team if they went for the rickshaw market.

Faisal Sherjan's advice was all they needed to pivot their business on to the new idea especially as different people had advised them to venture into the same market. They conducted a research on the potential as well as the challenges before finally entering the rickshaw space.

Phata Poster, *Nikla* Rickshaw

Translation: The poster was ripped and out popped a rickshaw, a Travly marketing campaign tagline

The Travly team met over 1,500 rickshaw owners in two months. Initially, when asked about the various facets of their work, such as the LPG consumption during the rides and how they get customers, the drivers took them for government officials out to penalize them. They had to approach the rickshaw drivers as students working on a project. They collected data in the form of recordings and other resources. As they analyzed the data and began to understand the market, they started working on a system. The app was redesigned. The solution was simple:

create a platform that connects commuters to rickshaws that were close by and available.

The team identified three major issues the Travly app would solve: fare, convenience and security. The fares are not regulated in Pakistan so rickshaw drivers charge at whim. The second thing that Travly tackled was convenience. Also, normally people would have to walk up to a rickshaw stand. Then there was the security concern, as people did not always trust the person driving the rickshaw.

They came up with a system-fares were standardized and the rickshaw would arrive at the commuter's doorstep. Comprehensive background checks on drivers before recruitment included a physical address check and driving license and identity card verification using the recently digitized criminal records system by the PITB.

The frontend is automated and customers can order a ride from Travly's website, using the app or by calling in. However, the rickshaw drivers were either semi-literate or illiterate, generally not tech savvy. Only five to 10 percent possessed smartphones. Therefore, Travly decided to operate their backend through a call center, keeping their dispatch system manual for a starter.

Travly installed trackers in all rickshaws and integrated their locations into the system-a low-cost solution as compared to giving smartphones to the driver. This also ensures a faster response time. Whenever a request comes in, the system identifies the nearest available driver and dispatches the vehicle to the client. Drivers are trained to use the system and learn different aspects such as how they will receive a request, how to reach their destination on time and how to deal with clients.

"Smartphone penetration is increasing by the second in Pakistan. I was going through a study which said that in the beginning of 2016, there were nine million smartphones in use in Pakistan. By the end of 2016, the number is expected to rise to a whopping 40 million. People are becoming accustomed to using different apps. They are becoming familiar with this technology, so we do not have to train the users," explains Shahmir.

Another technical glitch was that as soon as they started processing close to a 100 rides per day through the call center, the system began exposing its limitations. The number of call center operators had to be increased. The team realized that moving towards automation was a more cost-effective solution. Shahmir says, "We knew that if the system wasn't automated now, everything we've built up will die."

Travly started working towards automation. Even though smartphones have not been incorporated yet, the automated dispatch software has been developed. The phones have been tested and have shown excellent potential. "It's going to be amazing. We have also included some wow-factors at the driver's end too," reveals Shahmir.

Har Gali. Har Chowk

Translation: Every street. Every crossing.

Travly launched on October 14, 2015. On the first day, the team waited excitedly for calls, but they only got one booking, from their friend Murtaza. Their excitement waned especially since Murtaza lived right across from the Travly office. Initially, the team suspected that he was pulling a prank and told him off, but he insisted that he really did want a ride to Johar Town. Murtaza used Travly to go from DHA to Johar Town and paid PKR420 (US$4 approx.) for a route that normally cost him PKR610 (US$5.8 approx.). The next day, Travly received two bookings, of which one caller was Murtaza again.

Only one blog, ProPakistani, talked about the new app. On their second day of operations, Faisal Qureshi, a famous TV anchor, messaged the team on Facebook and asked for their contact information. He was interested in talking to them. He called asking about their product and promised to visit them in a day or two to give them coverage on his show. Faisal Qureshi was publically critical of the Bollywood actor Saif Ali Khan and his film Phantom, which had attracted a great deal of attention from the public. A day after Faisal Qureshi covered Travly, they found several news channel representatives waiting outside their office. Others such as Agency France-Press (AFP), one of the world's largest news agencies, interviewed them and Travly was featured in Dawn, Khaleej Times, The Daily Mail UK, the Telegraph Pakistan, Express Tribune as well as in Chinese and French newspapers.

A sudden spike in calls happened after the media hype. International investors showed a lot of interest. The dream was finally coming true.

In order to cater to the growing demand, the team has to add many more rickshaw drivers to the system. It was difficult in the beginning, says Talaal, but the first batch of inducted drivers helped streamline the recruiting process, bringing in their brothers and uncles. The rickshaw drivers are now coming to Travly, instead of Travly going to them. Talaal says that the drivers talk to other drivers about Travly and say that the company gives them rights and also guarantees business. A typical Travly driver now makes nearly PKR50,000 (US$476approx.) per month, "He parks at DHA Phase 5, Lahore, and knows that Travly is going to give him rides. He does not need to burn fuel searching for passengers."

Keeping Travly Going

The team had been bootstrapping since the start. Every month, they would take on website development jobs worth PKR200,000–300,000 (US$1900–2800 approx.) in order to run their operations. It all started from Plan9, says Shahmir. Plan9 was paying the team PKR20,000 (US$190 approx.) per person, most of which used to flow back into the company. The money they won from entering startup competitions was also ploughed back into Travly.

Faisal Sherjan was the first person to inject cash into the project. Since June 2015, he had mentored and advised the team until Travly was launched. At this point, he told the team, "You have a good product-market fit. I am ready to invest."

Talaal says the team decided not to draw salaries from the investment Faisal had committed but use it to build the company and its equity value. The money was also spent on social media campaigns.

Travly is still not cash-flow positive, although it has made money since day one. They keep a certain percentage of the fare generated through the platform; however, they are using manual collection methods at the moment. The cable-collection mechanism was not very prevalent in Lahore at that time and the telecom companies are working in this area. Money transfer services such as EasyPaisa have also been effective for collection.

Travly is still fine-tuning its payment and collection solution and that is a challenge that they have to overcome. For the time being, Travly has a weekly collection setup. It has around 500 rickshaw drivers in its system. The rickshaw drivers come in for training every week and give Travly its commission. Some rickshaw drivers have realized that business has picked up because of the app and submit the money themselves. A Travly employee also goes to collect money from the drivers who live far away. Shahmir believes that if they had not been strict about collection times they would have suffered as the rickshaw drivers do not save money and spend everything that they earn. The model works if collection times are short and a weekly plan works best.

Another revenue stream is the advertisements on rickshaw's backs. Travly places advertising panaflex panels for different companies on the back screens. Due to high profit margins, after paying the rickshaw drivers their share, Travly ends up saving a lot of money. There are two types of advertisements: simple panaflex and panaflex with backlit lights. The advertisements are put up for a fixed time and for specific routes.

In future, the team is also looking to break into local deliveries. "We have a good network and we can move things around," says Talaal. Customers have now started using their rickshaws to transport things. Customers have also built up trust with Travly, says Talaal. The service has come in handy several times in a city with notoriously long traffic jams and congested roads.

Future Plans

Travly team's target is to be cash-flow positive by 2018. They plan to expand in a big way and reach at least 22 more cities. Five years down the road, Travly aims to become Uber for the bottom billion.

A big problem in operating startups is that no technical platform will cater to all the requirements. Shahmir and his team are focusing on developing the technical platform in Pakistan and a major chunk of the investment is directed into this.

The team has made aggressive plans to integrate 100,000 rickshaws into their system in the next five years. Shahmir explains, "There are over 200,000 rickshaws in Lahore, out of which more than 500 are integrated into Travly's system. We are planning to integrate around 5,000 more rickshaws here before expanding to other cities." They are also piloting out-of-the-box ideas such as the Rickshaw Rani project, providing female driven rickshaws exclusively for women.

The processes are streamlined to the extent that when Travly takes the service to a new city they will only need to hire two employees there, one for recruitment and the other for setup. "The call center will be based in Lahore," explains Shahmir.

Moving steadily towards their goal, the team has recently signed an investment agreement with CresVentures and Faisal Sherjan for a further US$200,000 to support their expansion plans.

Travly's ultimate vision is to improve the low-end commuter experience in the global market. They observe that this market segment does not just exist in the emerging economies but also in developed countries, like the United States. With a tried-and-tested model, the operation can be duplicated in other markets where rickshaws are used commonly. Travly is next planning to expand to Bangladesh and is looking for contacts to evaluate possible partnerships for expansion into other economies.

Advice for Entrepreneurs

Importance of Market Research: Shahmir believes that thorough market research is the most important part of setting up a business. One cannot tell how the market works by talking to 10 or 50 people. You need to approach a large number of people, both customers as well as those already operating in that field. The research for the bus model was based on the input of around 300 people, and the team felt that even this was not an extensive enough sample.

For the rickshaw model, the team met their drivers across Lahore. Shahmir warns though that an entrepreneur may approach many people but may end up asking the wrong questions, which is what had happened with Travly's bus model. The potential customers were not asked whether they would be willing to pay for a service like Travly.

Persistence: Shahmir advises young people to be persistent. It took the team three extra months to set up the rickshaw model. The first month was spent on market research after which the system was developed. He says that the bus model cannot be compared to the rickshaw one, as both are different products. In its present form, Travly is a service that had to be set up from scratch. Shahmir's message is that if you do not do your homework at first, you will soon be forced to start from scratch.

Writing A Business Plan: The team strongly advises writing a business plan and prevent any straying from the path. Normally people suffer because they do not document the transaction identifier or transaction code, nor do they put together a clear business plan.

Scalable Product Development: Talaal suggests that young entrepreneurs should create a scalable system that can easily accommodate growing needs of the customers. It should be designed by a good system architect. Talaal also suggests that young entrepreneurs should bring discipline to their startups. He reiterates the importance of learning from mistakes and adapting quickly. If Travly had insisted on continuing with the bus model, the startup would have folded a long time ago. An executive needs to be more receptive to both negative and positive feedback.

Mentors: Faisal Sherjan is Travly's strategy officer and advisor as well as a partner. His entrepreneurial experience and industry expertise has been immensely valuable for the team.

Competition in the Market: Shahmir feels Careem or Uber, cab services that have entered the Pakistan market, are doing a great job but Travly is the leader in its own niche. He says Careem is targeting the top 20 percent of the population, those who may already have cars at home but do not want to use them and so order a cab. Travly, on the other hand is targeting the bottom 80 percent, who either do not have cars or have only one that cannot serve everyone in the family through the day. Travly's target market is those who need to pick their children up from school or reach universities and offices on time or go grocery shopping.

Team Building: The Travly team was a group of friends who knew each other, but not too well. They had never worked together before. So they outlined responsibilities and tasks in advance and distributed the work according to their expertise. Mehmood was a hardware programmer, Talaal was responsible for brand development, Faizan did the research and analysis, Shahmir built the Travly app and Zohaib took care of the operations. The early division of responsibilities has helped them operate well as a team.

Financing: Shahmir says a startup needs funds before you begin working on the idea. Talaal believes that one should start looking for investors as soon as the idea is validated, because the process takes a minimum of six to seven months. Both agree that it is difficult to attract finances in the early stages, especially in Pakistan. "You need to build up some traction before you can go out asking for money," Shahmir observes.

21

Harvesting an Agricultural Vision

Zaraei Ootaque
Umair Malik, Abdul Samad Sahito
Co-founders
Khairpur, Sukkur
www.facebook.com/zaraeiootaque

Our mind is like a field, and performing actions is like sowing seeds in that field. ~ Kelsang Gyatso, monk, author, meditation teacher and scholar

The Zaraei Ootaque team proves that there is a huge scope for entrepreneurship in rural Sindh. They started from scratch at the IBA-Sukkur incubation center, working to develop higher yield farms through their one-window farming consultancy and collective farming unit since May 2012. Today, the student led venture has graduated from the incubation center and is earning a revenue of PKR50 million annually (US$500,000).

Author's Note: Zaraei Ootaque is a company founded by a group of young students at IBA Sukkur, I met this team in the summer of 2012 at a preparatory workshop of the NUST-Discover Business Plan Competition. They got hold of me around 7 pm after the training session. We sat on the school lawns, which was abuzz with mosquitos. I had already had a long day and was ready to leave. However, this team was determined. We sat down to discuss their idea of establishing a consultation service for large-scale farmers in Sindh. While I liked the idea, I asked them to focus on small-scale farmers. The team accepted this challenge and started working on the project.

For almost five months, they worked on the project with their Sukkur Office of Research Innovation and Ccommercialisation team headed by my dear friend Ali Akbar Rizvi and other faculty members, and were able to launch the service. They came second in the competition and were awarded incubation at IBA Sukkur. Their business services started attracting small farmers (with farms under 10 acres) for vet services, soil testing, etc. Soon they had 600 farmers with approximate landholdings of 6,000 acres in their client base. This was when large suppliers of fertilizer, seeds and other goods and services start noticing Zaraei Ootaque and offered them partnerships. It was not feasible to approach every farmer individually, on the other hand collaborating with one entity, who was a strategic partner, made a lot of sense. Today they are running a showcase farm and have revenues of over PKR 48 million (USD 458,000) demonstrating the value of tapping the small-scale market and build the organization.

Umair Malik and Abdul Samad Sahito, young students at IBA Sukkur, dreamt of improving the lives of farmers. By increasing their agricultural output, they thought they could help farmers break the cycle of poverty that has ensnared rural Sindh for centuries. While in their second year at IBA Sukkur, they came up with the concept of Zaraei Ootaque. The concept was validated in 2012 when they participated in IBA Invent. They obtained seed funding and incubation at IBA Sukkur and piloted their concept while still in university.

Zaraei Ootaque provides agricultural products like seeds, fertilizers and pesticides regardless of whether the farmers have money or not. Zaraei Ootaque also guides farmers on modern agricultural methods to increase their yield through consultation.

When they presented the same concept a year later, they went on to win the NUST Discover. By the time Umair and Abdul Samad graduated in 2014, Zaraei Ootaque's annual revenue was PKR20 million (US$190,800 approx.) .In 2016, their revenue swelled to PKR48 million (US$457,900 approx.). Zaraei Ootaque has a headcount of 70 employees and provides consultation to 600 farmers and 114 farmhouses with a total area of 6,000 acres.

An Exploitative System

Agriculture contributes about 19.8 percent to Pakistan's gross domestic product (GDP) and employs 42.3 percent of the national employed labor force (Pakistan Economic Survey 2016). A major part of the economy depends on farming through production, processing and distribution of major commodities.

As per statistics, about 60 percent of Sindh's population is dependent upon the agriculture sector. However, Sindhi farmers have not been able to avail modern farming techniques to increase their land's productivity. As a result, the land remains idle, uncultivated, unproductive, and always at risk of foreclosure. The agriculturists' low crop yield per acre at majority of the farms can be attributed to outmoded farming practices, costly farm inputs, unpredictable weather, erratic water supply, intermediary profiteering and lack of farm credit at reasonable rates. As a result, the pressure on the small farmer remains acute and he stays stuck in a vicious cycle. He purchases inputs on credit, but when the time comes to sell his crop, the middleman, also known as *aarhti*, eats up a large portion of margins, so that the farmer is forced to borrow again to purchase inputs the next year.

Finding Their Feet

Umair Malik's father had been a farmer by profession since the early 1990s. He had worked at a multinational fertilizer company as a sales representative for a while in order to understand how to improve his agricultural output. While he did well in sales, his heart was always in farming, even though life as a farmer was harder. He spent the next several years in the agricultural sector learning and trying new things.

At times, life was hard in the Malik family. Compelled by necessity, Umair learnt to flex his entrepreneurial muscle at an early age. He shares a memory from when he was 10 years old, "I used to get up at five in the morning every day and head out holding a basket, selling tea from door to door. This was the kind of life that we needed to live to survive."

In August 2009, Umair gained admission into the IBA Sukkur on a need-based scholarship. He was not academically bright and had a poor foundation in education, so he struggled to get through four semesters.

However, he performed exceptionally well in extracurricular activities and would often get involved in multiple projects.

During this period, Umair met Abdul Samad Sahito who became his best friend at the university. Abdul had hope in his eyes and a strong faith in God. He wanted to upgrade the lives of the poor, because he had experienced poverty closely himself. He never talked about his deprivation and always asserted, "I do not need people's sympathy. God is testing me. I have to be successful to prove my worth."

In February 2012, while Umair was in his second year of BBA, IBA Sukkur announced a Business Plan Competition. Umair and Abdul Samad started working on the idea that would later mature as Zaraei Ootaque.

The venture aimed to help make agriculture prosper and to empower farmers to improve their standards of living through consultation. They pitched the idea of conducting workshops for farmers to allow them to increase their yield. While it was an interesting concept, the IBA Sukkur management rejected it as too grandiose and asked the two to work on something more realistic.

Taking Up The Challenge

Unfazed by the rejection, Umair and Abdul Samad took it up as a challenge and persisted with the project. They first identified and listed the problems that Sindh's farmers commonly faced. They found out that Sindh's farmers were less educated and poorer than the farmers of other provinces. They often lived from hand to mouth, were not able to increase their yield, and unlike Punjab's farmers, they did not use modern farming methods. There was a scarcity of water, but also lack of awareness of newer less resource-hungry farming methods. Inputs like seeds and fertilizer were provided to them on credit at higher interest rates. To top it all, even the seeds supplied were often of low quality. After harvest, the farmers earned less because the *aarhti* were eating the lion's share of profits.

According to Umair, "Having grown up in an agricultural society, I am aware of the hardships and injustices faced by farmers. From the very beginning, I had decided that I will pull them out of the Dark Ages and will light their inner confidence through awareness, technical knowledge and fairness in the market."

The premise of the boys' project was to offer good quality inputs at interest-free credit to farmers and pare down the role of the intermediary so that the actual producers could receive higher profits. In addition, if they could convince the farmer to improve their methods, their output would also increase. The boys worked day and night to launch their consultancy project. The idea was to open a shop that was more equitable for the farmers. In addition to this, if they could even marginally optimize farms, the output would also increase. Umair's father, Mian Nazir Ahmed, did not just offer moral support to the boys; he also showed an inclination to support the venture with his agricultural knowledge, skills and experience of 20 years.

The two students invested the money received from Mian Nazir and planned to open a one-stop shop in April 2012. The lack of business management skills, specifically, cash flow management created another major problem. Only a couple of days before the launch of Zaraei Ootaque on Saturday April 14, 2012, they realized that they were short of funds to meet the expenses of the launch ceremony. Umair and Samad were left with just PKR300 (US$3 approx.) in their pockets while they needed another PKR100,000 (US$950 approx.) for the inauguration.

Abdul Samad was not ready to give up just yet. He remembers, "We had lost almost all hope. But then we recalled the reason we had started. I recharged my cell phone and made calls to everyone from whom we could expect assistance." Help came from the Director, IBA Sukkur, Nisar Ahmed Siddiqui who supported the project and arranged seed money.

Zaraei Ootaque opened its doors on April 15, 2012 at Peerano Patan near Sikandarabad, Taluka Nara, District Khairpur, approximately 82 kilometers from Sukkur on the right bank of Nara Canal. The Director, IBA Sukkur, became the chief guest at the launch ceremony and farmers and landowners from all over Sindh were invited.

At the launch, Zaraei Ootaque received a very positive response from the farmers. A large number registered their farms. In its first season, Zaraei Ootaque attracted more than a 100 customers, more than 30 registered farmhouses (farms that are over 100 acres) and recorded sales of PKR12 million (US$115,000 approx.). It delivered services and products that increased productivity from 15 to 30 maunds per acre within a six-month period. Zaraei Ootaque earned approximately PKR5.2 million (US$50,000 approx.) in profits from the sales of fertilizers and seeds alone.

Registered farmers purchased on credit and received free training through workshops and advice on improving yield. "We also receive seeds and other materials at subsidized rates, which means that we are not exploited [by the middlemen] anymore," says Zahid Bux Bhambhro, a farmer from the Choondko area.

Providing Support And Service

Zaraei Ootaque works as a production entity, intermediary and distribution channel for agricultural inputs and offers credit services. Its social objective is to advance the living standard of individual farmers by creating opportunities for them to educate themselves.

As a production facility, Zaraei Ootaque produces 50 varieties of cotton and wheat on 6,000 acres of land. It has leased 300 acres while owning the remaining of the cultivable land. The farm is used as a model farm and test case for other customers. Average per acre output is 45 maunds of cotton and the average rate per maund is PKR2,500 (US$24), far better than its competitors.

Zaraei Ootaque also works as a distributor and retail channel. It has three retail shops and three franchises in Tarai, Saleh Pat and Pirano Patan. It provides different varieties of fertilizers, seeds and pesticides of various companies to the customers. The company's retail channels are tailored to the needs of the customers that include both large and small farm owners.

Once a customer registers, the organization not only provides credit and raw material, but also a team of consultants headed by the partners. Field officers visit the farmhouses of the registered farmer daily to monitor the progress. This special treatment helps provide timely information to farmers ensuring better crop output. Apart from the daily visits, Zaraei Ootaque arranges seminars, conferences and events on diverse topics like crop diseases, proper use of water and modern farming methods. The conferences are called Zaraei Ootaque *Gadjani* and Zaraei Ootaque *Kachehri*. Farmers are invited to these events from all across Sindh. The company has around 40 model farms and 1,000 individual customers today.

As an intermediary, Zaraei Ootaque purchases the farm produce, adds value to it in terms of quality, variety and segregation of various types, and markets it at a reasonable rate. By doing so, the consultancy is able to cut out the intermediary and filter down a larger margin to the farmer.

Offering Credit Services

According to Umair, the prime cause of poverty amongst Sindh's farmers is the exorbitant interest being charged on loans-as high as 48 percent to 60 percent at times-trapping them in the vicious circle of poverty. Farmers often find that their entire output goes into paying off the interest. Zaraei Ootaque is offering interest-free credit terms to registered farmers that fulfill certain criteria. Loan officers first evaluate the financial position of the farmers. If they can afford inputs on cash, they pay cash. Those who cannot pay cash are given credit. At the end of the season, the farmers pay Zaraei Ootaque either in cash or in the form of their produce.

Getting Recognition

After the launch, Zaraei Ootaque started getting a lot of recognition for its concept. First, IBA Sukkur presented Umair and Abdul Samad the 'Young Entrepreneur of the Year Award'. Then in 2013, Zaraei Ootaque participated in the Discover 2013 Business Plan Competition, in which 60 universities and more than 200 teams had participated. Their business plan was selected for the second position and awarded PKR300,000(US$2,800 approx.) as cash prize. It was a great honor for the team as the President of Pakistan and the Chief of Army Staff gave away the prize.

The award brought more visibility to Zaraei Ootaque and they received more business in turn. The director of NUST asked the team to register his land and cultivate crops for him. The team went on to win other prizes and accolades with write-ups appearing in national newspapers. In 2014, when the team members completed their BBA, they were ready to devote themselves fully to the business.

Franchising The Model

While still in college, the partners had started working on an expansion plan for the business. In February 2013, Zaraei Ootaque launched its first franchise in Pirano Patan. In November 2013, the company established its second franchise near Saleh Pat. On popular demand, in March 2014, Zaraei Ootaque went for its third franchise at Tarai.

Integrating backwards, Zaraei Ootaque produced its own cottonseed in the same year. Workers collected cotton and carried it to the ginning factory. However, carelessness on the part of the staff at the facility led to seed impurity. That was a challenging year for the company as the defective product brought down the sales.

By May 2014, the company underwent more trials. Zaraei Ootaque had 6,000 acres of farmland that they had leased from Prince Mir Mehdi Raza who cancelled the lease contract without prior notice or information. The hard work that the Zaraei Ootaque team had put into developing the model farm seemed to be going down the drain. This news was a blow not only for the management, but also for the farmers and the laborers who feared losing their work. The management tried to renegotiate the contract but failed.

After two weeks, Abdul Samad, the company CFO, announced to the workers, "Zaraei Ootaque was created to help farmers. You are all assets for the company, not expenses. We will not leave you alone during hard times. No one will lose their jobs. We have plans for a better future." The announcement increased staff motivation and renewed their commitment to the company.

In January 2015, they managed to lease a farmhouse near Rohri for the next ten years and worked hard to reconstruct their infrastructure.

Future Plans

The Zaraei Ootaque team now has seven employees at the management level and 25 trainers. The trainers work on the Zaraei Ootaque farms to improve their yield and conduct relevant experiments.

A field officer visits the farms of registered farmers and determines the impact of their advice. In addition, approximately 45 people work on the Zaraei Ootaque farm. They had nearly 80 employees in 2016.

Umair reports that 114 farmhouses, spread across 6,000 acres of land from Tajal to Rohri, have registered with Zaraei Ootaque so far. Six hundred customers buy material from them. "Farmers registered with Zaraei Ootaque are producing [up to] 80 maunds of cotton per acre, while others produce [up to] 25 maunds."

Apart from increasing sales, Zaraei Ootaque is also providing farmers high quality seeds at prices below market rates. Currently, there are only three seed plants in Sindh and the demand for good quality seeds is high. Zaraei Ootaque is also exploring the possibility of setting up a seed plant as a collective effort by the farmers.

The company is also looking into the option of opening its retail outlets and franchises in Sadiqabad, Multan and Vehari because of growing requests from farmers from Punjab. They are also planning to work on the seed plant in collaboration with Invest 2 Innovate (I2I). Together they are planning to open many branches of Zaraei Ootaque in different cities of Sindh. The company is also planning to open a chain of schools to educate the farmers' children.

Talking about the future, Umair says, "At present, we are working with those who grow cotton. But next year, we will provide modern techniques to those who grow wheat and other commodities."

22

No Speed Limits

XGear
Muhammad Ahmed Khalid
Co-founder
Lahore
www.xgear.io

"You have to be burning with an idea, or a problem, or a wrong that you want to right. If you're not passionate enough from the start, you'll never stick it out." ~ Steve Jobs, Co-Founder, Chairman, and Chief Executive Officer of Apple Inc

The XGear team revived a student project that collected real-time statistics about a vehicle and using that data can recommend corrective action. They improved upon the initial idea to create a product that extends the life span of the car, saves lives and saves millions of dollars.

Author's Note: XGear's story is of a typical high tech journey. I would classify this team as a hybrid between researchers and entrepreneurs. Had this team been in the developed world, they would have ended up in the R&D lab of an automobile manufacturer researching and be producing new technologies. They came up with the idea to develop an automobile monitoring device that would connect directly with the car engine and give vital statistics of the engine and other parts of the car. They failed once, but kept going and finally tasted success despite limited resources. When they came to MIT-BAP, their idea was at conceptual level only but showed great promise. My role was to help them understand the market potential, then convert the idea into proper market segments and based on that, develop a sound product strategy. The XGear team is a great example of the entrepreneurial spirit, as it continues to work hard under any circumstances. XGear has several key accounts as their customers now and are exploring international markets

Globally, road transport is the primary means of connecting people to their destinations-be it for transporting goods or carrying people to their places of work, schools, hospitals or markets. More than 50 million people are injured on the world's roads every year and 1.2 million people are injured each year due to road accidents (World Bank) some of which may be due to poorly maintained vehicles. It is said that the medical bills for accidents caused by these vehicles top billions of dollars each year. Even if a poorly maintained vehicle avoids accidents, it causes a significant reduction in the life span of the vehicle, wastes time and adds to pollution.

Ahmed Khalid has been fascinated with cars ever since he was a child. With the help of two of his friends Usman Riaz Ahmed Khawaja and Kamran Shahid Butt, he transformed this passion into a student project at his university and came up with XGear, an IoT (Internet of Things) project. The project is a data aggregation and predictive analysis platform. It gathers details about the car such as the RPM (revolutions per minute), temperature and speed, runs diagnostics, analyzes driving behavior and the state of the vehicle as well as offering corrective recommendations.

In 2006, the team was able to develop this prototype model as their final-year project. However, they dropped the idea after graduation, as no one was willing to invest in it at that time. However, in 2013 they revived XGear after a chance query by a fellow team member who wanted to use the product to diagnose a fault in his own car. Since there was still no substitute in the market, the team decided to work on the product.

In 2016, XGear was launched successfully. The system participated in an international Series A round and won US$40,000 at Startup Chile. It now boasts a growing customer list of companies such as Nestle, Pepsi, Toyota and Honda that are using the tool for fleet tracking and management. Currently, XGear has 4,000 registered customers and is growing to an annualized revenue of US$500,000.

Early Love for Cars

Ahmed loves two things with a passion. The first is his love for cars. "I have loved cars since I was three years old," remembers Ahmed, "Members of my family would gift me cars and I would collect them with great care."

The other thing he loves, for as long as he can remember, is engineering. Ahmed studied at the St. Anthony's School and the Government Islamia College, Civil Lines in Lahore. His grades were average and he was never interested in school. Unable to get into the highly competitive engineering colleges, he opted to pursue a BSc degree at the COMSATS Institute of Information Technology instead. However, his love for engineering was strong and in his four years, Ahmed and his friends participated in all the national-level electronics-based competitions. Ahmed participated in more than 50 competitions during this time and won at many of them.

The Project

In 2005, while he was in his Bachelor's final-year, Ahmed convinced his friends Usman Khawaja and Kamran to work with him on a car project. They explained to their advisor that they would develop software that would collect data such as the RPM, temperature and speed from the car and run analytics on it. The advisor objected that their project needed to be software-oriented, while what they were proposing contained an element of automotive engineering. It took a few meetings to convince the advisor to approve the project.

Ahmed and Usman worked on the hardware, while Kamran tackled the software programming. They created an analogue to digital converter and a small circuit to connect to the RPM, temperature, speed and other gauges. They wrote the analog to digital conversions and developed a small circuit that took the data to the computer through a serial port. A rough draft of the prototype was ready after a month.

In his research online, Ahmed came across Onboard Diagnostics (OBD) Technology, a vehicle's self-diagnostic and reporting capability. The OBD is present in every Electronic Fuel Injection (EFI) car manufactured internationally since 1996 and was introduced in Pakistan after 2002.

The three friends did not own cars. They were unaware of EFI or Electronic Control Unit (ECU) cars and their mechanisms, and much less about an OBD port. Each OBD has an interpreter ELM 323 which converts data streams into standard ASCII characters. They figured that they could attach every OBD with an ELM 323 and obtain data. They ordered some ELM 323 chips from abroad and designed hardware. After six months, the design was ready, but they did not have a vehicle to test it.

They approached friends and family who cringed at the thought of handing their cars to young students for experimentation. Eventually, Ahmed was able to convince his uncle to let them test the prototype on his car. The team plugged the cables into Ahmed's brand new HP laptop bought specifically for this purpose only to learn that its serial port had short-circuited.

"It was really scary. We connected our system and something zapped. We were not sure whether we had burnt the circuit board in my uncle's car or the laptop. Fortunately, it was not the car."

The cash-strapped teenager got the laptop fixed with great difficulty. After innumerable prototype iterations, night and day development and testing, the team persuaded other car owners to let them experiment with their cars. "The Mall Road car wholesale market became like a second home to us for those six months," Ahmed recalls. The system was finally stabilized. When plugged into a car, the hardware prototype would find the relevant data. They had also developed a user friendly application on .NET technologies that would display relevant data related to speed, temperature, quarter mile, and RPM and run analytics. "It was fascinating to see the data being generated," Khalid remembers.

Considering the high processing power, the team decided to add a voice control feature-Windows SDK- that would enable listening to songs and browsing items by voice. A Bluetooth feature was also added so that individuals could talk on the phone while driving.

For a final-year project, it was phenomenal. The car was multifunctional and had songs, data, browsing and a call option. It earned the students an A grade. This was back in 2005 when there were no Android or iPhones and cars were not modeled in this manner.

"We were fascinated by the Honda Accura Concept Car which was not in production yet, but had voice control features. It was still a very distant concept. We wanted to replicate all those features. The ultimate prototype was quite cool for a student project," says Ahmed.

The Prototype

The team graduated in 2006 and contemplated selling their prototype to the big names in the automotive industry. Their advisor from university introduced them to Hyundai. After assessing the prototype, the Hyundai team mentioned that though a useful gadget, too many wires and a laptop inside the car made it cumbersome and impractical. Toyota Motors were also not interested. Honda Motors offered to buy the diagnostics model for PKR5 million but, they made it clear that the team would not be involved with the gadget after the sale. "It was a lot of money for kids right out of college. But we couldn't imagine parting with our project, our baby," remembers Ahmed. The XGear team turned down the offer. Moving on, Ahmed secured a job at Nexlinx (Pvt) Ltd, Kamran started working in a software house and Usman pursued an MBA.

The Beginning – One Step Solutions

In 2008, Usman had completed his Master's and Kamran and Ahmed had found office work monotonous. The three decided to launch their own company, One Step Solutions.

One Step Solutions' core capabilities comprised creating scalable solutions including e-commerce, web-development, multimedia, groupware and databases. Their first potential client was the government, requiring a proposal for a project that would monitor the water levels in rivers and streams. The team designed the hardware prototype and discussed every aspect-coding and components- with the officials. However, the institution declined the team's offer and took their well-developed idea and workings to another party.

The team worked on small freelance and informal, mostly software projects that sold for between US$500 to US$2,000 in order to keep the company's revenue stream flowing.

In 2009, they landed a few big projects that stabilized One Step Solution's cash flow. The Combined Military Hospitals (CMH) was looking for solutions for their entry test. The One Step Solutions team pitched to automate the process according to their criteria, landed the project and obtained substantial revenues. Another project with Avicenna Medical College was for network design and monitoring and yet another with the Pakistan Telecommunication Company Limited (PTCL) asked for a single-platform solution to monitor its extensive network. This was a great opportunity and the One Step Solution team worked to consolidate and streamline the traffic. They also created a software for PTCL's call-centers that was deployed at over 1,200 locations across Pakistan.

In the beginning of 2010, Ahmed decided to pursue a Master's degree at the University of London focusing on wireless networks and infrastructures. Ahmed was in the UK for a year-and-a-half and wrote papers on wireless networking and protocol optimization, as well as a book on Protocol Optimization, which is available on Amazon. After Ahmed's graduation, the team took on optimization projects.

XGear Reignited with Plan9

In 2013, Ahmed's cousin and an employee at the company, Usman Ahmed, notice an odd issue with his car that would stop abruptly. Using XGear, the team analyzed the data identifying an anomaly with the radiator and a leakage in the hosepipe.

After this episode, Ahmed decided to develop a product around XGear. He bought some available automatic devices to build his product around but found shortcomings in each. The team identified the need for an autonomous app that did not require human action for collecting data. So, in 2013 Ahmed decided to focus on XGear. From the software point of view, XGear was strong; however, its financial viability remained questionable. Plan9's Jawwad Farid and Nabeel Qadeer met Ahmed at breakfast for a demonstration of the prototype. They were very enthusiastic about the product and advised him to apply for Plan9.

For the next three months, Ahmed focused on participating in various competitions. XGear did not win many, but Ahmed gained a lot from the networking opportunities. One of the most important contacts they made through the MIT Business Acceleration Plan was Idris Kothari, founder of California-based Vertical Systems, Inc. The judges of the Business Plan Competition gave critical feed back on their business plan. They vetted and refined it over four months with local and international mentors. Idris Kothari, a seasoned entrepreneur in the US, was the international mentor assigned to the XGear team. A tough taskmaster, Idris would sometimes call the team at 8 PM and ask them to have a business plan ready the next morning, spurring them into action.

Usman devoted himself fully to XGear product development in December 2013. Meanwhile, Ahmed finally convinced Usman and Kamran to apply to Plan9. In 2014, he connected with Kevin Langley from Entrepreneurs Organization (EO) after winning the Startup Weekend. The prize was a year-long mentoring engagement. Kevin introduced the team to contacts working in the American automobile industry. There they met representatives of General Motors who were working in telematics, the branch of IT which deals with the long-distance transmission of computerized information. They also met people from Ford who were interested in doing a similar project.

Finding The Market

In 2014, there was a session at Plan9 by Saad Fazal, who introduced the team to the ride sharing service Careem in Dubai at the time. In February 2014, the CEO of Careem invited them for further discussions. Ahmed and Usman flew out to Dubai with just the 2006 prototype version. Both of them spent the day before the meeting in developing a product close to the new and improved version that they had pitched.

The Careem representatives requested the team to hook up the device to a car and give them a live demonstration. Ahmed and Usman explained how the data and device works and convinced the Careem management to give them three days after which they would run the product in three of their cars to see how it would actually work.

For two days, Ahmed and Usman worked round-the-clock to reduce the loading time from 500 seconds to 15 and refine the product. The demo was a success. However, the challenge the team faced was that while Careem was ready to work with them, XGear required a

Telecommunications Regulatory Authority (TRA) license to proceed further. To obtain the license you had to be a Middle East-based entity and have a registered company. It had to be deferred for lack of finances.

At this point, they considered using crowd funding to bring their product into the market. They had a fully functional hardware and software platform. The Indiegogo campaign helped them get shortlisted for NextWeb, which is the biggest conference for startups in Europe. They planned an elaborate campaign in front of 6,000 people to raise US$10,000 in about two hours and spent a month preparing. Unfortunately, Ahmed's visa was rejected at the last minute. All their money had been spent on the campaign. The stall and the space were already booked and since plans had changed at the last minute, NextWeb could not refund. This was a tremendous setback for the team. In spite of this, they made their campaign at Indiegogo live, managing to raise half the amount.

Then XGear applied for other competitions and were finally shortlisted for Startup Chile. This promised them their first round of seed funding of US$40,000 as non-equity. The team was asked to move to Chile for the next six months. However, at the same time, Pepsi contacted them to install XGear in 40 vehicles, at US$8.5 per vehicle per month. Having landed the first customer, the team made the tough decision to stay back and refuse moving to Chile. Soon after, they bagged their second customer, LMKR, a petroleum technology company based in Islamabad, for whom they installed devices in 45 vehicles.

They realized that a lack of sufficient funds was slowing down their product development. Additional resources for R&D and up grades was also needed. Their second application to Blackbox Connect was successful and they travelled to the Silicon Valley. On their return, the team worked on a concrete strategy, defined a clear set of goals and outlined the targets for the next few years.

Next Generation Fleet Management Solution

In December 2014, the XGear team pitched to Nestle Pakistan and convinced them to install the devices in 10 of their vehicles for a month with money-back guarantee. When one of these vehicles had met with an accident, the Nestle management requested XGear for a report based on the data and insight into the accident.

The data confirmed that the chances of the driver being in an accident were high, compared to the rest of the drivers because of the way he was driving. When the Key Process Indicators (KPIs) were mapped with the rest of the vehicles in the pilot, it showed that the driver did not follow the standard operating procedures. The standard recommended speed was 40 km/hr, while he drove a 50-feet-long truck at 60 km/hr. The analysis and simulation of the trip was presented to the management. Since Nestle Pakistan reports every accident to their headquarters in Switzerland, they attached the XGear report to be sent to the head office.

The Nestle management was impressed and contracted XGear to track their vehicles' movements from one factory to another. In addition, their sales team requested them to do the same for movements from factories to distributors. The Nestle management requested an additional feature to track all vehicles from the distributors to the retailers. On doing this, the team realized that a great amount of data was being generated. It was possible to use this data for the optimization of Nestle's entire supply chain process, production planning, logistics, loading base and movements.

Nestle liked the proposed solution and agreed to have the system installed for their countrywide movements. By adding handheld devices for their sales persons, the team was also able to help the management with consumer analytics, product learning and product launches.

Having consolidated the Nestle project, the team discussed this with the management of Pepsi to figure out if the challenges they faced were the same. Their answer was positive. Pepsi Pakistan had five different software, SAP and Analytics; but their analysis was manual. The team had hit a gold mine by discovering a market gap that they could fill.

Pivoting The Model-The New Paradigm for Fleet Management

XGear has two teams now. One handles supply-chain management while the other is entirely vehicle centered. Ahmed thinks that there are three things missing in essentially all forms of behavioral analysis of fleets in the market: Context, maintenance and hardware.

Context: Currently there are hundreds of different applications collecting information about vehicle and storing either online or in their system within the vehicle for later download and inspection. These are simple programs gauging the engine performance and driving speed etc. However, with the advent of internet's connectivity with moving vehicles, several new avenues for fleet management have opened. XGear has added several variables for external conditions like weather, road safety and traffic. It compares them with all the empirical factors that need analysis to give a contextual view. Now you may be driving at a speed within the allowed limit of say 120 KM per hour but the fog, heavy rains or similar weather conditions may require you to drive at 40 KM or less. XGear will alert the driver as well as the fleet management team at the office to engage with the drivers online real time to control their speed.

Maintenance: There are two types of vehicle maintenance: scheduled and unscheduled. Scheduled maintenance includes oil and filter changes and brake changes, etc. which occur after every 5,000 kilometers. However, the team believes that this method is flawed. They feel that a lot of factors must be considered including where and how the vehicle is driven. They have created an algorithm that provides a predictive analysis on unscheduled maintenance as well as insight into when the car is likely to break down.

Hardware: The team believes that the current hardware systems are becoming obsolete. Some companies are now deploying APIs and XGear is in talks with them to bring different cars' data on a unified platform: BMW, Mercedes, Toyota, Porsche, General Motors, Volvo and Renault to name a few.

The XGear dashboard now provides an integrated system that generates real-time data to help track close to 150 points in a vehicle. It provides a mobile and web-based interface for monitoring and improving driving behavior, increasing fuel efficiency, pre-emptive car maintenance, geo-fencing, vehicle tracking, forensic audits and safer driving. Combined with external conditions, the data provides recommendation to enhance driver safety, reduce costs and improve productivity of the fleet. It charges US$28 per vehicle per month for its analytics services.

Outlook for XGear

XGear has pivoted to supply-chain optimization and is in collaboration with Microsoft. It is also penetrating quickly into the European, Pakistan and the US markets. The team was incorporated in Belgium to reach the European automobile market. Device fabrication and their back office operations are based in Lahore. Faisal Sherjan is working as their Chief Strategy Officer and Hina Munir heads their global sales department. Clients are delivery, FMCG, insurance and automobile companies.

In 2016, they earned revenues of US$250,000 and installed 4,000 devices. So far, they have analyzed over 400 million data points and their cars have logged in more than 3.5 million kilometers.

Key Advice for Entrepreneurs

Timing a Product Launch: There is a time for a product to be successful. Sometimes, it is better to wait if the market is not ready to accept your solution and then try again after a while.

CrowdFunding: Crowdfunding is a great platform to raise small funds particularly for consumer products where there is a tangible result.

Pivoting Your Model: Do not be afraid to pivot your business model if it makes sense and if it promises to give you more customers.

23

The Need for Speed

Omni Motorsports
Dr Syed Ovais Masud Naqvi
CEO OMNI Motorsports
Karachi
www.fb.com/OmniRacing/

"A smooth race never made a skillful driver" ~Anonymous

A doctor by profession and an auto racecar driver by passion, Ovais dreamt of bringing professional motor sports culture to Pakistan. He is currently involved in a Greenfield project developing the first of its kind Formula One racing tracks in Pakistan. Today, he has proved that audacious dreams are the only ones worth striving for.

Author's Note: I was introduced to Ovais a while ago while he was developing his business plan for the karting track and looking for some advice. Six months later, I had a team from NUST who were trying to build a solar racing car. I recommended them to go meet Ovais who is one of the few people who are from this field. Ovais was kind enough to entertain this bunch of kids who later got funding from Bank Alfalah. A few months later, two of the students came back to Ovais when perhaps he was planning to pack it all in. Funny thing was that the same students had a key to the missing piece of puzzle that Ovais was not able to solve. The story is interesting because it demonstrates the importance of understanding the power of networking. Today because of a series of chance encounters and a good deed he did a while back, he is on the brink of making his dream come true.

Standing at the edge of the track, a little boy watched in wonder at the go-karts whizzing around the track. As he readied himself for his own race, he thought, "I am going to be the best." Excitement coursed through his body as he watched the flagman raise the flags,

"Ready. Set..."

In 2006, Dr Syed Ovais Masud Naqvi's childhood passion became an obsession as he trained to become an A1 Grand Prix driver. In 2010, Ovais decided to set up a local club where go-kart racers could congregate and pursue their passion for racing.

While Ovais' story is mainly about the struggle and hard work that goes into getting support for a new project, it also underscores the power of networking. Just when Ovais had become dejected and felt that the project could not proceed, a group of young boys from NUST whom he had mentored, appeared unexpectedly and helped pull him to the finish line. Knowing that a little networking could have a big impact on their mentor's dream project, the boys connected Ovais to the right people who jump-started the project.

Work has begun on the motor sports facility, which will be spread over 12 acres and will meet international standards. It is located adjacent to the Airmen Golf Course and Recreation Park and will be completed by the end of 2017.

Despite the hardships that he has endured, Ovais' passion remains unchanged from when he was a young boy, standing at the edge of the track, watching the flagman drop the flags and shouting: *"Ready, Set, Go!"*

Reimagining Life

Born in Karachi and raised abroad, Ovais experienced the expatriate life as a child. He lived in Muscat, Oman and the Cayman Islands in the West Indies where his father worked as a banker. Later, he returned to Pakistan and completed his high school education at the Karachi American School, proceeding to graduate from Baqai Medical University in 2001.

After medical school, Ovais decided to sit for the United States Medical Licensing Examinations (USMLE). He had cleared one of its Steps, and was on his way to attaining a medical residency in the US when he saw a news report about the launch of the A1 Grand Prix, the World Cup of Motor Sports, and along with it the launch of A1 Team Pakistan. The drivers would represent countries, rather than teams owned by corporations. Twenty five national teams were participating and each team had sponsors, the driver, the pit crew and management.

Ovais contemplated participating in the championship and decided that he could put his medicine career on hold for a couple of years. He saw this as an opportunity to pursue his dream to be a racer in an international event. He was determined to become Pakistan's first professionally licensed racer.

The A1 Team Pakistan was owned and funded by the managers of the series. The management had recently changed hands from Emiratis to a South African businessman. It was ironic that even though the managing director of the event was a Pakistani, no Pakistani racecar drivers participated in the event.

Ovais was determined to represent A1 Team Pakistan. Two other drivers-one a British Pakistani and the other a Pakistani American-were also eyeing the same slot as Ovais. These two had already been taken onboard, as at the time no local Pakistanis were up for the race. Both the racers had more experience and exposure than Ovais. The only track he had ever raced on was the First Karting Centre near Baqai Medical College and, so far, he had treated racing only as a hobby and not as a serious professional sport.

Car Wars

Motorcar racing is an expensive sport and takes years of practice, commencing when the racer is very young. Ovais did not have millions stashed away, nor had he started out young. In the early 2000s, most Pakistanis had not even heard of Formula Racing, and so there were no local corporate sponsors. In 2006, Ovais started visiting several corporations to present marketing plans and discuss the cost of sponsorship. He managed to sign the TV channel GEO Super as a media partner. Under the agreement, GEO Super agreed to air Ovais' races live and create a show on the first Pakistani race car driver. The A1 Grand Prix was just one level below Formula 1 and so, at US$2 million, the cost of participation was high. Ovais thought that if divided between four or five big multinational corporations, the sponsorship amount would be easier to put together. However, funds could not be raised in time and hopes of participating in the event were abandoned. Ovais was unable to take part in that race, but he still managed to participate in some of the smaller ones.

For three years, from 2005 to 2008, Ovais worked on acquiring credentials to obtain a racing license. He even worked at a call-center for six months at a time in order to pay for his trips abroad for this purpose. In June 2008, Ovais qualified for the license. But, because of the worldwide financial crisis in August 2008, the team managers and sponsors pulled out. However, Ovais did not lose hope and continued to participate in other more affordable races and events.

The Birth of An Idea

In 2007 and 2008, as these events unfolded, Ovais began a research about different aspects of media, marketing and motorsports, and the commercial viability of the sport. He started working on a plan. If a motor sport facility were built near the target population in the Clifton and Defence areas, it would be possible for Karachi to have its first international standard car-racing track, provided it was marketed properly.

The go-kart track that he went to was near Baqai Medical College on the outskirts of Karachi. Its distance from the city, and the lack of proper facilities had kept it unpopular. Ovais believed that with proper management and facilities, a new track could be a successful business venture providing a sports and recreation opportunity for motor racing aficionados.

In 2007 and 2008, Ovais test-drove his idea. He imported 17 second-hand go-karts from Singapore and scoped out a makeshift location on a private property near Karachi's National Highway. The dirt track was smoothed and, for the first time in the history of Pakistan, a racing championship series was held. The Pakistan National Karting Championship had Tapal Tea as its major sponsor and Shell and Toyota Motors as co-sponsors. CNBC Pakistan and FM 91 were the media sponsor. Seventeen teams took part, backed by other big brands, like DHL, Telenor and Caltex.

Despite the old cars and the makeshift facility located in the middle of nowhere, Ovais managed to generate PKR5 million (US$48,000 approx.) per event, totaling PKR15 million (US$143,000 approx.) for three. He generated PKR3 million (US$29,000 approx.) per event from the three sponsors and a total of PKR1.7 million (US$16,000 approx.) from the 17 teams. At the end of the event, Ovais walked away with around PKR3 million (US$29,000 approx.) in profit.

The success was a go-ahead signal to Ovais to convert his dreams into reality. All he needed after that was a state-of-the-art motor sports facility built on a piece of land that was accessible to the target market. He could back it up with an appropriate marketing strategy and a few equity partners and give Pakistan its first international standard racing track.

Formulating The Business Model

In 2009, Ovais toured the US, Europe and the Middle East to research racetracks. He picked the best aspects of each one of these and incorporated them into his plans for the racetrack in Karachi.

Trained to be a doctor, Ovais had no idea how to go about making a business plan. However, he has cultivated a vast network of people from different spheres of life whom he could contact whenever he required help. One such friend sent him the sample business plan of a plastic resin company for guidance to develop a business plan for his venture. Using the sample as a guide, Ovais produced a business plan that integrated all financial aspects, ratios, market compatibility, proper structuring and marketing strategy.

Acquiring Land

With the proposal in hand, Ovais started looking for the right piece of land. It was an uphill task, as many factors would fail his attempts. Sometimes potential partners would just not buy into the idea. At other times, they would back out at the last minute. Even if Ovais felt that a location was perfect or the coverage of the land was just right, things would fail to move forward. Still, his enthusiasm for his project would never wane. He remained highly motivated to fulfil his passion of inaugurating a top-notch sporting arena in the country.

Ovais had pursued the Defence Housing Authority (an upscale residential area in Karachi managed by the armed forces) for about ten months for land. He even approached the Corps Commander personally who assured him of granting his request through proper channels. However, an officer at a lower level blocked his case out of spite. Then he approached authorities like the KMC, KPT, Army Welfare Trust, Emaar and every single property owner in that region but did not get the land he wanted. His high spirits were now failing as all doors were shutting on his face.

In 2011, Ovais got in touch with the Pakistan Air Force that offered him a piece of land at the PAF Base Korangi. Ovais went to look for investors as equity partners. He searched high and low for shareholders and managed to raise PKR100 million in equity investment. But when he went back to PAF, the deal fell through.

In 2013, Ovais was introduced to someone who owned a vast tract near Korangi. Ovais struck a deal for a 10-acre property as well as additional funding as debt financing of PKR 60 million and land rent at PKR100,000 (US$950 approx.). The deal was to be signed in 2014, but dragged until 2015. After two years of intense negotiations, one of the two landowning-partners backed out of the deal on the day of the signing ceremony. Ovais had lost another opportunity. He was now depressed beyond limits and thought that all his efforts of so many years had gone to waste.

The Silver Lining

An unexpected breakthrough happened. One of his mentors Azhar Rizvi sought his technical assistance for a group of students from the Pakistan Naval Engineering College (PNEC), National University of Science and Technology (NUST) in developing an automotive engineering project that required technical assistance-Pakistan's first solar racing car. Ovais guided the students on marketing, racing and other associated dynamics.

In April 2015, during their interaction, Ovais mentioned his project in passing. He told them that he had still had not been able to obtain land. The PNEC NUST team offered to help and encouraged Ovais to try the PAF again. Though skeptical, he decided to give it another shot. It turned out that the resourceful team connected Ovais to the people with the authority to provide exactly the piece of land he had his eyes on. This was a major turning point.

"It was fantastic how it worked out. Just when I thought nothing was going my way, I received help from a place I had least expected it from. It was just fate that I kept going back to the same location," recalls Ovais.

On May 17, 2016, Ovais received the official written approval for the Korangi land, on even better terms and conditions than before. Where a door had been shut, another had opened.

A Dream Fulfilled

Finally, his dream looks achievable. Investment for the project has been arranged. A detailed agreement has been signed to signal the start of the construction. If things go according to plan, his dream will become a reality in 2018. Following the inner voice that was always calling him towards his passion, one of Pakistan's first professional motorcar racers, Ovais will be inaugurating an international standard go-kart racing track in Karachi.

The motor sports facility is spread over 12 acres and will meet international standards with a go-kart track, a drag strip, auto cross and a wide track, which will accommodate up to 40 go-karts. Pit garages, dressing rooms, exclusive members' lounges, walking paths and natural scenery will be included. Exclusive members of Omni Motor Sports, members of the Airmen Club and the public will be able to access the facility.

Members will receive benefits such as access to an exclusive lounge, a rooftop deck, an 8,000 sqft conference hall, a bicycle track, priority booking for races, and the ability to purchase their own go-karts. From a business point of view, Ovais has provided a value proposition for the Pakistan Air Force and the Omni Motorsport members, at the same time proposing attractive offers for the general public. He plans to sell memberships to corporations and private individuals. The initial founder membership fee during the construction period is PKR 500,000(US$4,750 approx.).

Ovais has grand plans that go beyond holding the championship racing series: The club will also host high-profile events such as fashion shows, book launches, new car launches and corporate events.

Ovais struggled through his entrepreneurial efforts during his early years, but he did not lose hope. He stumbled, and fell, but he always got up again. Syed Ovais Naqvi's dream has turned into reality and he continues to strive so that his passion for racing becomes popular in Pakistan.

Advice for Entrepreneurs

On Failure: If at first you do not succeed, try, try again. You never know when the time is ripe for success. Persistence is essential. Keep your eyes on the prize even when your goal seems far off.

Planning: Take pains to do research before plunging into any project. Have complete command and knowledge over all aspects of your business plan and project. Learn to create a comprehensive marketing plan. You can do it even if you have not been to business school. Be resourceful and ready to adapt to any situation.

Leave No Stone Unturned: Check out all leads and contacts, even the unlikely ones. One never knows who will be the person to help you. In the same spirit, help others out. Someone may decide to pay you back at a future date.

Principles: Always maintain integrity and honesty. Do not compromise on your principles.

24

The Bazaar of Story Tellers

Emperor's Bazaar
Muhammad Ahmad Ibraheem, Usman Khan, Haroon Baig

Co-founders
Peshawar
www.emperorsbazaar.com

"Everything you possess of skill, and wealth, and handicraft, wasn't it first merely a thought and a quest?" ~ Jalaluddin Rumi, 13th-century Persian poet, jurist and Islamic scholar

With extreme pride in their heritage and culture, three young technology entrepreneurs realized the need for highlighting Pakistani handicrafts to the global market. So, they built an online marketplace that not only connects artisans to the market but also provides training and development to bring them at par with quality expectations of international customers.

Authors Note: From Peshawar, we have the Emperor's Bazaar team. They were avidly competing in business plan competitions while in school. Right after graduation, they launched The Emperor's Bazar, an online portal selling ethnic handicrafts. The team realized the potential of a large market for the stunning creations by local artisans both in Pakistan and globally. They are in the second year of their operation and have now reached break-even. I noticed them when they pitched at the Peshawar 2.0 event and later at Pakathon. Personally, I believe that it is the team that matters the most while the product or service comes later. This is a good team to keep an eye on as I am sure they will soon become a very successful venture from Peshawar.

From the Indus Valley Civilization to the remnants of the Greek and

Central Asian invasions in the northwest to Islamic and Mughal influences, Pakistan has an eclectic culture more than 5,000 years old. The artistic and cultural legacy of indigenous artisans is diverse and steeped in ethnic history. Their rugs, carpets, woodwork, brassware, leather products, precious and semi-precious stones, jewelry, handicraft and embroidered work have always been in demand in the international market.

Global handicraft exports are expected to grow at a 12 percent Compound Annual Growth Rate (CAGR) by 2019. However, in Pakistan, 22 percent of the working population employed in handicraft and related services have a per capita income of only PKR11,000 (US$108 approx.) (Pakistan Bureau of Statistics 2013-14). Dwindling tourism and outdated market mechanisms have contributed to the shrinking of the business for handicraft export market.

Realizing the need for a digital platform promoting Pakistani handicrafts in the world market, three friends, Muhammad Ahmad Ibraheem, Usman Khan and Haroon Baig decided to change things around. They developed an online portal that highlights local crafts and Pakistan's artisans. They represent some of the finest handicrafts in the country and are working to highlight the history of the craft and the artisans.

Since they started their venture in 2014, they have been going from success to success towards their goal of putting Pakistan handicrafts on the map of startups.

In 2014, a New Zealand based Tech Blog, Brave New Coin featured Emperor's Bazaar as the first Pakistani e-commerce startup with Bitcoin payment integration.

In 2015, they were finalists in MITEFP's BAP Competition and inducted into the I2I cohort.

In 2016, TechinAsia named Emperor's Bazaar with seven others as the Most Innovative startups of Pakistan.

The US State Department selected Emperor's Bazaar to represent Pakistan in Global Entrepreneurship Summit 2016 in

Silicon Valley, California.

Emperor's Bazaar also won the Best Startup in Social Entrepreneurship category of Startup Magazine's Expo 2016.

Qissakhawani Bazaar (the Storytellers' Bazaar)

Located on the eastern side of the Khyber Pass, the walled city of Peshawar is among the oldest cities in Pakistan, and perhaps even in South Asia. With history dating back to 539 BC, Peshawar was once known as the Crown Jewel of Bactria and an important trading stop on the Silk Route. In the older part of the city is an ancient market known as the *Qissakhwani Bazaar,* or The Storytellers' Bazaar. A fascinated Rudyard Kipling has described this market in a ballad.

The *Qissakhwani Bazaar* is the most vibrant handicrafts market in the region. Magnificent carpets, shiny copperware, intricate wooden and marble wares, silver jewelry and other traditional items abound in its narrow lanes. Created with profound precision and incorporating diverse cultural influences-some drawn from the Indus Valley Civilization-these wares charmed three local students Ibrahim, Usman and Haroon who decided to share these with the world.

Once a key stop for tourists proceeding to the mountains in the north of Pakistan, Peshawar is facing dwindling tourism because of security concerns. Talented artisans have suffered. While the region's security has improved and returned to relative normalcy in recent years, the revitalization of these crafts and the livelihood of the craftspeople is yet to happen.

Joining Hands

Muhammad Ahmad Ibraheem, Usman Khan and Haroon Baig grew up and went to school and college in Peshawar. They all studied at the University of Engineering & Technology (UET), Peshawar from where Ibraheem and Usman graduated in 2012 with Bachelor's degrees in electrical engineering and Haroon from the computer science program a couple of years later.

After graduation, they went their separate ways. Usman co-founded an Interactive Media Studio called Sweet Pixel Studios, which develops creative web and mobile products for consumers as well as businesses. Ibraheem joined a UK-based technology startup called The Appography, where they made a mobile application for the BPO (Business Process Outsourcing) industry.

In January 2014, Code for Pakistan (a non-profit organization building a non-partisan civic innovation ecosystem) and the World Bank organized Peshawar's Civic Incubation Program, Peshawar 2.0. It was at the event that Ibraheem and Usman reconnected and also met Haroon. Ibraheem and Haroon were participating in the hackathon and were paired together. Haroon was majoring in Computer Sciences. He was also working with Microsoft Pakistan, Mozilla Firefox and a US-based company, 'Messiah'. Usman was at the event as a mentor.

Haroon and Ibraheem's project was called 'No Kunda', which monitored electricity theft. The entry went on to win the Best App for Government prize. Later the two paired up for more projects and the three started to think about working together.

Hacking Emperor's Bazaar at Pakathon 2014

In the fall of 2014, a team of young Pakistani expats announced a global online hackathon competition under the Pakathon banner. The goal was to bring together diverse startups over a three-day period to create solutions to local problems.

The three friends took it as the perfect opportunity to tackle a problem close to their hearts. They had already been thinking about the problems of trade and commerce in the local arts and crafts sector. In the run-up to the event, the friends brainstormed why a country of over 180 million, with an agricultural and manufacturing-based economy, fails to contribute to the online trade and e-commerce sectors. Research showed that around 15 percent of Pakistan's total workforce operates in the handicrafts industry, a largely unregulated sector.

They identified three reasons for the lag in the online trade and e-commerce sectors. First, investment into building the required infrastructure was lacking; Second, online banking had not been widely adopted, and international payment processing and digital currencies had not taken off in Pakistan; Finally, a lack of mutual trust existed among local businesses, as well as between local and foreign businesses.

The trio signed up for the Pakathon event from a local partnering university. They came up with a proposed solution to the problem, which became the initial idea for Emperor's Bazaar. They envisioned an online e-commerce marketplace highlighting the very best handmade, bespoke and luxury products sourced from the most skilled artisans and independent brands across Pakistan. Emperor's Bazaar was set up to celebrate the artistic prowess and artisanship of Pakistan's craftspersons and display it for a global audience.

The team was extremely passionate and motivated about the idea. The almost impossible task of setting up a viable prototype, the frontend, backend and payment processing on the website was completed within the 72-hour Pakathon deadline. The team also worked on developing various options for payments including integrating the online payment options using bitcoin, a type of digital currency gaining popularity globally.

In the last few hours before the demo, they fine-tuned their first pitch-deck for Emperor's Bazaar. Their business model and a working prototype of Emperor's Bazaar, which included a listings page, checkout and the successful transfer of bitcoins, was received enthusiastically. The international Pakathon team of judges seemed impressed by Emperor's Bazaar and judged them to be among the top five most innovative ideas pitched during the event. This was extremely motivating for Ibraheem, Usman and Haroon.

At the same time, they realized the need to understand the industry and explore Pakistan for the right products, before their idea could turn into reality. It was obvious that they required help and guidance along the way. So, they began pursuing all possible leads as well as started applying to the best startup incubation programs.

Connecting to the Entrepreneurship Ecosystem in Pakistan

In May 2015, the World Bank collaborated with the Khyber Pakhtunkhwa IT Board (KPIT Board) to organize the annual Digital Youth Summit Peshawar. The summit was the biggest startup gathering of its kind across the region, bringing together mentors, investors and startup veterans from around the globe. The Emperor's Bazaar team was extremely excited to meet all the experienced individuals and share their passion for the startup with them. They also met Kalsoom Lakhani at the event who heads the social impact accelerator called Invest 2 Innovate (I2I). She was immediately responsive and asked them to apply to her program's latest cohort. After a detailed application process, they became part of that year's cohort.

A couple of months later in July 2015, MIT Enterprise Forum Pakistan announced its annual Business Acceleration Program. The Emperor's Bazaar team took part in the introductory event, where they met Azhar Rizvi and Zahir Syed. The mentors and judges liked the Emperor's Bazaar and urged the boys to become a part of the program.

The team knew that they were very fortunate to have been accepted in all of these programs. They were one of the first startups from the KPK region to take part and successfully make it to these competitions. The programs offered the team great learning opportunities to refine the portal's startup plan, maximize the social impact and also become cash flow positive.

Haroon says, "All of us are from technical backgrounds. The MITEFP team pushed us to rethink our business, and guided us on a wide-range of considerations such as financial modeling, market research, market analysis, finding the correct product market fit, strategizing a good go-to-marketing strategy, all the way to raising funds and defining viable exit strategies for the business venture."

It was the first time that the core team composed and drafted a comprehensive 60-page business plan. Their dedicated mentors enabled them to win the proceeding rounds and they made it to the list of the top six startups in Pakistan. Even though they did not win the competition, the team returned with rekindled motivation and passion towards their startup.

Usman says, "We entered MITEFP and other programs with nothing more than a rough idea and a prototype, but we emerged a much stronger business with unique insights, connections and partnerships with some of the most trusted individuals and enterprises around the country.

Soon after the I2I and MITEFP programs, Usman was selected for the Emerging Leaders of Pakistan 2016 program. As part of the cultural exchange program, he visited the United States to explore business opportunities, learn from and personally meet other technology companies that were having a social impact internationally. In addition, the team was selected for the Global Entrepreneurship Summit 2016 in Stanford University, organized by the US State Department. Prestigious organizations like the US State Department, USAID, Pak-Afghan Women Artisans and UNESCO saw and appreciated Emperor's Bazaar.

Reviving The Crafts Sector

The experiences and learning over the course of that year helped the young team members pivot the Emperor's Bazaar business plan each step of the way. By the time Emperor's Bazaar graduated from MITEFP and I2I, they were not just looking at the problem from a technological lens, but also through a social lens.

Their early pitches were very techno-centric. The team had been stressing on it being a bitcoin based e-commerce website. Soon, their focus shifted from the bitcoin-based payment technology (which they discovered to be less viable in Pakistan) to other online and offline payment options, including a sharp operational refocus towards a customer-oriented approach, with the local Pakistani online market as the initial go-to market.

However, in the months of interaction with artisans and women from some of the most remote regions of Pakistan, they realized that the problems not only existed at a technical level but also at the social level. With this knowledge, the team knew that they had to change their mindset significantly in order to face these issues. They decided to take a two-pronged approach towards solving the problem.

Developing a Vendor Network

Since handicrafts and bespoke products are experience driven and high value, the team was fastidious about creating an online marketplace to display local brands. The brand offered an experience reflecting immense attention to detail. Their brand identity incorporated refined tastes and a luxury feel attracting collectors and connoisseur of fine products.

They carefully selected their first set of vendors from only the best independent brands from across the country that measured up to strict quality standards.

Usman says, "It was a consuming yet crucial process of discovering the best brands across each province of Pakistan. The products could potentially stand out as masterpieces of creativity and craftsmanship of Pakistani manufacturing."

Currently, one can find the best quality bespoke product lines on the platform. These include:

- Handmade shoes from Gomila Intersole
- Leather bags from Bear Necessities
- Ethically-made women's accessories from interior Sindh by Inaaya
- Iconic Peshawari sandals from Tribal Culture
- Traditional furniture inspired by the Mughal era by Kalamkaar
- Traditional and contemporary carpets from Miaco Carpets
- Luxury home accent furniture pieces made from stone, brass and marble in lay by LÉL Collections
- Bespoke Mont 5 leather jackets
- Antiques from the old bazaars of Pakistan

Quality And Fair Trade

The team realized that local craftsmen and small businesses needed to understand how to scale to the international market. Therefore, Emperor's Bazaar also started working on educating and facilitating small businesses for which they arrange exhibitions and workshops.

These broad and diverse efforts are essentially tied to the greater goal of reviving the handicrafts and manufacturing industries of Pakistan. Emperor's Bazaar's long-term goal is to develop a platform that would enable every artisan and small-scale business in Pakistan to take their business online.

The team envisages that their portal can contribute to making the 'Made in Pakistan' label, one of trust and quality.

Going Places in 2016

The core team has grown to include three more people who are developing the marketplace and the brand stories around the products that they carry. So far, they have mostly bootstrapped the company and have only just crossed breakeven. The team continues to plow into their earnings to expand the portal and channel relationships.

They are also developing partnerships in major cities in Pakistan, like Karachi, Lahore and Islamabad to streamline customer services and bring on more vendors. There are now 12 companies on board and vendor relationships are growing fast.

The team adopts a storytelling approach on the website. Each of the brands are in the process of developing their own stories about how the artisans work to give global buyers a flavor of their painstaking efforts.

The team also works with partners to develop the local artisan market and make them more tech-savvy. In 2015, they collaborated with USAID to conduct a workshop for Pakistan-Afghanistan Women Business Opportunities conference. Currently, they are in talks with a mobile payments solution provider for connecting to artisans who do not have access to the internet.

Another new backend initiative that they have developed is a technology called Merchant Connect. This is a facility for someone without access to the internet to run an online store using SMS.

Ibraheem says, "We realize that Emperor's Bazaar is still very much in its infancy and although we have been fortunate enough to make significant strides and partner with some of the most high-impact organizations in our very short journey, we still have a long way to go."

Usman adds, "We have to continue working hard towards our goal to create the perfect platform for our best and the brightest artisans, craftsmen and small businesses across Pakistan, so that they can showcase their amazing products, inspiring stories and masterful processes for the global audience online. This will garner the much needed focus and attention that their earnest efforts deserve."

Advice for Entrepreneurs

Get Your Hands Dirty: Handicrafts are produced in tiny, cottage and small sector manufacturing units scattered across the country, particularly in the interior of the provinces. It was difficult to bring them together, make them aware of the export potential in the world market. The team had to do a lot of research and visit many of the facilities to understand the business. It is very important to understand the intricacies of the business you are getting into, focus on understanding the market and ultimately the needs and behavior of your business' end consumers. The more you refine your understanding, the better positioned your startup will be in gaining consumer trust and loyalty.

Where to Focus: Focus on building a holistic experience around your product and/or service. In our opinion, the best product or service is one that solves or mitigates a problem and it should do that effectively and seamlessly.

Link into Mentor Pools to Learn Quickly: The Emperor's Bazaar team was able to connect to relevant people more quickly because they were constantly participating in exhibitions, hackathons and competitions. If they had not done so, they might have run out of steam soon. Each meeting with a mentor always makes the business model stronger. Advisors play a crucial role in a startup's success especially when all of the founders are young and not adequately experienced in the industry. The team dedicates their success to their advisors from MITEFP and Kalsoom Lakhani from I2I. Their unconditional support and personal guidance not only shaped the team members' careers as better entrepreneurs, but their motivation early on was also a key factor in helping them to take Emperor's Bazaar forward with a clear focus.

Learn to Wear Multiple Hats: Invest in learning new things and always be ready to wear several hats. Entrepreneurship is not an easy career choice and the beginning is by far the most difficult phase. You will not have enough financial freedom to begin with, so dedicated founders should know every aspect of their business; from customer support to supply chain management, financial modeling, down to dealing with common chores in the workplace. It takes a certain level of commitment to achieve business success.

Do not Compromise on Principles: Always negotiate a deal with mutual interest. Young founders can sometimes be manipulated into taking a deal, which is not ideal, especially in markets like Pakistan where investment capital is not flowing freely. Do not fall for a less than ideal offer. Take your time, be patient and try to put yourself in a position to negotiate your terms. Sometimes confidence in one's abilities can go a long way.

Failure: The biggest asset of any young entrepreneur is their time. Failures early on are valuable experiences, although this does not mean that entrepreneurs should take uninformed decisions. If they fail, they should take failure head-on and reinvest the learning from previous experiences to gain success.

Pakistan as A Startup Environment: Contrary to popular belief, Pakistan is one of the best places to start a business. The team realized this firsthand with the tremendous support they received for Emperor's Bazaar from very devoted mentors, advisors and the sheer number of opportunities for innovation that were available in the market. Almost 50 percent of the Pakistani population is under the age of 30, which is a tremendous opportunity in itself.

Learn from Competitions: At the Global Entrepreneurship Summit 2016 in Silicon Valley, the team witnessed the dedication of the US President Obama in organizing the summit. They realized how big an impact innovation and disruption has in our modern society. Entrepreneurs change the course of history and help shape the economic landscape of their countries. Sharing the stage with some 1500 entrepreneurs globally in Stanford University reassured the team that their work had significance and that they were on to something meaningful.

25

Cancer Killing Virus

ASAB-NUST
Tahira Khan

Researcher, ASAB-NUST
Islamabad, Khyber Pakhtunkhwa
www.nust.edu.pk/institutions/Schools/ASAB

"If you can let go of passion and follow your curiosity, your curiosity just might lead you to your passion."~Elizabeth Gilbert, American author, essayist

The cartoon show, Dexter's Laboratory, motivated Tahira to be a scientist. She is now working at the Atta-ur-Rahman School of Applied Biosciences (ASAB) at NUST todevelop a virotherapy cure for the 1.4 million cancer patients in Pakistan whose number is rising each year by 8 to 10 percent. Moved by her interactions with suffering cancer patients, one of whom was her own grandfather, Tahira was inspired to find a cure through her research-which has already shown in-lab success.

Author's Note: Tahira Khan is my mentee from NUST. I mentored her for five months at the NUST competition in preparing a business plan and enabling her to pitch the proposal at a big forum. She is developing a cancer cure using virotherapy and is working with a common local strand of Rani Khet virus. She is very hopeful about the initial results of her endeavor and is now proceeding to the next stage of testing. If all goes well, she will have a result in the next two or three years.

The biotechnology industry stands at the forefront of science. Inspired biotechnologists and life scientists are pushing boundaries to find cures for the most critical health problems facing humans today.

Tahira Khan belongs to this elite group of researchers. She is an ordinary urban Pakistani girl pursuing a Master's degree at the Atta-ur-Rahman School of Applied Biosciences (ASAB) at the National University of Science and Technology (NUST).

Her childhood inspiration was a cartoon character Dexter who owned a laboratory. Watching this cartoon as a child, she began wanting to work in her very own lab one day. With that vision in mind, Tahira embarked on a journey at NUST in the field of biotechnology to find a cure for cancer when a loved one passed away from this disease.

She is currently working on developing a virotherapy solution for liver cancer using a local strain of the Rani Khet virus. She has developed and tested the treatment under lab conditions with positive outcomes and is working towards testing it further before embarking on commercialization.

Roots

Tahira Khan comes from a military background. Her father was part of the aviation unit of the army. While most of her life was spent in Rawalpindi, her family also relocated to Multan, Karachi and Gujranwala from time to time due to her father's postings. Tahira began her education at the Iqra Army Public School. She completed her Matriculation from APS Westridge, after which she went to the Fauji Foundation College.

The groundwork of her career as a scientist was laid at the age of three when she could barely talk. When questioned by her grandfather about what she wanted to be when she grew up, she amazed him by saying 'scientist'. He often wondered where she had picked up the word. He could never guess that one of the biggest influences on Tahira's life was Dexter, the cartoon hero of 'Dexter's Laboratory.' She had a childhood dream of owning a laboratory just like him.

Intrigued by Viruses

Tahira pursued higher studies at NUST and enrolled in BSc (Honors) in Biology and Immunology program on September 20, 2010, a date she recalls clearly. The name of the program was later changed to Atta-ur-Rahman School of Applied Biosciences (ASAB). ASAB-NUST boasts of state-of-the-art teaching and research. The home of Pakistan's largest biotech cluster and pool of expertise, it is an invaluable resource that enables students to access biotechnological skills.

Tahira jokingly refers to her family as 'the NUST family' as they are connected to NUST in many ways. Her father completed his MBA from there; her younger sister is pursuing an undergraduate program in Applied Biosciences, and another sister is studying Industrial Design from the NUST School of Art, Design and Architecture.

The school is unique as it has established expertise across a broad range of biotechnology, and encourages innovative approaches to teaching and research. It is one of the top 400 universities in the world. Areas of expertise include healthcare biotechnology, industrial biotechnology, food and plant biotechnology. ASAB has dynamic interdisciplinary undergraduate and graduate programs that prepare the students for pursuits in research and teaching in pure molecular as well as applied biology. Additionally, it has local and international research collaborations that provide students the opportunities to work in joint research projects from around the world.

Tahira recalls that the first two years of her undergraduate degree were very intensive. She was intrigued by the ability of viruses to cause deadly diseases such as AIDS that cause wide-scale health problems despite being so tiny. Her favorite subjects were Virology, the study of viruses, and Immunology, the study of the immune system.

Reprogramming Viruses

Two of the most common ways of treating cancer are chemotherapy-treatment by chemical substances-and radiotherapy-treatment using ionizing radiation to control or kill malignant cells. As a common side effect, both these treatments damage healthy cells also while treating cancerous cells. This weakens the patient's immunity system making him/her susceptible to infections that can often be lethal.

Virotherapy is an alternative biotechnology treatment reprogramming viruses to treat diseases. It has three main branches: Anti-cancer oncolytic viruses, viral vectors for gene therapy, and viral immunotherapy. Viral immunotherapy simply uses a virus' ability to selectively replicate and kill cells, while stimulating a patient-specific immune response against cancer at the same time. This intervention leaves the healthy cells potentially unharmed.

Tahira is working on a cure based on this principle. She uses the Rani Khet Virus, globally known as the Newcastle Disease Virus (NDV). The Newcastle disease commonly attacks and kills chicken after producing flu-like symptoms. It is a contagious disease affecting many bird species. First identified in Java, Indonesia in 1926 and then in Newcastle-upon-Tyne, England in 1927 where it received its name, the virus is transmissible to humans.

When humans are exposed to the infected birds, for example, in poultry processing plants, they can develop mild conjunctivitis and flu-like symptoms. Other than that, the NDV poses no serious threat to human health. As an oncolytic virus, NDV selectively attacks and destroys only tumor cells as well as stimulates a body's immune system.

Consumed by A Passion

In her fourth semester at NUST, Tahira was sitting in a class on livestock development. "I remember, the lecture was very boring and the whole class was half asleep. Suddenly, the teacher mentioned cancer-killing viruses that made me sit up. I thought that was very interesting stuff." Tahira's curiosity was piqued so she started reading up more about the phenomenon. She keenly researched the cancer-killing virus and tied her coursework to it at every opportunity she could find.

"This was a personal thing for me, because my dear grandfather had died of liver cancer when I was 16," says Tahira. "I said to myself, 'Tahira, you can find a cure for cancer.' I know that finding a cure for cancer is a really big goal, but there could be some small aspect of it, which I could research and look into."

The next incident that had an effect on Tahira was during a research internship in her undergraduate years. This program was in the summer of 2013 at the H. Lee Moffitt Cancer Center and Research Institute at the University of South Florida in Tampa, US. Tahira recalls, "Whenever I passed by the chemotherapy department, I saw patients in so much pain that they could not even walk or talk properly. The torment was evident on their faces. You would not wish such pain on your worst enemy. It is such a depressing disease and very few survive it." This feeling served as further motivation for her to pursue a cure for this disease. Because of the internship at Tampa, Tahira was able to publish her first international paper on the genes involved in lung cancer and their role in the degradation of the immune system.

Researching A Potential Cure for Cancer

Her research project in Tampa was on the Rani Khet virus. Tahira believed that God has not created anything without a use, and wished to explore this virus as a potential cure for liver and ovarian cancer.

She signed an agreement with the Pakistan Poultry Research Institute in Rawalpindi, which supplied her with a virus strain extracted from infected livestock. The agreement covered the ethics and procedures involved in the handling of the strain, to avoid mishaps like the production of mutant strains that could threaten livestock.

Testing Out

In 2016, Tahira presented her idea at a contest at NUST called Finding Innovative and Creative Solutions for Society (FICS). She ranked sixth among hundreds of researchers. She plans to participate in more of these platforms to make her idea global. So far, NUST has funded her research and its Corporate Advisory Council has connected her with numerous doctors and individuals associated with the pharmaceutical industry who could be potentially interested in her idea. She is working on a business plan and currently doing market research to present a strong case to potential investors. Simultaneously, Tahira plans to pursue her PhD as it is a preliminary requirement for becoming a cancer researcher in the US or Germany, where most virus related research is being conducted.

Referring to her entrepreneurial journey, Tahira is still at the beginning. Her journey started by participating in Discover 2015 where she learnt that researchers also need to understand the basics of marketing, finance, and operations for the commercial success of their product.

After conducting experiments on mice based on this hypothesis, she plans on patenting the idea and collaborating with the pharmaceutical industry to conduct clinical trials. This is a long-term plan since it takes eight to ten years for a drug to develop from a model into a product ready for the market. Four to five years are needed for it to reach the clinical trials stage. Currently, Tahira is midway into the research and will be doing trials up to 2018 to refine her investigation.

The Journey Ahead

Tahira conducted experiments in her laboratory to study the molecular interaction of the virus with cancer cells. The aim of her research was to discover whether the virus actually eradicates cancer cells and if it can be used to make a sort of anti-cancer vaccine. She submitted her Master's thesis in October 2016, and on approval, she will submit it for international publication. She will develop the vaccine and test it on mice during her PhD.

Tahira is independently researching under the supervision of Anila Javaid, the clinical virologist and assistant professor at NUST. Her other mentors and supervisors are Nasir Jalal, her role model and inspiration who has encouraged her constantly, and Amir Baig, who ingrained in her the belief that she can handle any project successfully. Her entrepreneurial journey will start when her research is ready for commercialization.

Funding is crucial for her idea to succeed. Since Pakistan is a developing country, basic issues like primary healthcare and sanitation are priority areas for government. Hence, advance research is often ignored and research budgets are frequently slashed. Finding investors can be an uphill task, although there are various funding bodies. She plans to seek partnerships with pharmaceuticals after the completion of her Master's Degree.

Apart from contacting pharmaceutical companies, she plans to form a diverse team comprising individuals from a variety of backgrounds such as finance, marketing and medicine.

Many anti-cancer viruses are in the approval process for Virography, which has raised Tahira's hopes for proving her hypothesis. However, she still expects many obstacles along the way. She talks about the challenges of being a female from the Khyber Pakhtunkhwa (KPK) a place where women's education is not encouraged. She believes that the idea of a woman wanting to inject germs into cancer patients will meet with a lot of resistance in her home region where illiteracy and superstition are rife. She cites the example of her uncle, killed in an attack last year because of his organization's campaign to eradicate polio in KPK. Tahira does not see her idea gaining approval from the people who are mostly prejudiced, even against polio vaccines.

Some of the other challenges she foresees include societal and peer pressures, which obstruct an individual, especially a girl, from accomplishing all that they can. The stress placed on Pakistani girls to get married as quickly as possible is one of these. According to Tahira, "Marriage is just a part of life. It should not happen at the expense of one's dreams."

Fortunately, Tahira's parents possess a progressive outlook and fully support her in her career. She hopes to overcome all of these issues, as she believes, "God is always with the person who has good intentions."

Advice for Entrepreneurs

Curiosity for A Researcher: Tahira advises all the girls who plan on pursuing a career in research to be less curious about people and more curious about ideas. The field of research is very different from what is written in textbooks.

Being A Woman: She believes that women can achieve anything they put their mind to. She encourages women to, "Dream big and rock the world."

On Good Intentions: Good intentions provide a vital push towards achieving one's goals.

26

Embracing Indigenous Knowledge

Nanosmart
Faria Khan
Nano-biotech Researcher and Founder,
NanoSmart
Islamabad, Lahore

"Curiosity has its own reason for existing. One cannot help but be in awe when he contemplates the mysteries of eternity, of life, of the marvelous structure of reality." ~ Albert Einstein, German-American Theoretical Physicist and Nobel Laureate

A WHO internship set Faria on the research path. She is currently developing a nanoparticle-based hospital disinfectant-a patented product that will be commercially viable and more eco-friendly than other disinfectants in the market.

Author's Note: Faria Khan fell in love with nanoparticles. Her continued research has met with with early success and now she has a product: a disinfectant paint for the healthcare and hospital sector that is already being test-marketed. Through the NUST competition, I mentored her in preparing a business plan and gave a direction to her product development and marketing strategies. Though the final product is still under research, Faria now understands the purpose of marketing and financial sustainability. She is now test marketing a basic model and yes, making some money too. She made my day a few weeks back, when she asked me to join her startup, NanoSmart, as its CEO. These are proud moments for any parent or father figure!

Born in 1989, Faria Khan had travelled extensively in Pakistan while she was still a young girl. She was an inquisitive soul and loved nature. After being denied admission to a medical school on a

technicality, she joined the Virology and Immunology Department at NUST-Atta-ur-Rahman School of Applied Biosciences (ASAB).

While at NUST, Faria secured a two-month long internship at the World Health Organization (WHO) headquarters in Geneva, Switzerland in 2013. The internship helped her grow as a professional. When she returned to Pakistan, she began developing an innovative disinfectant formulation, which used Pakistan's indigenous herbs with modern nanotechnology tools to control hospital-acquired infections.

Faria completed her Master of Science degree in Industrial Biotechnology from NUST in 2016. The BS final-year project that she had begun in 2014 is now moving towards commercialization. Meanwhile, Faria has been working to improve the disinfectant formulation prior to its commercial launch. Under NUST's banner, her team is developing a patentable product, commercially viable and more eco-friendly than other disinfectants in the market.

Growing Up in A Military Family

Faria was born on November 13, 1989 in Rawalpindi. Her father, Khalid Iqbal Khan was an army officer. She travelled widely and lived all over Pakistan, moving wherever her father was transferred with his regiment. She did her first year of O level final and AS level in Multan and completed A levels from the Beaconhouse School in Lahore with straight A's in all subjects.

The flora of the places where she had lived fascinated Faria as a child. She observed herbs and other plants of different regions and was very interested in how they were being used as traditional medicine by the local people. This fascination has stayed with her throughout.

A Disaster, An Opportunity

As a straight A student, Faria had hoped to enter medical college. However, in 2009, the Government of Punjab introduced a new pattern of testing for A level students as part of the standard Medical College Admission Test (MCAT). When the question paper was handed out on the examination day, the students found it problematic. More than 90 percent A level students failed to acquire the required percentile due to a flawed test. Only a handful were able to get admission and only into second-tier medical schools. Disgruntled, the A-level students filed a case against the University Of Health Sciences and the MCAT authorities for setting a flawed exam. The High Court reprimanded the Controller Examination and Registrar but decided in favor of the system. Apart from a few news headlines and discontinuation of the experimental examination format, the students were left to deal with the life-long consequences of the judgment on their careers.

The incident proved to be a turning point in Faria's life. Her options were laid out in front of her. She had received admission offers from universities abroad for undergraduate programs; from NUST-ASAB; and from some average medical programs. Faria decided that instead of enrolling in a second grade medical college, she would study in an institute that could make a leader out of her. Her parents were hesitant sending her abroad. Therefore, she opted to pursue an undergraduate degree in Applied Biosciences at NUST, her best option in the country.

A Huge Gap

During her second year at NUST, Faria interned at PIMS (Pakistan Institute of Medical Sciences) where she collected breast cancer samples for genetic analysis. She noticed the short comings in Pakistan's health system firsthand and became determined about changing them. According to Faria, "The patients who had been diagnosed at different stages of cancer would hold our hands and ask for reassurances, thinking we were young house officers. Their pain made me realize how important it was to work towards finding a solution to this disease. I also realized the importance of biotechnological interventions which were required to control the spread of diseases as well as for early diagnosis."

Faria's professional career received a big boost when she earned an Internship at the World Health Organization (WHO) headquarters in Geneva, Switzerland in 2013. This was a life-changing experience for her. She was the first undergraduate student from Pakistan to get the opportunity to intern at the WHO. The internship was under the supervision of world-renowned epidemiologist, Dr Moazzam Ali. The two-month internship gave her the opportunity to meet highly experienced scientists, researchers, doctors, policymakers and healthcare professionals. From these interactions, she also learnt about their efforts to combat the problems in healthcare sectors around the world. This altered her perspective towards the field.

Faria evaluated the health protocols at PIMS against the standards proposed by WHO and saw the huge gap between the on ground situation and the recommendations by the global organization. "While collecting samples for our university with three of my batchmates, I realized that a big gap existed between the protocols that our best hospitals were following and the WHO recommended standards. The patients were not even counseled properly," Faria recalls, "It was a huge revelation for me."

As an undergraduate research student, she continued to volunteer and join societies on the side. As part of the community service program at NUST, she spent a lot of time with Thalassemia patients and orphans at the SOS Village. "I was brought up in a protected environment and it was heartbreaking for me to see how these children were suffering," says Faria. She felt the strong love of parents whose children brought them to

PIMS for blood infusions. She saw the determination of sick children who were pale and suffering, yet dreaming of a happy future. She drew inspiration from the orphans at SOS Village, who had nothing to give but love and respect. This made her realize how blessed she was and how much she could contribute through her profession and dedication. "The regular interaction with patients made me realize the value of the work that could be done," says Faria.

His Doubts Motivated Her

In her final-year of the BSc (Honors) program at the NUST-ASAB, she decided to focus on research that would address the prevalent issues of the healthcare sector through biotechnological interventions. She had observed that while patients were in hospital, a breed of strong drug-resistant bacteria was causing hospital infections. Even patients who walk in could pass on infections and contribute to the spread of disease in the hospital. The Multiple Drug Resistant (MDR) bacteria became the subject of her final-year project, under the supervision of Dr Hussnain Janjua, a PhD in Microbial Molecular Biology from Imperial College, London.

In her thesis, she focused on identifying the factors in clinical settings that contributed to the emergence of the MDR species a situation that increases the mortality rate and the per capita investment required in Pakistan's healthcare sector.

"I told my supervisor that I would need epidemiological data from the hospital as this was a study of disease in a specific region. I told him I need basic primary healthcare facilities' data. He said that it was an ambitious project and that I could not implement it in three or four months. But I was so determined."

The supervisor gave his go ahead grudgingly, but he doubted that she will obtain the relevant data. Faria remembers, "Instead of discouraging me, his doubt motivated me!"

Controlling Hospital Acquired Infections

Faria focused her research on countering infections and speeding up the wound-healing process. At NUST's Biotechnology Department, Faria met Dr Qasim Hayat, a professor in the NUST Plant Biotech department, who had an avid interest in medicine. He told Faria about a plant used for healing wounds and soothing burns in the Cholistan desert. This plant became Faria's primary area of focus. Her secondary interest was to prevent infections acquired in hospitals and curtail their spread. She collaborated with AFIP (Armed Forces Institute of Pathology) in her second area of focus.

By integrating indigenous knowledge of herbal medicine with modern nanotechnology, Faria developed an innovative disinfectant formulation that would control hospital-acquired infections."I collected highly infectious species of bacteria from AFIP on which no antibiotic worked. By the end of the project, I had created an effective formulation which used nanotechnology tools," Faria explains.

Talking about the formulation, Faria says, "By using nanotechnology tools, we can create antibacterial, antifungal or antiviral agents that can work against the pathogens. My work focused on silver and zinc oxide nanoparticles. I placed them between plant formulations and created silver nanoparticles. It is not something huge, but it was novel because I integrated Pakistan's indigenous knowledge of medicinal plants into my product."

Eco-Friendly And Safe

Her Principal Investigator at ASAB, Dr Hussnain Janjua, encouraged Faria to work on factors required to bring stability to her product as a part of her Masters research 2014-2016. For a lack of facilities at NUST, she had to carry out some of the lab analysis at the LUMS chemistry department, where the Chairman, Dr Irshad Hussain advised her in formulating a stabilized product.

The products that are currently available in the market use a chemical route during their synthesis phase requiring very high temperatures and certain hazardous conditions inside the manufacturing facility. Faria's product uses a biological route that is much safer for the environment and the workers.

Faria explains, "The industrial nanoparticles require increased temperatures, controlled pH and several other parameters. In contrast, my product can be made within a few minutes in a lab under simple lab conditions. It is just a basic plant extract in aqueous form and the process is quite simple."

Most silver nanoparticles cause skin problems. Faria's current lab product has not produced any allergies or irritation even after several experiments on mice, including primary safety and efficacy analysis. Therefore, even if Faria's organic product is released into the environment, the nanoparticles will cause no damage. The disinfectant uses herbal medicine that can speed up wound healing, offering extra benefit to recovering patients.

Seeing it Grow

By the end of her BSc (Hons), Faria had already started her journey towards becoming a competent scientist. However, her dream to make a difference had still not come true. The opportunity to link her professional goals with the real world arrived when she participated in the NUST Discover Business Plan Competition 2014-2015. Faria's team NanoSmart was among the top five finalists from hundreds of participating teams from across the country. In the judges panel sat many known Pakistani entrepreneurs, including Azhar Rizvi and Dr Zahir Ali Syed of MITEFP. While she was presenting the idea to her mentors and the judges at Discover, Azhar Rizvi asked her, "Do you want to take this project forward?"

"Yes," she replied without missing a beat. "The project is my baby and I would love to nurture it and see it grow and save lives." Impressed by Faria's passion, Azhar Rizvi said, "Then proceed with the same wisdom, passion and dedication that you have shown in developing it. Only you own this idea and so you are the only one who can turn it into a real business."

She pondered these words and pursued her research with unflinching courage and dedication. Her entrepreneurial skills were polished further when she participated in the UNIDO CleanTech program for Small and Medium Enterprises (SMEs) and Startups 2015. Her team was one of the semifinalists and received advice and training from many experts including the renowned mentor Paul deGive, MD of the deBarsy group.

Making It Commercially Viable

Never in her wildest dreams had Faria imagined that her final-year project would lead to anything more than a research paper. She had presumed that all her hard work would be put away along with other stacks of scientific papers and would never be used. She was grateful that she had the chance to further her research by exploring options to commercialize.

Faria's product is now ready for launch in Pakistan and is expected to be able to help control hospital-acquired infections, a common problem in local hospitals. Faria's product can be used in two or three different forms: As a spray and as a disinfectant for cleaning the hospital floors. Faria also says that it can be used to coat surgical instruments to ensure hygiene and safety standards.

She has been seeking financial support through grants and sponsorships. She is confident that her mentors and teachers will help her find funding at an international level.

There are three other members in the founding team. Two of them are Uzair Hashmi, who works with her in the lab and Muhammad Salim, a colleague from ASAB and a healthcare biotechnologist and pharmacist by profession. Salim is also her advisor on the required laws and registrations. The third member of Faria's team is Shayan Khalid, who studies at the NUST Business School and is the team's marketing and finance expert.

Key Advice For Researchpreneurs

Challenges of Setting Up A Biotech Company: The idea of a biotech company is still new in Pakistan. While starting a nanotech-based startup (NanoSmart) here, Faria understands that she might have to face several hurdles. She believes that challenges come in two areas, technical and social.

Participation in enterprise development programs and competitions exposed her to the basic framework required to accelerate a biotech-based startup and improve the product development and commercialization outcomes.

Family Support in Making Research A Career: Faria says her mother, Sana and father, Major Khalid, have played vital roles in motivating and supporting her towards this goal. Her father specially encouraged her to pursue the idea even to the extent of collaborating with venture capitalists across the country. She says that without family support, it would have been impossible for her to pursue the commercial aspects of the venture.

Becoming A Tech Entrepreneur: The journey from researcher to tech entrepreneur is never easy. For Faria, this was not a matter of months but years. Her journey is relatively new, but also a long one. She is optimistic about its success and believes that no matter how biased the society is towards women working in science and as entrepreneurs, she will succeed in commercializing her biotech product.

Women And Entrepreneurship: Faria wants to encourage women to take part in enterprise-based research and contribute to the healthcare sector. She feels it is time that society starts accepting women in science and entrepreneurship. Parents and families should be open to letting their girls decide their own career paths. It is imperative to understand that women who are confident of their family's support can contribute far more to the country than those that have to face resistance.

27

Running Towards My Dream

Maha Yusuf
PhD Student
Stanford University

Jhang, San Francisco

"The biggest adventure you can take is to live the life of your dreams"~ Oprah Winfrey, American media proprietor, talk show host and producer

A simple small town girl from Jhang, Maha dreamt of becoming the next Nobel laureate, like Dr Abdus Salam who also hailed from her hometown. This is the story of her struggle to reach Stanford University and become a doctoral researcher working in hydrogen-based fuels.

Author's Note: Maha Yusuf is a chemical engineer from NUST and is now a PhD student at Stanford University's School of Chemical Engineering. She is perhaps the most troublesome, but also my most favourite student. She is the first one to post a Father's Day message on my FB wall for the past five years now, sometimes annoying my other daughters. She uses the time difference to her advantage.

Maha Yusuf is also happily married to another dear student of mine, Nasrullah. They first came to the Discover Business Plan competition at NUST with the piezoelectric shoe. Soon she was among the best and moved on to win the competition. She kept working on the idea even after the competition had concluded.

After completing her education and refusing jobs from ICI, Engro and other blue chip firms, she chose to join Schlumberger in Colombia (Latin America) as a Field Rig Engineer. As the only woman on the rig, her 18 months there were a nightmare for her parents and myself as she used to call in case of emergencies, sometimes twice and even thrice a day. But hats off to Maha for her persistence! She attended the trainings and was again top of her class at the company. Soon she was given the sensitive task of handling radioactive substance for drilling etc.

Her Aha! moment came when she went to the US for a conference and later to Draper University for a three-month training program in entrepreneurship. She did well in the program, by pitching her social entrepreneurship project. When Draper University offered her investment for her project, she declined it and instead requested to spend a day with her ideal, Sheryl Sandburg of Facebook, which she did. Now Maha is at Stanford University doing research for a project funded by a major automobile manufacturer. She is finally happy with what she is doing and totally focused on her work—a fact I can well assume based on the number of phone calls I used to get from her. They have dwindled from several in a week to once every couple of months.

Maha Yusuf belongs to a middle-class family from the Jhang district in Punjab. Her journey began in a Pakistani village where women were encouraged to start a family as soon as they turned 15. She became the first girl in her family to reach O levels. She went on to NUST to complete her BS in chemical engineering and maintained an outstanding GPA of 3.92 on a 4.00 scale. Leaving fantastic job offers at ICI and Engro to join Schlumberger, her first assignment was to go to Bogotá, Colombia, where she spent over a year on an oilrig. Many a times, she was the only woman on the team.

After her stint in Colombia, Maha went to Draper University on a prestigious entrepreneurship program, where she got a chance to meet her hero, Sheryl Sandberg, COO of Facebook and Founder of Leanin.org.

Today, Maha has proved to everyone, including herself that women can have it all. Having pushed cultural, gender and social boundaries, Maha is currently pursuing her PhD at Stanford University. She is also part of a research group at Stanford working on clean energy technologies.

Small Town, Big Dreams

Maha Yusuf is from a small city called Jhang in the province of Punjab in Pakistan. Her father is a small landowner who used to work in government. Jhang is also the birthplace of Dr Abdus Salam, Pakistan's first Nobel Laureate. Like many families in Punjab, Maha's family was also very conservative. Her father was the only one in his generation to complete a Bachelor's degree while his five sisters, Maha's aunts, were married off right after they had completed high school.

Breaking with this family tradition, Maha's father encouraged her to study and pursue her dreams. She studied at the Chenab School in Jhang and got nine A's in her O levels in 2007.

Maha started receiving marriage proposals at the age of 15. But she had different goals for herself. She participated enthusiastically in science competitions and numerous projects in school and had known for a long time that she wanted to pursue the sciences. Due to an exceptional academic record, she was selected to represent Pakistan at the International Geofest in India in 2007, her last year of school. The only girl from her school and one of the few girls participating in the competition, Maha won her team a medal from among 76 international teams.

Changing Track

After completing her O Levels, Maha went to visit her aunt in Faisalabad during the summer holidays. Her aunt was a coordinator at the local Beaconhouse School. She decided that she wanted to take up A levels there because of a shortage of science teachers at Maha's school in Jhang. Maha was in fact one of the very few students to take up science in school.

She asked her parents to let her continue her education in Faisalabad. In a country where most women leave the home only when they marry, her parents were not too eager. Maha's mother was already talking about her marriage and her father was apprehensive about her moving to a bigger city.

Her parents eventually relented, realizing that Maha would be unhappy if not allowed to explore her talents. She was granted permission on the condition that she would live with her aunt only. Therefore, at the age of 16, Maha packed her bags and moved to Faisalabad. Based on her O level grades, the Beaconhouse School offered Maha a full scholarship. She continued to participate in science competitions and won in the National Chemistry Contest.

Even though Maha had moved to Faisalabad for education, she remembers the extended family objecting to her parents. "It was hard moving far away from my parents, living by myself, and traveling in buses in a bigger city. Despite of all these pressures from my extended family, I wanted to do it because science was my passion. For me there was no choice," says Maha.

Aiming High

Living in Faisalabad gave her the chance to interact with students from all over the country and from abroad and opened her eyes to the world. Maha had already heard of Cambridge and Oxford and decided to apply to universities in the UK for higher studies. She achieved stellar A Level results and was offered admission into the prestigious Oxford University; but there was no scholarship or financial assistance. She went back to her parents to try to convince them to let her go to Oxford. This time, they put their foot down and she could do nothing to change their decision. She had to stay in the country.

She continued to dream of going abroad and studying at a top university. She recalls, "I didn't know about other opportunities in other countries like the US. I did not know if I could apply to other countries for scholarships. I had no idea."

The question of marriage continued to loom. All her female cousins were either getting married or preparing to tie the knot. Maha's mother was always worried that she would not be able to find a good match. "I sat my mother down and told her that studying science made me happy. I told her that I would get married, but I was also going to follow my dreams," says Maha. Seeing her daughter's determination, her mother gave in and told her that she will support her in the pursuit of her dreams.

Maha took the entry test at NUST and LUMS, and eventually

decided to attend NUST (National University of Science and Technology). Her mother accompanied her to NUST. "If Allah has chosen this place for me then I believe it is the best place for me. I have to believe in Him," Maha said to herself about her admission in NUST.

She joined the second batch of School of Chemical and Materials Engineering (SCME) at NUST. One of the top 400 universities in the world and one of Pakistan's best engineering universities, NUST offered a stimulating environment. With renewed optimism, Maha made the best of the opportunity. She believes that positivity and optimism is very important in life and a prerequisite for success. This belief supported her during her time at NUST. It also whetted her appetite for learning and motivated her to excel at everything.

Designing The Piezoelectric Shoe

In her third semester at NUST, Maha led a team of three in designing the prototype of the piezoelectric shoe. The shoe converts mechanical energy generated from walking into electrical energy and can charge mobile batteries of up to three volts. At that time, this was an innovative concept. The project won the third prize and the Best Science Project Display award at the EME Olympiad 2010 and NASTEC 2011, respectively.

The project called 'A Piezoelectric Solution to Pakistan's Energy Crisis', was among the 25 semifinalists from 43 countries in the GISTech-I (Global Innovation through Science and Technology Initiative) at the Second Global Summit on Entrepreneurship, hosted by the Prime Minister of Turkey and the US Vice-President, Joe Biden, in December 2011. It reached the semifinals at the Global Social Venture Competition (GSVC) at the Haas Business School, University of California, Berkeley, and at the London Business School in the EMEA (Europe, Middle East and Asia) finale.

This project opened many doors for Maha. She founded a club called Brains, a club for nerds, at NUST. After participating in the GISTech-I, she also met a number of mentors who helped her crystallize her future goals.

Maha did her internship in Jhang at the Shakarganj Sugar Mills in 2011. This was the same year that she was invited to attend the second

Global Entrepreneurship Summit in Istanbul where she met experienced mentors and people from MIT, Stanford, and Silicon Valley. When she came back to NUST, she started working online for a Malaysian startup. She was also doing social media marketing and research for a startup. In the summer, she did an internship at Engro Fertilizers at Daharki in Sindh.

Introduction To Nanomaterials

In her final year, Maha was offered a scholarship by the US Department of State to attend a course in chemical engineering at the University of Mississippi for a semester. It was a fantastic experience for her being exposed to different cultures, living with diverse people and learning from them. While there, she started a research project on nanomaterials (nanographene for carbon capture) with Professor Wei Yin Chen.

Nanoscience and nanotechnology are the study and manipulation at the atomic, molecular and supramolecular scale for use across all the other scientific fields, such as chemistry, biology, physics, materials science and engineering. This includes manufacturing nanomaterials, made from a single layer of atoms. One such material is graphene, a single atomic layer of graphite. Under the guidance of her supervisors, Maha used this as a base to develop a carbon-based sorbent (a material used toliquids or gases) for capturing carbon dioxide.

This was a great learning experience. When she returned to Pakistan, apart from a 4.0 GPA, she brought enough research experience to continue this as her final-year project at NUST. She worked under the supervision of Mohammad Mujahid, Dean of SCME, and Professor Habib Nasir.

At the same time, she continued her extracurricular activities with the same enthusiasm and vigor. She also met the Founder of Engineers Without Borders (EWB), Professor Bernard Amadei, in Islamabad in 2013. Later, she joined the Pakistan-US Alumni chapter of EWB. In 2013, She was awarded the Emerging Leader Award at the US Embassy in Islamabad. She was also invited to talk about women empowerment and education in a discussion as a panelist with representatives of all UN agencies in Pakistan on UN YouthPak Day. She has also been a panelist with the US Secretary of State, John Kerry, the US ambassador to Pakistan, and the Vice-Chancellor of Fatima Jinnah Women's University, speaking about the role of women in engineering, during the Secretary's visit to Pakistan.

Working in Colombia on Oil Rigs

In August 2013, Maha graduated from NUST. She wanted to continue to work and explore the world of science. A number of marriage proposals were waiting for her and it was becoming increasingly difficult to convince her family to let her continue her education. Once again, Maha sat her mother down and told her, "Ammi, this really makes me happy. I promise that I will marry when the time comes." Once again, Maha's mother tacitly agreed to let her continue her pursuit of goals.

She accepted a job offer as a trainee field engineer at Schlumberger, a leading provider of technology in the oil and gas industry. While this was a dream assignment for any chemical engineer, it was by no means an easy job. She was assigned the Colombia and Peru geo market and had to work on oil rigs.

This was her first official job after graduation and it proved to be quite challenging for the girl from Jhang. At US$5,000 a month, the pay was great; however, the conditions were tough. She worked long hours at the oil rig. She was often required to visit forests and conflict zones to check on the rigs. Many a times, she had to share living space with men and sleep in cramped spaces. She worked at the rig for over a year.

"It was really difficult. While everyone was really nice to me, the only female on their team, working on oil rigs was undoubtedly out of my comfort zone. I thought I would be happy if I was independent and doing what I had studied. But while it was interesting, life was hard," she shares.

When she met an old mentor at the Women Engineers' Conference in the US, Maha shared her unhappiness. The mentor advised her to quit her job and go home. So Maha resigned and booked the next flight home.

Home Again

Maha came back to Pakistan. However, she could not get a job because of limited opportunities for female engineers in Pakistan. She had gone from being a field engineer in Colombia to being unemployed in Pakistan."I was getting great money in Colombia, and doing good work, even while I was miserable because of the living conditions. Back home, I could not find a job worth even a fraction of what my old job was paying me," remembers Maha sadly. It was difficult for her to accept this new reality.

The only silver lining during that period became that her college mate Nasrullah Khatri proposed to her. Nasrullah was her classmate from NUST and a fellow team member of the school projects. Later they had worked for Schlumberger, but in different locations. When they met again, they found that they had a lot in common and Maha found Nasrullah easy to get along with. Talking about Nasrullah, Maha says, "I was always friends with him since college. I was on vacation and had gone to attend his sister's engagement. While I was there, Nasr's parents insisted that we become engaged."Maha's mother was ecstatic that her daughter was finally getting married to a nice young man.

Around the same time, Maha was selected for the prestigious Draper University's seven-week, world-class entrepreneurship boot camp in Silicon Valley, designed and run by the preeminent venture capitalist, Tim Draper. She received fourth prize out of 40 international pitches on Pitching Finale. As a reward, she got her wish to meet Sheryl Sandberg, the Chief Operating Officer of Facebook.

Onwards to Stanford

After finishing her entrepreneurship diploma, Maha received the news that she had been accepted to the prestigious Stanford University's PhD program. She went home to Jhang to get married to Nasrullah and then moved to Stanford in August 2015.

Currently, Maha is working as part of the Jamarillo Research Group at Stanford in the area of clean-energy technologies. While this research is not directly related to her previous work, Maha feels that she has been guided throughout her life to reach this point. For now, she is very happy in research. She shares, "I am not sure any more whether I am meant to be an entrepreneur, or an engineer or a researcher. I am happy doing what I am doing now. I am not sure what I will be doing two, three or five years from now. But I do know that I will be at the intersection of science and research."

About her marriage, she says, "The journey to follow my dreams has not been easy. It still isn't easy because Nasrullah and I live in different countries and we meet only once in three months when he comes to the US for training. However, I am content because I am following my heart and living my dream."

Key Advice

To Women and Young Girls: "Be passionate. Do not give up on your passion or the dreams that you want to fulfill. Passion is infectious and it will take you everywhere." Maha advises girls to give everything a chance, take every single opportunity they get, and choose the best for themselves.

"Every girl has to marry one day. But do not let it kill your dreams." Maha believes a girl should marry someone who supports her and her dreams, not someone who restricts her for unreasonable cultural norms. It is difficult, but can be done if one really tries.

To Men Who Influence Women: Educate women. As a father or a life partner, support her in pursuing her dreams. If she wants to study, or wants to explore the world, do not restrict her ever. That is how change will happen.

For Parents: Maha believes education and work are equally important for women. "Be friends with your daughters and sons. Listen to them and guide them. Be a support system for them. That's how they will achieve what they want to."Maha Yusuf has a friendly relationship with her parents. She believes that her parents grew up with her and learnt a lot about life that they did not know before.

GLOSSARY

A

A1 Grand Prix, A1GP: An auto racing series in which national teams competed against one another, also known as the "World Cup of Motor Sports"

Ad Server: The server system that enables advertisements to be displayed and managed on the web. The ad server also monitors the progress of the advertising campaigns.

Acquired Immunodeficiency Syndrome, AIDS: A disease that causes severe loss of cellular immunity. This lowers the body's capacity to resist infection and malignancy

Android: A popular open-source operating system developed by Google and Open Handset Alliance for smartphones and tablet computers

Antibiotics: Powerful medicines used to fight bacterial infections

Asia Pacific ICT Alliance, APICTA: An network of national ICT organizations of the Asia Pacific that work to promote technology innovation, capability and adoption, and encourage the development of local ICT solutions for global markets

Application program interface, API, APIs: A set of routines, protocols and tools for building software applications that specify how software components should work with other systems, applications or services

Armed Forces Institute of Ophthalmology, AFIO: Dedicated Ophthalmology Hospital in Rawalpindi, Pakistan

Atta-ur-Rehman School of Applied Biosciences (ASAB): A school at NUST that provides university education in Applied Biosciences, Healthcare Biotechnology, Industrial Biotechnology and Plant Biotechnology.

B

Biometric: Authentication techniques based on physical characteristics of the person. It includes technologies to scan fingerprints or iris. It has widespread use in identity and security systems.

Biotech, biotechnology: Technology that uses living systems and organisms to develop products or processes

Bitcoin: A type of digital currency used as a replacement for cash

Board for Control of Cricket in India, BCCI: The national governing body for cricket in India

Business Incubation Centers, BIC: An office that provides business support services to startup and early-stage companies. Service offerings range from office space to management training.

Business Intelligence, BI: Software applications and techniques used to analyze and interpret organization's raw data--which is often unstructured--to create new strategic business opportunities. Data mining, analytical processing, querying and reporting are all BI activities.

Business Process Outsourcing, BPO: The process of contracting a third party provider to perform business activities such as payroll, human resources (HR), accounting and customer/call center relations. These activities come under the ambit of IT-enabled Services (ITeS).

C

Campus Management Solutions, CMS: A system to manage students and alumni on a campus

Cash on Delivery, CoD: The system of paying for goods in cash at the time of delivery

Centre for Advanced Studies in Engineering, CASE: A private research college in Islamabad affiliated with the University of Engineering and Technology, Taxila

Chemotherapy: Treatment, especially of cancer, by chemical substances, especially by cytotoxic and other drugs

Chief Commercial Officer, CCO: The top management executive who sets strategies to grow business through activities related to marketing, sales, product development and customer service

Chief Executive Officer, CEO: The senior executive who leads an organization

Chief Information Officer, CIO: The top management executive who sets information technology (IT) strategies to drive an organisation's goals

Contract Research Organization, CRO: Organization that conducts research projects from pharmaceutical, biotechnology, and medical companies

Chief Technology Officer, CTO: Atop management executive who sets and manages the technology requirements of a company

Clean Energy Technologies: A process, product, or service that provides energy efficient and environmentally responsible solutions with sustainable or environment-friendly resources

College of Electrical & Mechanical Engineering, CEME, NUST, EME College: The college at NUST that provides undergraduate and postgraduate degrees in Electrical and Mechanical Engineering

Commercialization: Process by which a research idea, product or service is introduced to the market

Computer Society of Pakistan, CSP: Professional Association of Technology Professionals in Pakistan

Content Management System, CMS: A computer application used to manage digital content on a website being updated by a team

Crowd Funding: Funding a project or venture by raising many small amounts of money from a large number of people. This is usually done through common internet platforms.

Crowd-funded platform: An organization, system or technology that can coordinate and channelize funds through crowd funding.

D

Diabetic retinopathy, DR: A diabetes complication in which high blood glucose damages the blood vessels of the retina

E

EasyPaisa: An online payment solution in Pakistan enabling customers to send and receive money

E-commerce: Trading or facilitating sale of products or services online

Economies of Scale: The economic phenomenon in which mass production reduces the overall cost per customer

Ecosystem, Entrepreneurship ecosystem: The network of people, organizations and support institutions constituting the overall environment for an entrepreneur. Also known as business support environment

EDP--Entrepreneurship Development Program at MIT: A week-long entrepreneurship program hosted by MIT for candidates from around the world

E-Governance: The set of information and communication technology (ICT) used by the government to deliver services, exchange information or communicate more efficiently.

Electronic Control Unit, ECU: A generic term for any embedded system in an automobile that controls one or more of its electrical systems

Electronic Fuel Injection, EFI: The computer system that controls the fuel delivery system to provide optimum power and fuel efficiency. An electronic control unit (ECU) controls the EFI system.

Electronic Medical Record, EMR: A digital version of the patient's medical history. An EMR typically contains data such as patient visits, appointments, vaccinations, treatments and tests tracked over time, and measured against standard parameters.

Elevator Pitch: A short summary (verbal or written) to convey the idea, business or value proposition quickly and simply usually under 30 seconds to a minute

Enterprise Resource Planning, ERP: An ERP management information system integrates many areas of the value chain to simplify sharing of information between departments.

F

FAST, FAST-NU, FASCT National University of Computer and Emerging Sciences: The Foundation for Advancement of Science and Technology is a private research university that played a role in introducing software engineering degrees in Pakistan. It has multiple campuses in many cities of Pakistan.

Fellowship of the College of Physicians and Surgeons, FCPS: A postgraduate degree awarded by the College of Physicians and Surgeons, Pakistan

Fleet tracking, vehicle tracking system: A tracking system that automatically monitors vehicle location and aggregates this as comprehensive fleet data for all the vehicles in the fleet

G

Gartner: Gartner, Inc. is an American research and advisory firm providing information technology related insight.

GBP, Great Britain Pound: The currency is equal to approximately Pakistani Rupees PKR130 per GBP1 as of March 2017.

General Headquarters of Pakistan Army, GHQ: The headquarters of Pakistan Army located at Rawalpindi

Ghulam Ishaq Khan Institute of Technology and Sciences, GIK/GIKI: A private research university located in Topi, Khyber Pakhtunkhwa, Pakistan

GITEX: An annual consumer computer and electronics trade show, exhibition, and conference that takes place in Dubai, United Arab Emirates at the Dubai World Trade Centre

Global Entrepreneurship Summit: The US government program hosts an annual summit focused on supporting and empowering entrepreneurs in Muslim communities

Global Innovation through Science and Technology (GIST): A US government program on innovation and entrepreneurship for young innovators to develop startup solutions addressing development challenges

Government of Pakistan, GoP: Official website: www.pakistan.gov.pk

Greenfield: A term used to denote a project to be developed in a new environment without the need to consider any prior work

Groupware: An application software designed to help people collaborate in executing a common task. This may include communication, coordination, emails, project management, workflow management, knowledge management and bookmarking.

GCC countries: Gulf Cooperation Council Countries include Bahrain, Kuwait, Oman, Qatar, Saudi Arabia and UAE.

H

Higher Education Commission, HEC: Institution in Pakistan responsible for primary funding, overseeing, regulating and accrediting the higher education efforts in Pakistan

Hospital Acquired Infections: Infections caused by prolonged exposure to hospital; commonly caused by viral, bacterial, and fungal pathogens

Hospital Management Information System, HMIS or Health Information Management System, HIMS: A system designed to support planning, management and decision-making in health organizations

I

Immunology: The study of the body's immune system

Information and Communication Technology, ICT: Also Information Technology (IT). The terms broadly includes telecommunications, hardware and software that enable users to access, store, transmit and manipulate information.

Incubation programs: Programs designed to help young businesses grow by providing them with necessary support and financial and technical services

Incubator: An organization that provides business support resources needed by an entrepreneur to accelerate the growth and success of his company

Information Technology Enabled services, ITEs: Also called web enabled services or remote services. These businesses use Information Technology to improve efficiency.

Information Technology, IT: The application of computers and the internet to store, retrieve, transmit and manipulate data or information, often in the context of a business or other enterprise

Institute of Cost and Management Accountants of Pakistan, ICMAP: A professional body offering qualification and training in management accountancy

Institute of Electrical and Electronics Engineers, IEEE: A global professional association of engineers, scientists and allied professionals dedicated to advancing technological innovation

International Labour Organisation, ILO: A United Nations agency dealing with labor issues, such as international labor standards, social protection, and work opportunities for all.

Internet of Things, IOT: The network of physical objects (smart devices, connected devices) that collect and share data through sensors, electronics or software

iOS: A mobile operating system created and developed by Apple Inc. for its mobile devices, such as iPhone, iPad, and iPod touch.

IP Address, Internet Protocol Address: A numerical label assigned to each device (e.g., computer, printer) that is in a computer network and uses the Internet Protocol for communication. The IP address signifies the origin of the data.

J

J2EE: A Java based platform for developing, building and deploying Web-based applications

K

Kids Blood Diseases Organization, KBDO: A charity based in Mansehra that mainly caters to poor children, maintains a blood donation base for thalassemia patients and creates awareness about HIV, Hepatitis B, Hepatitis C, Thalassemia and other blood related-diseases

Khyber Pakhtunkhwa Information Technology Board, KPITB, KPK IT Board: The Government of Khyber Pakhtunkhwa body responsible for the promotion of Information Technology (IT), IT-enabled Services (ITes) and IT enabled Education (ITeE).

KRL, Kahuta Research Laboratories: Also known as Khan Institute. APakistan Government's multi-programnational research institute. It is one of the largest science and technology institution in Pakistan that conducts research in fields such asnational security,space explorationandsupercomputing.

L

Limited Partner: A partner of a company whose liability is legally limited to the amount of the money invested

Lahore University of Management Sciences, LUMS: A Lahore based private university

M

Maintenance Data Processing System, MDP: The system that interprets data to analyze use of machines or execution of processes and provides suggestions for improvement

MATLAB, Matrix laboratory: A programming language that allows matrix calculations, plotting of functions, and implementation of algorithms

Matriculation: Standardized examination at the end of Grade 10

Maund: Local measure of capacity or of weight, equivalent to about 38 kilograms

MBBS: Bachelor of Medicine, Bachelor of Surgery

MCPS : Member of College of Physicians & Surgeons, Pakistan

Microfinance: Financial service for entrepreneurs and small businesses lacking access to banking

MIT Enterprise Forum of Pakistan Business Acceleration Program, MITEFP-Business Acceleration Plan, MITEFP-BAP: An annual business plan competition for technology companies in Pakistan

MIT-EFP: MIT-Enterprise Forum of Pakistan

MoIT: Ministry of IT and Telecom

Multiple Drug Resistant (MDR) bacteria: Multi-drug resistant tuberculosis (MDR-TB, also known as Vank's disease) isa form of TB infection caused by bacteria that are resistant to treatment with at least two of the most powerful anti-TB drugs.

N

Nanographene: Nanostructuresmade fromgraphene

Nanoparticles: Particles between 1 and 100 nanometers in size

Nanomaterial: A material having particles or constituents of nanoscale dimensions, or one that is produced by nanotechnology

Nanotechnology: Nanoscience and nanotechnology are the study and application of extremely small things--about 1 to 100 nanometers.

National College of Arts, NCA: College in Lahore specializing in Arts

National Database and Registration Authority, NADRA: An agency under the Ministry of Interior and Narcotics Control,Government of Pakistanthat regulatesgovernment databasesand statistically manages the sensitive registration database of all thecitizensofPakistan

National Database Organization, NDO: The precursor to National Database and Registration Authority (NADRA)

National Defence University, NDU: A publicly funded military institution located in Islamabad, Pakistan dedicated to the study and research in military science, geo-strategy and international relations.

National ICT R&D Fund, NICTRDF: A government supported Research & Development Fund for projects proposed by industry and academia

New York Over-the-Counter Market (OTC): Refers to stocks that trade via adealer network as opposed to on a centralized exchange. It may also refer to the debt securitiesand otherfinancial instruments, such asderivatives, which are traded through this dealer network.

Non-Governmental Organization, NGO: A private, not-for-profit organization formed to create some social impact. Usually funded by donations and mostly run by volunteers

O

Office of Research Innovation and Commercialization, ORIC: Offices at universities/higher education institutions under the ambit of HEC to manage research activities

Onboard Diagnostics Technology, OBD: A system installed in vehicles that monitors and reports data from the various subsystems of the vehicle allowing the vehicle owner or repair technician to gauge their condition

Optical Character Recognition, OCR: Technology that can photoscan text and convert the photo to ASCII character codes

Organisation of Islamic Countries, OIC: An international organization consisting of 57 member states with Muslim majorities

Organization of Pakistani Entrepreneurs of North America, OPEN: A voluntary, not-for-profit organization lead by the Pakistani-American community, dedicated to the promotion of entrepreneurship and business leadership

P

P@SHA ICT Awards: The annual P@SHA ICT Awards is an annual award event for IT and ITES companies in Pakistan.

Pakathon: An organization for engineers, business professionals, designers, researchers. Pakathon conducts a global hackathon and many mini events engaging Pakistani diaspora around the world to solve social problems of Pakistan.

Pakistan Poultry Research Institute: Research institute in Punjab focused on developing the poultry industry

Pakistan Software Export Board, PSEB: An government body mandated to promote Pakistan's IT Industry in local and international markets through programs in infrastructure development, human capital development, company capability development, international marketing, strategy and research and the promotion of innovation and technologies.

Pakistan Software Houses Association, P@SHA: Association of Software and ITES companies in Pakistan

Pakistan Telecommunication Authority, PTA : Governmentagencyresponsible for the establishment, operation and maintenance oftelecommunicationsinPakistan

Piezoelectric Effect: Some materials produce electricity in response to a mechanical stress.

Presidential Award: Civil Awards presented by the President of Pakistan on the Independence Day, August 14.

Punjab IT Board, PITB: A body of the Government of Punjab province that aims at modernizing governance and increasing the digital literacy of the citizens

Q

Quality Assurance: The systematic process of testing a product or service that it is meeting specified requirements

R

Radio Frequency Identification, RFID: A technology that uses electromagnetic or electrostatic coupling of radio frequency (RF) to uniquely identify an object

Radiotherapy: Treatment that uses ionizing radiation to control or kill malignant cells

Rani Khet virus: Also known as Newcastle disease virus. A contagious bird disease affecting many domestic and wild avian species. It is transmissible to humans.

Real Time, RT: A computer system that responds immediately or enables the computer to keep up with some external process

Revolutions Per Minute, RPM: Revolutions per minute (abbreviated rpm, RPM, rev/min, r/min) is a measure of speed counting the number of rotations of a mechanical component around a fixed axis in one minute.

Role-playing game, RPG game: A game in which players act out roles within the game

RWR Radar Warning Receiver: The system that detects the radio emissions of radar systems and issues a warning when a signal is detected as a threat

S

SAAS Software As A Service: A software licensing and delivery model in which software is licensed on a subscription basis and is hosted centrally

SAAS-based cloud solution: A model of software distribution in which a third-party provider hosts applications and makes them available to customers over the Internet

Scalable solutions: The capability of a system, network, or process to handle growing amount of work

School of Chemical and Materials Engineering, SCME: The NUST school which offers undergraduate and postgraduate degree programs in the twin disciplines of Chemical Engineering and Materials Engineering.

SDK (software development kit): A set of software development tools that allows the creation of applications. Also called devkit

Secure Access Control Systems: Systems that control permissions to use a place or resource. These systems work for physical, informationand authorizations.

Series A round: A company's first significant round of venture capital financing

Silverpreneur: Silverpreneurs are the category of entrepreneurs who have had a previous career and are now moving towards an entrepreneurial career, post-retirement or after midlife.

Sitara-e-Imtiaz: Star of Excellence in English. It is the third highest honor and civilian award conferred by the State of Pakistan.

Social Stock Exchange: A concept in which businesses, investors and donors pool resources to make a positive social and environmental impact

SOFTEC: An annual event held atFAST-NUCES,Lahore,Pakistan to recognize talent, exchange ideas and provide opportunities for students

Space and Upper Atmosphere Research Commission, SUPARCO: The space agency of the Government of Pakistan responsible for the country's public and civil space program and aeronautics and aerospace research

Symbian: The operating system used primarily by Nokia for its mobile phones

T

Technopreneur: A person who sets up a technology related business

Telecommunications Regulatory Authority, TRA: The federal telecommunicationsregulatory agencytheArab Emirates

The GIST Tech-I Global Pitch Competition: An annual competition for science and technology entrepreneurs from emerging economies worldwide in which aspiring innovators produce videos to pitch their ideas and startups. GES, GIST Tech-I finalists make connections and gain international exposure.

The Indus Entrepreneurs Pakistan, TiE: Founded in 1992 by a group of successful entrepreneurs, TiE is a non-profit, global community welcoming entrepreneurs from all over the world.

The International Defence Exhibition and Seminar, IDEAS: The largest defence exhibition and seminar held biannually in Pakistan

U

The United Nations Educational, Scientific and Cultural Organization, UNESCO: A United Nations' (UN) agency to promote international collaboration through educational, scientific, and cultural reforms promoting universal respect for justice, the rule of law, and human rights along with fundamental freedom.

United States Medical Licensing Examinations, USMLE: A three-step examination for medical licensure in the United States

University of Engineering and Technology in Lahore, UET: A public research university in Lahore specializing in STEM subjects

US State Department: A US federal executive department responsible for foreign policy

USAID Small Grants and Ambassador's Fund Program, SGAFP: A seven-year program of the United States Agency for International Development (USAID) Pakistan that provides grants to NGOs and grassroots/community-based organizations to support their self-help initiatives

The United States Agency for International Development, USAID: The United States Government agency primarily responsible for administering civilian foreign aid

V

Venture Capital Fund, VC Fund: A type of fund pooled by individual and institutional investors who are interested in equity stakes in startups and small- to medium-sized enterprises with strong growth potential

Venture Capitalist, VC: Investor who provides capital (equity or debt) to a startup

Virology: The study of viruses

Virotherapy: An alternative treatment of cancer using biotechnology to reprogram viruses for treating diseases. There are three main branches of virotherapy: anti-cancer oncolytic viruses, viral vectors for gene therapy and viral immunotherapy.

Voice of America, VoA: A United States government-funded multimedia news source and the official external broadcasting institution of the United States.programming for broadcast on radio, television and the Internet outside of the, in English and some foreign languages.

W

Water and Power Development Board of Pakistan, WAPDA: An autonomous statutory body that regulates water distribution policies in Pakistan under the administrative control of the federal government

Women 2.0 Startup Competition: Open to women owned early-stage ventures around the world who have received less than a million in funding

Women 2.0: Association for women in technology. A for-profit, for-good company hiring, founding, investing and leading women in technology

Z

Zakat: A form of alms giving which is a religious obligation for Muslims who meet the criteria of wealth

BIBILIOGRAPHY

BOOK 1: TECHNOPRENEURS

Aftab, Hassan. *CoVenture, Pakistani Owned Startup, Raises $3 Million in Funding.* Propakistaniwebsite. www.propakistani.pk/2015/02/20/pakistani-venture-firm-coventure-raises-3-million-in-funding. 2014. Accessed September 15, 2016.

CoVenture. Angel List website. www.angel.co/coventure. Accessed September 15, 2016.

CoVenture. Crunch base website. www.crunchbase.com/organization/coventure#/entity. Accessed September 15, 2016.

D'Onfro, Jillianand Robinson, Melia. *This Cornell Student Went From Sleeping In Starbucks To Investing In More Than A Dozen New Companies This Year.* Business Insider website. www.businessinsider.com/ali-hamed-coventure-most-impressive-cornell-2014-3. Mar. 27, 2014. Accessed September 15, 2016.

Gartner lists Kualitatem as top ten mobile testing service providers. Kualitatem website. www.kualitatem.com/news/gartner-lists-kualitatem-as-top-ten-mobile-testing-service-providers/. December 7, 2015. Accessed September 15, 2016.

Husain, Osman. *Despite dropping out of college, this inventor was recognized as one of the world's brilliant minds.* Tech in Asia website. www.techinasia.com/inventor-recognised-brilliant-minds. July 15, 2011. Accessed August 15, 2016.

Noc Team.*A Quality Assurance Success Story. Codeweek Website* Www.Codeweek.Pk/2010/12/Jamil-Goheer-. December 28, 2010. Accessed September 15, 2016

Slade, Hollie. *How CoVenture's Founder Went From Sleeping In Union Square To Investing In 20 Companies.* Forbes website. www.forbes.com/sites/hollieslade/2013/12/19/comeback-kid-how-coventures-founder-went-from-sleeping-in-union-square-to-investing-in-20-companies/#17f61d716812. DEC 19, 2013. Accessed September 15, 2016.

Tapinator, Inc. (TAPM). Yahoo!Finance website. finance.yahoo.com/quote/TAPM?ltr=1. Accessed October 13, 2016.

Techjuice. *This Pakistani Startup is tapping the multi-billion dollar industry beyond biometrics.* Techjuice website. www.techjuice.pk/this-pakistani-startup-is-tapping-the-billion-dollar-biometric-devices-market/.July 14, 2015. Accessed August 15,2016.

Thompson, Lisa .Zacks Small Cap Research. Yahoo!Finance website . finance.yahoo.com/news/tapm-q1-beat-progress-social-150000520.html. May 17, 2016. AccessedJune 17, 2016.

Time Magazine Names Tapinator's "Burn It Down" as A Top Game of the Week Tapinator's Newest Release Also Featured by Apple and Is Top 50 Game. PR Newswire website. www.prnewswire.com/news/releases/time-magazine-names-tapinators-burn-it-down-as-a-top-game-of-the-week-300075047.html. April 27, 2015, 08:00 ET. accessed July 27, 2016.

Why Soloinsight. Soloinsight website. www.soloinsight.net/website/#why_soloinsight. Accessed August 15, 2016.

Williams, Chris. 33: *Farhan Masood – Innovative hope for Pakistan, Chicago and China.* Isharehope website. www.isharehope.com/interviews/33-farhan-masood-innovative-hope-for-pakistan-chicago-and-china-isharehope/#sthash.9C3W5nRD.dpuf. June 11th, 2015. Accessed August 15, 2016.

Williamson, Alastair. *Tapinator To Capitalize On Untapped, Celebrity-Focused Mobile Gaming.* Seeking Alpha website. www.seekingalpha.com/article/2664275-tapinator-to-capitalize-on-untapped-celebrity-focused-mobile-gaming, Originally published Oct 10, 2014. Accessed July 27, 2016.

Zafar, Quart. *Farhan Masood Scores another Achievement for Pakistan!.* Techjuice website. www.techjuice.pk/farhan-masood-scores-another-achievement-pakistan. December 31, 2013. Accessed August 15, 2016.

Bilytica (Business Intelligence & Analytics). Linkedin website. www.linkedin.com/company/bilytica-private-limited. Accessed June 20, 2016.

Erpisto Software. Software Advice website. www.softwareadvice.com/erp/erpisto-profile.Accessed June 20, 2016.

Definition of e-commerce. Wikipedia website. en.wikipedia.org/wiki/E-commerce. Accessed July 9, 2016.

Cricket Companion website. www.cricketcompanion.com. Accessed 9 July 2016.

Web desk. *P@SHA ICT Awards 2012 held in Lahore.* The Express Tribune website. www.tribune.com.pk/story/450647/psha-ict-awards-2012-held-in-lahore. October 12, 2012. Accessed July 9, 2016.

Pradeep, Neal. *Cricket Companion Introduces Ball By Ball Cricket Update On Mobile.* Telecomtalk.info website. www.telecomtalk.info/cricket-companion-introduces-ball-by-ball-update-mobile/21098/, telecomtalk.info. March 7, 2010, Accessed July 9, 2016

Nokia App Summit concludes on positive note for local developers. The Express Tribune website. www.tribune.com.pk/story/409621/nokia-app-summit-concludes-on-positive-note-for-local-developers. July 18, 2012. Accessed July 9, 2016.

Anon, John. *Top 10 Cricket Apps.*Android Headlines website. www.androidheadlines.com/2015/06/featured-top-10-cricket-apps-android.html, Android Headlines, June 18, 2015, Accessed July 9, 2016

Arslan Khakwani (Pakistan) – Developer of The Week. Vserv website. www.vserv.com/arslan-khakwani-pakistan-developer-of-the-week/. May 28, 2013, accessed July 9, 2016.

Dalrymple, Jim. *Apple Sued Over Screen Rendering Technology in IPhone.* PC World from IDG website. www.pcworld.com/article/159553/article.html.Feb 13, 2009. Accessed July 10, 2016.

The Nest i/o . *Speaker Series with Shahzad Qureshi: 'The Brand Story of Tohfay'.* vimeo.com/152118762. February 2016. Accessed June 8, 2016.

Mamoo in Pakistan website. www.mamooinpakistan.com. Accessed June 8, 2016.

Baloch, Farooq. *E-Commerce: Major players see increase in size of pie.* The Express Tribune website.

Www.tribune.com.pk/story/765303/e-commerce-major-players-see-increase-in-size-of-pie/. September 22, 2014. Accessed June 8, 2016.

Webiz Media - Fastest Growing Arabia 500. Webbizmedia website. webizmedia.com/webiz_media_-_fastest_growing_arabia_500_event14. . Accessed 15, June 2016.

By 2020: Pakistan's e-commerce market to surpass $1 billion. The Express tribune website. www.tribune.com.pk/story/1016706/by-2020-pakistans-e-commerce-market-to-surpass-1-billion/. December 27, 2015. December 27, 2015

Ahmad, Junaid. *The encouraging future of e-commerce in Pakistan.* The Express Tribune website. www.tribune.com.pk/story/975430/the-encouraging-future-of-e-commerce-in-pakistan/. 19 October 2016. Accessed June 15, 2016.

Hamariweb.com Traffic Statistics . Alexa website. www.alexa.com/siteinfo/*Hamariweb.com*. Accessed August 25, 2016.

Shadman, Adil. *It Is About Time We Create Standardized and Internet-Ready Urdu Fonts.* Propakistani website. propakistani.pk/2016/03/29/it-is-about-time-we-create-standardized-and-internet-ready-urdu-fonts/. June 2016.

Tricast Media website. www.tricastmedia.com.pk. Accessed July 9, 2016.

GenITeam website. www.geniteam.com. Accessed June 17,2016.

Bilytica website. www.bilytica.com. Accessed June 20, 2016.

Cloupital website. www.cloudpital.com. Accessed June 20, 2016.

Erpisto website. www.erpisto.com. Accessed June 20, 2016.

Evamp and Saanga website. www.evampsaanga.com.Accessed August 1, 2016.

Tapinator website. www.tapinator.com. Accessed October 13, 2016.

Kualitatem website. www.kualitatem.com. Accessed September 15, 2016.

Book 2: Socialpreneurs

Akhuwat website. www.akhuwat.org.pk. Accessed July 24, 2016.

Baloch, Farooq. *Pakistan 3rd-highest user of freelancer as self-employment rises.* The Express Tribune Website.

www.tribune.com.pk/story/516239/pakistan-3rd-highest-user-of-freelancer-as-self-employment-rises/. March 5, 2013. Accessed July 26, 2016.

Chhichhia, Bandini. *The Rise of the Social Stock Exchanges.* Stanford Social Innovation Review website.www.ssir.org/articles/entry/the_rise_of_social_stock_exchanges. January 8, 2016. Accessed July 29, 2016.

CNBC Catalyst Content Studio. *CNBC: Change Makers Episode 5: Meet Maria Umar.* Vimeo website. vimeo.com/108800210. October 13, 2014. Accessed July 20, 2016.

DoctHERs secures spot in MITEF programme. The Express Tribune Website. www.tribune.com.pk/story/993403/women-entrepreneurs-DoctHERs-secures-spot-in-mitef-programme/. November 18, 2015. Accessed September 8, 2016.

DoctHERs website. www.DoctHERs.com. Accessed September 8, 2016.

Ehsan, Shariq. *Interview with Maria Umar, Founder and President of Women Digital League.* Propakistani website. www.propakistani.pk/2015/02/25/interview-with-maria-umar-founder-and-president-of-women-digital-league. 2014. Accessed July 20, 2016.

Famous Dadar sanatorium turns into a ghost house. Dawn website. www.dawn.com/news/1177916. Apr 24, 2015. Accessed September 8, 2016.

Fellows Bio – Humaria Bachal. Emerging Leaders of Pakistan website. www.elpak.org/fellows/humairabachal/. Accessed May 25, 2016.

HCP (Hazara.com.pk*). Maria Umar.* Dailymotion website. www.dailymotion.com/video/x2uxwth. 22 July 2015. Accessed July 20, 2016.

Illyas, Ferya. *From 'doctor brides' to practicing physicians.* The Express Tribune Website. www.tribune.com.pk/story/969805/DoctHERs-from-doctor-brides-to-practicing-physicians/. October 9, 2015. Accessed September 8, 2016.

Khan,A.J. Si.*Scope Of Medical Colleges In Private Sector .* Ayub Medical College website. ayubmed.edu.pk/JAMC/PAST/16-1/AJKhan.htm. Accessed September 8, 2016.

Khurram, Sara. *DoctHERs: Mind the Gap.*The Express Tribune

Website. www.tribune.com.pk/story/969081/DoctHERs-mind-the-gap/. October 11, 2015. Accessed September 8, 2016.

Lifebuoy partners with 'doctHERs' to improve healthcare access in Pakistan. Unilever Pakistan Website. www.unilever.pk/news/press-releases/2016/Lifebuoy-partners-with-DoctHERs-to-improve-healthcare-access-in-Pakistan.html. June 23, 2016 Accessed September 8, 2016.

Mahre, Mahim. *What the Hitchhiking Women of Moach Goth Can Teach the Sindh Government.* The Friday Times website. www.thefridaytimes.com/tft/what-the-hitchhiking-women-of-moach-goth-can-teach-the-sindh-government. April 3, 2016. Accessed May 25, 2016.

Mehmood, Mohsin. *Pakistan's Freelancing Future Looks Bright.* propakistani.pk/2015/12/16/pakistans-freelancing-future-looks-bright/. Nov 2015. Accessed July 26, 2016.

Mehsud, Rafiuddin. *The Lost Culture of South Waziristan Agency, Fata.* Daily Times website. www.dailytimes.com.pk/blog/24-May-16/the-lost-culture-of-south-waziristan-agency-fata. May 24, 2016. Accessed July 20, 2016.

Muhammad Yunis. Wikipedia website. en.wikipedia.org/wiki/Muhammad Yunus. Accessed July 29, 2016.

Najeeb, Faryal. *A Charitable Nation We Are.* The Express Tribune website. www.blogs.tribune.com.pk/story/6317/a-charitable-nation-we-are/. Accessed July 24, 2016.

Online Work Report: Global, 2014 Full Year Data. Upwork website. www.elance-odesk.com/online-work-report-global. Accessed July 26, 2016.

Pakistan: Health spending per capita. The Global Economy.com website. www.theglobaleconomy.com/Pakistan/Health_spending_per_capita/. . Accessed September 8, 2016.

PDX Facebook. page www.facebook.com/Pakistan-Development-Exchange-431919930326058/. Accessed July 29, 2016.

PDX website. www.pdx.com.pk. Accessed July 29, 2016.

PSX You tube channel. You tube website. www.youtube.com/channel/UCp1HYxXf5ifs0VkzY6jbYfQ. Accessed July 29, 2016.

Quddus, Munir. *Book Review - Building Social Business by*

Muhammad Yunus. Emel website. www.emel.com/article?id=109&a_id=2309. Issue 78 March 2011. Accessed July 29, 2016.

Rabtt website. www.rabtt.org. Accessed July 24, 2016.

Safire. *Humaira Bachal – The light of Moach Goth, Karachi.* www.sapphirical.wordpress.com/2011/07/20/humaira-bachal%E2%80%99s-small-dream/. Accessed May 25, 2016.

Saleem, Farrah. *doctHERs: Remote patient care with female doctors at the fore.* Dawn website. www.dawn.com/news/1234694. May 12, 2016. Accessed September 8, 2016.

Shamsi, Amber. *Are Pakistan's female medical students to be doctors or wives?.* BBC News website. www.bbc.com/news/world-asia-34042751. August 28, 2015. Accessed September 8, 2016.

Shorish, Hafsa. *Working Hard for the Money.* www.technologyreview.pk/working_hard_for_money. Accessed July 26, 2016.

Social stock exchanges: A new instrument in the international development toolkit? Devex website. www.devex.com/news/social-stock-exchanges-a-new-instrument-in-the-international-development-toolkit-77593. Accessed July 29, 2016.

South Waziristan. Wikipedia website. en.wikipedia.org/wiki/South_Waziristan. Accessed July 20, 2016.

Springer, Jon. *Pakistan's Educator Madonna Wants You To Know.* Forbes website. www.forbes.com/sites/jonspringer/2014/11/25/pakistans-educator-madonna-wants-you-to-know/#7c9557273e9a. NOV 25, 2014. Accessed May 25, 2016.

Statistics. Pakistan Medical and Dental Council website. www.pmdc.org.pk/Statistics/tabid/103/Default.aspx. Accessed September 8, 2016.

Transforming healthcare by empowering women: doctHERs wins Young Entrepreneur Award. Unilever Pakistan Website. www.unilever.pk/sustainable-living/sustainable-living-news/transforming-healthcare-by-empowering-women-DoctHERs-wins-young-entrepreneur-award.html .May 2016. Accessed September 8, 2016.

UNREASONABLE.IS, *DoctHERs: Pakistan's 'Doctor Brides' Inspire Confidence — And Better Health — For Women.* Impact

Alpha Website. Impactalpha.Com/Pakistans-Doctor-Brides/. MARCH 14, 2016 . Accessed September 8, 2016.

*Women's Digital League: Digital Livelihood Training-Peshawar, Khyber Pakhtunkhwa March 9, 2015- May 29, 2015.*Women's Digital League website.womensdigitalleague.com/wp-content/uploads/2015/05/small-spreads.pdf. Accessed July 20,2016.

BOOK 3: SILVERPRENEURS

Biomisa website. www.biomisa.org. Accessed July 10, 2016

Case Study NADRA. Information System Reforms for Improving Governance. WorldBank website. www.siteresources.worldbank.org/PSGLP/Resources/InformationSystemReformsforImprovingGovernance.pdf. Accessed July 18, 2016.

CASE University Website. www.case.edu.pk. Accessed July 10, 2016.

Chairman NADRA resigns. The Nation website. www.nation.com.pk/politics/08-Aug-2008/Chairman-NADRA-resigns. August 8, 2008. Accessed July 18, 2016

*Crunchbase website.*www.crunchbase.com/person/sajjad-kirmani/timeline#/timeline/index. Accessed August 2016.

Development of a Net Enabled Retinal Image Analysis & Screening System for Grading & Diagnosis of Diabetic Retinopathy and its Integration in i-telemedicine System. Funded Projects. ICTRND website. www.ictrdf.org.pk/index.php/component/tprojects/project/56, Accessed July 10, 2016.

Dr. Shafaat Ahmed Bazaz Profile. CASE University website. www.case.edu.pk/FacultyPortal/DetailInfo.aspx?id=ydRRTTxkdt6Trx91pX1%2bcA%3d%3d. Accessed 10 July 2016

Dr. Shafaat Ahmed Bazaz Profile. LinkedIn website. www.linkedin.com/in/shafaat-bazaz-587b691b. Accessed July 10, 2016.

Infogistic website. www.infogistic.com. Accessed August 2016

Jan, Zia Ahmed. *Catalysts for Change- The Unique Culture Behind NADRA's Success- A Case Study.* Presented Pakistans 10th International Convention on Quality Improvement. PIQC website. www.piqc.edu.pk/casestudies/Prof_Maj_Zia_Ahmad_Jan_Catalys

ts_for_Change_the_Unique_Culture_Social_Quality_Case_Study_PIQC.pdf. Nov 27, 2006. Accessed July 18, 2016.

National ICT R&D Fund website. www.ictrdf.org.pk. Accessed July 10, 2016.

Netsol Technologies. Sajjad Kirmani Talks About NetSol's Beginnings. Youtube website www.youtube.com/watch?v=vMVF6ZOMGls.Feb 9, 2011. Accessed August 2016.

Pasha ICT Awards -2015 winners. PASHA –ICT awards website. www.pashaictawards.com/winners-2015. October 12, 2015. Accessed July 10, 2016

Profile Brigadier Saleem Moeen. LinkedIn website. www.linkedin.com/in/saleem-moeen-71753311 .Accessed July 18, 2016.

Secure Tech Consultancy website. www.securetech-consultancy.com. Accessed July 18, 2016.

Stoten, Philip. *Interview with Brig. Saleem Ahmed Moeen at Wise Media's sixth EMEA Summit.* ID People website. www.id-world-magazine.com/id-people/?p=848. Accessed July 18, 2016.

World Health Organization. *Developing health management information systems: a practical guide for developing countries.* WHO website. www.wpro.who.int/health_services/documents/developing_health_management_information_systems.pdf. Accessed July 18,2016.

BOOK 4: FUTUREPRENEURS

Agriculture Problems in Pakistan And Their Solutions. CSS Forum website. www.cssforum.com.pk/css-compulsory-subjects/pakistan-affairs/43470-agriculture-problems-pakistan-their-solutions.html. January 14, 2011. Accessed August 2016.

Agriculture, Pakistan Economic Survey 2015-16. Ministry of Finance Website. www.finance.gov.pk/survey/chapters_16/02_Agriculture.pdf. Accessed August 2016.

Allahwala, Rehan. *Interview with Maha Yusuf.* Vimeo website. vimeo.com/120126076. 2014. Accessed August 29, 2016.

Azeemullah. *Meet XGear, a First of its Kind Car-Human Communication Link, Developed by Pakistanis.* Propakistani website. www.propakistani.pk/2013/09/30/meet-xgear-first-kind-car-human-communication-link-developed-pakistanis/. 2015. Accessed 2016

Bukhari, Syed Waseem. *Zaraei Ootaque*. Slideshare website www.slideshare.net/sayedwaseembukhari/zaraei-ootaque. January 10, 2014. Accessed August 2016.

Global Handicrafts Market 2015-2019. Technavio website.www.technavio.com/report/handicrafts-market. November 25, 2015. Accessed August 2016.

Handicrafts of Pakistan. Pakistan Defence website. www.defence.pk/threads/handicrafts-of-pakistan.75973/. Oct 10, 2010. Accessed August 2016.

Imran, Tanzila. *Pakistan startup hopes for a global hit with xGear, brings 'quantified self' to your car.* TechinAsia website. www.techinasia.com/pakistan-startup-hopes-global-hit-xgear-brings-quantified-self-car. Apr 24, 2014. Accessed August 2016.

Kelly,Elizabeth and Russell, Stephen J.. *History of Oncolytic Viruses: Genesis to Genetic Engineering. Molecular therapy : the journal of the American Society of Gene Therapy.* 15 (4): 651–9. doi:10.1038/sj.mt.6300108. PMID 17299401. Accessed August 2016.

Mithal, Muhammad. *Report on Zaraei Otaque Nara & Al-Noor Rice Millls.* Love With –Blogspot website. www.knowpanhwar.blogspot.com/2014/01/zaraei-otaque-nara-al-noor-rice.html. January 8, 2014. Accessed August 2016

Nanomaterias. . Wikipedia website. en.wikipedia.org/wiki/Nanomaterials. Accessed August 2016.

One Step Solutions website. www.onestepsolutions.biz/xgear/. Accessed August 2016

Report Buyer. *Global Handicrafts Market 2015-2019.* PR Newswire website. www.prnewswire.com/news-releases/global-handicrafts-market-2015-2019-300187146.html. Dec 2, 2015. Accessed August 2016.

Science Round. *Science Documentary: Graphene, Nanomaterials, a Documentary on Nanotechnology.* Youtube website. www.youtube.com/watch?v=UEd1Z-eIXsQ.Jul 6, 2015. Accessed August 29, 2016.

The Higher Education Commission of Pakistan website.

www.hec.gov.pk/. Accessed July 2016.

Travly website. www.travly.io. Accessed August 2016.

Viruses: The new cancer hunters. IsraCast website. www.isracast.com/article.aspx?id=15. March 01, 2006. Accessed August 2016.

What Is Lung Cancer - Non-Small Cell. American Cancer Society website. www.cancer.org/cancer/lungcancer-non-smallcell/detailedguide/non-small-cell-lung-cancer-key-statistics. Accessed August 2016.

XGear Drive smart. Slideshow. www.hkdworld.net/doc/XGearProfile.pdf. Accessed August 2016.

XGear Facebook page. www.facebook.com/xgeario/. Accessed August 2016.

XGear Website. xgear.io. accessed August 2016.

XGear. Crunchbase website.www.crunchbase.com/organization/xgear#/entity. Updated May 5, 2015. Accessed August 2016.

Yusuf, Maha. *SWE'14 Annual Conference Talk: 'Engineering, Leadership and, Entrepreneurship ~ A Journey from Pakistan to Latin America'* . Slideshare website. www.slideshare.net/mahayusuf9. Accessed August 29, 2016.

Zaraeei Ootaque Facebook page. www.facebook.com/Zaraei-Ootaque-284526748307625/. Accessed August 2016

WHERE TO GET MORE HELP

CAMBRIDGE ADVISORS NETWORK: Cambridge Advisors Network (CAN) is a consultancy that aims to support the entrepreneurship ecosystem of Pakistan. We provide consultancy and training to universities, entrepreneurs, startups, early stage companies and students. We also work with entrepreneurial support organizations to build and sustain the Pakistan's entrepreneurial ecosystem. Our services include design and execution of Business Plan Competitions, technology and incubation policy and development, R&D commercialization, startup programs, Enterprise Growth Consulting, Technology Adoption and Change Management Consulting, Development of Policy Guidelines.

For more information and updates about our activities, trainings and current project please visit **CambridgeAdvisorsNet.com**.

AZHAR RIZVI.COM: To learn more about Azhar Rizvi and his work, access his blog or visit www.AzharRizvi.com and www.entrepreneuringpakistan.org

Entrepreneuring Pakistan

www.ingramcontent.com/pod-product-compliance
Lightning Source LLC
Chambersburg PA
CBHW020625220526
45464CB00001B/34